BIOGRAPHY IN LATE ANTIQUITY

THE TRANSFORMATION OF THE CLASSICAL HERITAGE

Peter Brown, General Editor

I

Art and Ceremony in Late Antiquity
by Sabine G. MacCormack

II

Synesius of Cyrene: Philosopher-Bishop
by Jay Alan Bregman

III

Theodosian Empresses: Women and Imperial Dominion in Late Antiquity
by Kenneth G. Holum

IV

John Chrysostom and the Jews: Rhetoric and Reality in the Late Fourth Century
by Robert L. Wilken

V

Biography in Late Antiquity: A Quest for the Holy Man
by Patricia Cox

PATRICIA COX

Biography in Late Antiquity

A QUEST FOR THE HOLY MAN

UNIVERSITY OF CALIFORNIA PRESS

Berkeley Los Angeles London

University of California Press
Berkeley and Los Angeles, California
University of California Press, Ltd.
London, England

LIBRARY OF CONGRESS CATALOGING IN PUBLICATION DATA
Cox, Patricia (Patricia L.)
Biography in late antiquity.
(The Transformation of the classical heritage; 5)
Bibliography: p.
Includes index.
1. Biography (as a literary form) 2. Classical literature—History and criticism. I. Title. II. Series.
PA3043.C6 808'.06692 82-4946
ISBN 0-520-04612-9 AACR2

Printed in the United States of America
1 2 3 4 5 6 7 8 9

For my mother, and in memory of my father:
Each a "hidden person of the heart."

1 Peter 3:4

Contents

Acknowledgments

Several friends and colleagues have graciously given helpful suggestions during the years when this study was written and rewritten, and to all of them I owe true gratitude. However, there are a few to whom I would like to offer special thanks.

Robert M. Grant, Professor in the Divinity School of the University of Chicago, presided genially and with scholarly acumen over the first version of this work.

Jonathan Z. Smith, Professor in the University of Chicago, convened an informal seminar on the holy man during an important year. Gene Gallagher, Jim Tabor, and Bruce Woll, fellow-members of the seminar, infused the sharing of ideas with "spirits."

Professor Peter Brown of the University of California, Berkeley and Ms. Doris Kretschmer, editor at the University of California Press, gave hearty and consistent encouragement.

Finally, in the spirit of "The Comedian as the Letter C," I thank my colleague and friend, David L. Miller: he helped me "round my rude aesthetic out." The "jagged lops of green" which remain are mine alone.

Introduction

"A slight thing like a phrase or jest often makes a greater revelation of character than battles where thousands fall."[1]

So Plutarch remarked about the telling ways in which we speak in spite of ourselves. As he goes on to say, it is precisely this kind of speaking—the mute eloquence of our quirks and gestures—that interests the biographer and distinguishes his vision from history's focus on the grand and illustrious sweep of events. For Plutarch and the ancient biographical tradition generally, a man's actions, whether illustrious or ignominious, were significant insofar as they revealed his character; as Plutarch says, biography was revelatory discourse, aimed at disclosing a man's inner self. The biographer's task was to capture the gesture which laid bare the soul.

The art of biographical narrative reflected this task. Ancient biographies are constellations of such gestures, carefully selected and assembled not to chronicle a life's history but to suggest its character. These character-revealing gestures are presented in the biographies primarily by means of images and anecdotes, and they show the free play of the biographical imagination as it works in the service of history's "meaning." If the facts of history form the "landscape" of a man's life, character is its "inscape," the contours and hollows which give a landscape its individuality. Biographies are like caricatures, bringing landscape and inscape, event and character, together in a single moment of evocative expression.

This is the overriding perspective guiding the present study: that ancient biographies of holy men were caricatures whose aim was to evoke, and thus to reveal, the interior geography of the hero's life. Baldly stated, this seems quite simple. Yet for the group of Graeco-Roman biographies with which this book is primarily concerned, capturing the gesture that reveals the soul entailed a complicated act of the biographical imagination. As a glance at

1. Plutarch *Alexander* 1.1–2.

any political cartoon will show, caricatures speak their truth by lying, that is, by exaggerating, typifying, stylizing, idealizing, and so on. One could discuss ancient biographies as sustained narrative series of such pictures. Biographers like Porphyry and Eusebius, however, had something more to contend with, for they saw God at work in their heroes' lives. Thus when they set about to "capture the gesture," they were negotiating the intersection of the human and the divine. Their caricatures speak, not with the voice of buffoonery or satire, but with the voice of myth. That mythic voice is the central concern in what follows.

"Holy man" names the mythic perspective which this study engages, and that mythic perspective has its locus in what I have called the free play of the biographical imagination. The myth of the holy man is here considered to be an imaginal[2] "place between" where the history of a man's life and his biographer's vision of human divinity meet and mingle. Biographies of holy men are the literary expressions of this play between fact and fantasy; they are the "place between" come to life as embodied ideal, imaginal history.

As we explore these biographies, we will emphasize a style of thinking—even a style of consciousness—rather than a method of composition. This style seeks images of character that give a man's history an abiding significance while taking care not to divorce the imagistic from the historical. *Style* is used here in its root sense of "stigma": the way one chooses to construct reality betrays how and where one has been struck and deeply touched by the world.

Our authors had been struck by an affinity between the mundane world of everyday life and the unseen but equally real realm of the spirit. This affinity is, of course, difficult to express directly. As Plutarch noted,[3] the gods speak to man in poetic circumlocutions—in image and metaphor—and, conversely, as Plotinus said, human speech about the divine world must always carry within it a metaphoric "so to speak."[4] Thus it is not surprising to find Eusebius, Porphyry, and other biographers expressing a willingness to read poetic truth as historical fact, and vice versa.[5] Indeed, that willingness is at

2. In this book, I have used the word "imaginal" not only as the adjectival form of "image" but also to avoid the pejorative connotation of the words "imaginary" or "imaginative." For a discussion of this word, see Henry Corbin, *Corps spirituel et terre céleste* (Paris: Éditions Buchet/Chastel, 1979), pp. 7–19.

3. Plutarch *Pyth. orac.* 26, 407e.

4. Plotinus *Enn.* 6.8.13: "Everywhere we must read 'so to speak'."

5. See chapter 3 for a discussion of this issue.

the heart of the biographical style to which this study is devoted. Biographers of holy men did not "translate" or "represent" their heroes' lives; like Plutarch, they were engaged in revelation. Their biographies succeed in exposing the inner radiance of the lives of their heroes precisely because biographical writing is evocative, not descriptive.

The voice of myth is supremely indirect; in ancient biographies of holy men, the heroes come alive in the biography's allusions, images, patterns, and themes. These are the interpretative "gestures" of the biographer himself, and they make possible that interplay between the mundane and the ideal, the earthly and the heavenly, by which the soul-revealing gestures of the hero are captured. In keeping with the evocative, allusive working of biographies of holy men, I often employ images of light to describe how the biographers proceed in their delicate task of "laying bare the soul." Yet, because of the idea of mythic indirection, which I think to be crucial for an understanding of these ancient writings, the imagery is not that of brilliant sunlight, but rather of shadows, shadings, and reflections.

Especially in chapters 4 and 5, which explore biographies by Eusebius and Porphyry in detail, I will refer to particular characterizations of Origen and Plotinus as, for example, "reflected images" or "shadowed distortions." Such images have been used to describe both how the biographer thinks and what he has written. Our interest lies not only in the enigmatic holy man but also in his enigmatic biographer. We are looking for the inner radiance of the biographical process itself, an inner radiance which, in honor of the free—and mischievous—play of mythic discourse, I will finally characterize as a "law of shadowing."

Various perspectives will help us understand how ancient biographers went about making imaginative worlds out of the lives of their heroes. Part I considers Graeco-Roman biographies from the standpoints of generic tradition and literary analysis and attempts to account for continuities and discontinuities within the biographical tradition. Basically, the argument of this section is that in the course of its long history, dating from the fifth century B.C., Greek biography developed characteristics that continued as hallmarks of the genre in Late Antiquity and made possible the kind of interplay between the mundane and the ideal that later biographers utilized.

Biography was unique in concentrating on the life of a single personality and in its panegyrical tendencies to exaggerate the account of that person's achievements. History, by comparison, spurned idealized narratives, concentrating instead on chronological reports of political and military events.

Biography was thus a halfway house between history and oratory, and biographers often consciously set themselves against the historians.[6] Biography was also unique in its interest in types of individuals. Hellenistic and Graeco-Roman biographers wrote systematic series of lives of politicians, emperors, generals, philosophers, and so on. Lives of politicians and military men, however, tended to remain close to political history, whereas lives of philosophers were idealized and often used by one school of philosophy as propaganda against competing schools.[7]

In the Graeco-Roman era, biographers sustained the idealized, contrahistorical mood of the genre, strongly emphasizing the achievements and personalities of the various philosophical masters and putting forth their lives not only as models to be used for the perpetuation of particular philosophical schools but also as polemics to be employed in furthering one tradition at the expense of others. In the third and fourth centuries, when the pagan philosophical schools and Christianity were vying with each other for recognition as the reigning spiritual guardian of the empire, biographies assumed the character of cultic hagiographies.

Biographies like Philostratus' *Life of Apollonius of Tyana*, Porphyry's *Lives* of Pythagoras and Plotinus, and Eusebius' "Life of Origen" all serve an old typological interest, the traditional sage of philosophy. But this venerable figure had been transformed by the religious temper of the times and was endowed with specific qualities and talents linking him to divinity. A mythology of the holy man could be used by the philosophical schools because philosophy itself, which had once resisted the incursions of religious speculation, came increasingly to denote the search for God.[8] Thus while biography had formerly been used in the battle of school against school, it was now used by cult against cult in the rivalry between paganism and Christianity, a rivalry whose intensity had reached a feverish pitch by the time these biographers were writing. Scrambling to gain adherents,

6. See the comments of Plutarch *Alexander* 1.1–2.

7. The earliest known practitioner of propagandistic biography was Aristoxenus of Tarentum, a fourth-century B.C. Pythagorean whose life of Pythagoras, accompanied by a description of the Pythagorean community's lifestyle and school, was written in conscious opposition to the Platonists.

8. On the equation of philosophy with religion, see E. R. Dodds, *Pagan and Christian in an Age of Anxiety* (New York: W. W. Norton, 1970), p. 92, who quotes the Hermetic *Asclepius* 12: "Philosophy consists solely in learning to know the deity by habitual contemplation and pious devotion."

each side produced biographies of its "patron saints" in an endeavor to crystallize belief and so win converts. One has only to consider the amount of space given over to discussions of disciples, teaching methods, and publications in biographies like Eusebius' of Origen and Porphyry's of Plotinus to understand that they are a form of propaganda for a way of life and a body of beliefs.

Part II is devoted to intensive studies of two biographies, Eusebius' "Life of Origen," and Porphyry's *Life of Plotinus*. Both characterize the hero as "godlike" rather than as a "son of god" (see chapter 2 for a discussion of this typology). They have been chosen for intensive analysis because they were written by men close in time and philosophical sympathy to their heroes and so show more clearly than other biographies an interaction between fact and fantasy that I think is the major characteristic of ancient biographies of holy men.

While chapters 4 and 5 both focus on the mythic world created by biographies of holy men, they provide two distinct ways of entering that world—two different approaches to the myth-making of ancient biographies. Both, however, attempt to imagine exactly how biographers went about "capturing the gesture."

The difference between the readings in these two chapters reflects the tension in the biographical tradition generally between *praxeis* (acts) and *ēthos* (character) which, in the context of biographies of holy men, we have called "fact and fantasy," or "the historical and the divine." Chapter 4 emphasizes the biographer's ability to evoke character from a reconstruction of his hero's acts or history. By showing how Eusebius "patterns" the various aspects of Origen's career, one can see how Eusebius' thematic structuring of history carries his vision of Origen's holiness. The focus in this chapter is on the biographer's historical imagination in order to show that one way to read an ancient biography is to investigate how the author has read character *as* history.

In chapter 5 the emphasis is reversed. Here we suggest that another way to read an ancient biography is to examine how the author has read history *as* character. Whereas in chapter 4 emphasis is placed on the thematic concerns of the biographer as historian, in this chapter the imagistic concerns of the biographer as poet are stressed. Again, whereas in the study of Eusebius' biography the "mystery" of historical reconstruction occupies center stage, in the study of Porphyry's work the mysterious process of embodying ideals of character is highlighted. The perspective developed in chapter 5 entails a more poetic, allusive approach to the material, since fantasies about a man's character cannot, after all, be reconstructed from sources in the way that his historical activities can.

Both chapters take the anecdotal mode of biographical narration seriously; but chapter 4 shows how anecdotes come together to give a biography thematic coherence, while chapter 5 takes anecdotes singly as evocative poetic images. Perhaps the difference can be stated quite simply. If, as we remarked earlier, biographies of holy men occupy a mythic "place between" fact and fantasy, then they can be viewed either as imaginal histories or as historicized mythic ideals. Chapter 4 is a reading of Eusebius' "Life of Origen" as imaginal history, while chapter 5 is a reading of Porphyry's *Life of Plotinus* as embodied poetry.

Finally, whether the entrée is by way of historical theme or poetic trope, both studies aim to show that the biographical portraits of holy men are neither solely fact nor solely fancy: they are, rather, both fact and fancy at once. Therein lies the persuasive power of their mythic appeal. As Porphyry said of the Delphic oracle's interpretation of the life of Plotinus, "We knew ourselves that he was like this."

PART I

Biography and Tradition: The Myth of Genre

CHAPTER ONE

Graeco-Roman Biography: Form and Function

In recent years, New Testament scholars have revived the search which began around the turn of this century[1] for a literary prototype of the gospels. This new quest, like the older one, has delved into Graeco-Roman literature to find a genre tradition that will elucidate the form (and, to a great extent, the content) of the gospels. The focus has been on ancient collections of miracle stories because the reigning hypothesis of both the old and the new quest is that at some point prior to the composition of the gospels, a literary form was developed that used as its basis these collections of miracle stories. This hypothetical genre has been labeled "aretalogy," since it is thought to have evolved from early cultic practices of reciting the virtuous and miraculous acts (*aretai*) of a divinity. The major interest of those involved in the new quest has been to extend the parameters of the genre to include any story of a man to whom marvelous activities or capacities are attributed. In other words, their goal is to substantiate the claim for the existence, early in the Hellenistic period, of a literary form that follows a fixed pattern for the life of a holy or supernaturally gifted man and so to

1. Representative works of the first phase of the search are Richard Reitzenstein, *Hellenistische Wundererzählungen* (Leipzig: B. G. Teubner, 1906) and Ludwig Bieler, *ΘΕΙΟΣ ΑΝΗΡ*, 2 vols. (Wien: Buchhandlung Oskar Höfels, 1935–36). For an exhaustive survey of the older works see Morton Smith, "Prolegomena to a Discussion of Aretalogies, Divine Men, the Gospels, and Jesus," *JBL* 90 (June, 1971): 174–99. Among modern scholars who have revived the interests of these older writers are Moses Hadas and Morton Smith, *Heroes and Gods* (New York: Harper and Row, 1965); David Tiede, *The Charismatic Figure as Miracle Worker*, SBL Dissertation Series, no. 1 (Missoula, Montana: Society of Biblical Literature, 1972); Helmut Koester, "One Jesus and Four Primitive Gospels," *HTR* 61 (1968): 203–47; Jonathan Z. Smith, "Good News Is No News: Aretalogy and Gospel," *Christianity, Judaism and Other Greco-Roman Cults*, Studies for Morton Smith at Sixty, ed. Jacob Neusner, 4 vols. (Leiden: E. J. Brill, 1975), vol. 1: *New Testament*, pp. 21–38; Howard Kee, "Aretalogy and Gospel," *JBL* 92 (September, 1973): 402–22.

establish a literary niche for the gospels. In marshaling evidence for this thesis, however, scholars have adduced biographies written long after the gospels as testimony to the developed form of earlier aretalogies, none of which are extant. Because of the assumptions underlying the aretalogy hypothesis, these later works, foremost among which are Philostratus' *Life of Apollonius of Tyana* and Porphyry's and Iamblichus' *Lives* of Pythagoras, have been considered primarily with respect to their treatment of miracles. The integrity of these biographies as literary works in their own right, written to confront issues and problems in their own societies, has thus been slighted in the effort to construct an earlier literary form from supposed later examples of it.

What makes "aretalogy" even more problematic is the existence in the same period as the works mentioned above of two biographies that clearly adhere to a schema of the divine sage yet do not use miracle working as a validating credential. These biographies are Porphyry's *Life of Plotinus* and Eusebius' "Life of Origen." Study of these two works and other biographies of the period has convinced me that it is impossible to define a stable literary pattern for the life of the holy man if miracles are posited as the organizing motif. Further, the attempt to construct from hindsight a hypothetical literary form does injustice to the literary works so used. The constricted notion of an aretalogical form based on a single motif leads to a distorted view of the divine sage; this figure cannot be equated with only one character trait. Also, the concentration on form has led to neglect of the social and philosophical contexts of the biographies. Meaning does not inhere in form alone; rather, form and content should be considered as interlocking features of the goals served by writing the biography. It is my contention that there is no need to postulate a new literary genre, "aretalogy," to explain the form and content of biographies that exhibit the "holy man" or the "divine sage." The historical development of Graeco-Roman biography provides a more suitable framework within which to consider these works. It gives a definite lineage for biography writing, and when later biographies are evaluated in the light of this lineage, the continuity in form, content, and function that the tradition fostered makes them more easily understood.

Early Formation of Biography

Jacob Burckhardt once vehemently accused Eusebius of being "the first thoroughly dishonest historian of antiquity" because of the historical misconceptions fostered by the idealizations in his *Life of Constantine*.[2] A similar charge could easily be made against Eusebius' biography of Origen—indeed, against any ancient biography. Though Burckhardt's observation that Constantine's virtues are given a lavishly panegyrical treatment by Eusebius is certainly true, his charge of dishonesty is misbegotten. Burckhardt's error was to judge Eusebius' biography according to the canons of history writing. The fact is, however, that in antiquity biography was not simply a subgenre of history. It had its own unique characteristics, and sustained historical veracity was not one of them. To impugn the integrity of a Graeco-Roman biography on the basis of factual discrepancy is to misconceive the literary tradition of the genre to which it belongs.

As early as the fifth century B.C., Greek writers made a distinction between historiography and erudite research. Historiography focused on political and military events and excluded any systematic treatment of religious and social phenomena. Its tone was didactic and proposed to be "useful" to posterity, and it insisted upon a strict adherence to chronology. Thucydides' straightforward dedication of the historian's craft to truth based on observable data defined the essence of historical methodology for centuries: "And with reference to the narrative of events, far from permitting myself to derive it from the first source that came to hand, I did not even trust my own impressions, but it rests partly on what I saw myself, partly on what others saw for me, the accuracy of the report always tried by the most severe and detailed tests possible."[3] With tongue in cheek, Thucydides regrets that the "absence of romance" in his history may result in rather dull reading. He strongly disapproved of incorporating traditions into historical narrative which might make it "attractive at truth's expense."[4] The writers at whom this scorn was aimed were what we would call antiquarians, whose erudite monographs, often systematic or topical rather than chronological in organization, dealt with religious ceremonies, art, manners and mores, and the history of lesser-known cities and nations. Unlike Thucydidean historiography, which depended heavily on oral testimony, erudite research looked to written sources, including archival documents, for its material.[5] Antiquarian scholars differed from classical histo-

2. Jacob Burckhardt, *The Age of Constantine the Great*, trans. Moses Hadas (New York: Pantheon Books, 1949), p. 283.

3. Thucydides 1.23.

4. Ibid., 1.20–22.

5. Arnaldo Momigliano, "Historiography on Written and on Oral Tradition," *Studies in Historiography* (London: Weidenfeld and Nicolson, 1966), pp. 216–17. Examples of erudite

rians in yet another marked respect: they took individual achievement into account, whereas historians concentrated on the activities of the collective body of the state.[6]

The predilections of Greek biographers were much the same as those of the antiquarians. Biography appears to have developed within the context of erudite research, reflecting its interest in phenomena apart from mainline Greek politics. The earliest known biographers, Skylax of Caryanda and Xanthus of Lydia, were older contemporaries of Herodotus. Although Herodotus labeled them *logopoioi*[7] and Thucydides considered them among the *logographoi*, the pioneer historians,[8] these writers actually share the logographers' preoccupation with mythographic treatises, geographical travelogues, and cultural histories of non-Greek civilizations; this places them rather in the antiquarian camp.[9] Skylax of Caryanda, for example, wrote a treatise describing his travels along the Indian coasts as well as an account of the life of Heraclides, tyrant of Mylasa; and Xanthus of Lydia, who composed a work on the life of the philosopher Empedocles, wrote his major treatise on the history of his native land.[10]

Though some form of biographical writing is thus attested early in the fifth century B.C., the genre was not distinguished by receiving a name, *bios*, until the Hellenistic period.[11] Scholarly attempts at ferreting out the obscure genealogy of ancient Greek biography have variously credited both the Academy and the Peripatos with the invention of the genre. Representative of the partisans of the Academy, Albrecht Dihle theorized that the necessary prerequisite for the subject of biography writing was a charismatic personality—for example, Socrates, whose force of character led to the collecting of his personality traits by the Socratic schoolmen. Friedrich Leo, advocate of the Peripatos, traced the invention of biography proper to the Aristotelian school and characterized two branches of biographical de-

---

works are: Hippias, list of Olympic victors and monograph on names of nations; Critias, study of different constitutions.

6. Arnaldo Momigliano, *The Development of Greek Biography* (Cambridge: Harvard University Press, 1971), pp. 39–40.

7. Herodotus 2.134, 143.

8. Thucydides 1.21.

9. See Lionel Pearson, *Early Ionian Historians* (Oxford: Clarendon Press, 1939).

10. Momigliano, *Development of Greek Biography*, pp. 29–31.

11. In *Development of Greek Biography*, p. 12, Momigliano notes that the term *biographia* is of a much later provenance. The earliest surviving reference to it is in Damascius' *Life of Isidorus* dating from the end of the fifth century A.D.

velopment: the "Plutarchian" type—chronologically ordered biography which grew from the early Peripatetics' desire to characterize statesmen in the way that their master had characterized states; and the "Suetonian" type—systematically arranged biography developed by antiquarians to portray literati and artists.[12] Though both of these theses are open to objections, what remains true of their interpretations is the important role attributed to the Academy and the Peripatos in the gradual evolution of biography.

The long-standing interest of the Greeks in preserving traditions surrounding such mythical heroes as Heracles, Theseus, and the Seven Wise Men received its complement in the fourth century when the Socratic school memorialized an historical hero, Socrates. The apologies produced after Socrates' death by Plato and Xenophon, while not biographies in full flower, contain elements that became standard features of later biographical portraits. The *Apology* and the *Memorabilia* create a charged atmosphere in which neither fact nor fiction prevails. Plutarch once wrote that "when history descended from its poetical chariot and walked on foot, it distinguished between myth and truth."[13] In contrast to history, these apologies present an intermingling of fantasy and historical reality with the intent of capturing the ideals suggested by the actual life. The reader is confronted with a conflict between earthly and supramundane truth, a tension that later biographers will exploit for the benefit of their own particular philosophical visions.

Among Socratic contributors to biography, the foremost was Xenophon. His "apology" for Socrates, the *Memorabilia*, was written to counter the *Accusation of Socrates*, an attack on Socrates by the Sophist Polycrates written shortly after the death of the philosopher. Xenophon's work was not, however, a pugnacious counterattack but rather a favorable commentary on Socrates' philosophical principles and corresponding behavior. Xenophon's presentation is not what we would normally expect in a biographical work since there is no systematic ordering of the events in Socrates' life from birth to death. His method is to develop Socrates' character by presenting illustrative (and imaginary) dialogues pertaining to Socrates' social and moral

12. Albrecht Dihle, *Studien zur griechischen Biographie* (Göttingen: Vandenbroeck and Ruprecht, 1956); Friedrich Leo, *Die griechisch-römische Biographie nach ihrer litterarischen Form* (Leipzig: B. G. Teubner, 1901). The theses of both of these works are discussed and criticized by Momigliano, *Development of Greek Biography*, pp. 17–20, 86–87.

13. Plutarch *Pyth. orac.* 24, 406e.

tenets. Interspersed with the dialogues are anecdotes and incidents that give indications of Socrates' personal traits. The *Memorabilia* thus contains basic ingredients of biography: the first two books give an account of the man's character, while succeeding books illustrate this by conversations and stories.[14] It is significant that the conversations that Xenophon presents are not, for the most part, authentic reproductions of Socrates' speeches. They are, rather, a distillation of the best of Socrates' thought, and represent what Socrates *could* have said, even if, historically speaking, he did not. This convention of presenting as fact something that could have taken place but did not is what rhetoricians would later define as myth.[15] The process of "mythologizing" a man's life by using fiction to convey truth became one of the enduring features of biography.

Another of Xenophon's biographical experiments, the *Agesilaus*, was based on a prose encomium model formalized by the Athenian rhetor Isocrates. In his *Evagoras*, Isocrates followed the custom of previous encomiasts, according to which the traits of the man considered were made to conform to preconceived notions of the virtues inherent in that man's particular occupation.[16] Thus the Cypriot Evagoras assumes the mantle of Isocrates' conception of the ideal monarch. The organizational scheme that Isocrates used, while basically chronological, was punctuated with descriptions of the hero's virtues apart from his acts.[17] It was this combination of a systematic review of virtues and a chronological narrative of the life itself, albeit in rudimentary form in the *Evagoras*, that Xenophon seized upon and developed in his *Agesilaus*.

Two features of Xenophon's *Agesilaus* are important for understanding subsequent developments in the composition of biography. The first is the bipartite division of the biography into *praxeis*, a chronological account of the life, and *ēthos*, a systematic treatment of character.[18] These two categories had been presented in a haphazard mixture in Isocrates' *Evagoras*, but

14. Duane Reed Stuart, *Epochs of Greek and Roman Biography* (Berkeley: University of California Press, 1928), pp. 33–34; Momigliano, *Development of Greek Biography*, pp. 52–54.

15. Aelius Theon, *Progymnasmata* 3, defined myth as *logos pseudēs eikonizōn alētheian*. See the discussion in Robert M. Grant, *Earliest Lives of Jesus* (London: SPCK, 1961), pp. 37–43, 121–22.

16. Stuart, *Epochs of Greek and Roman Biography*, p. 64.

17. See Leo, *Die griechisch-römische Biographie*, pp. 91–92; Momigliano, *Development of Greek Biography*, pp. 49–50; and Hadas, *Heroes and Gods*, p. 8.

18. Leo, *Die griechisch-römische Biographie*, p. 91.

Xenophon separated them into distinct sections. The interaction of *praxeis* and *ēthos* continued as the major focus of biographers like Plutarch and Suetonius. Although Xenophon's two-part format was not always rigidly adhered to, its significance lies in the fact that the hero's deeds were clearly viewed as a backdrop for his virtues: the historical elements of the man's life, while important, were subservient to the essence of his life, his noble character. Xenophon's *Agesilaus* thus illustrates the biographers' use of historical detail to lend credence to the ideal portrait they were concerned to develop. The second important feature of the *Agesilaus* is its emphasis on the youth and education of its hero. Historians were interested primarily in the military and political prowess of men at the height of their careers, but biographers, following the precedent set by Xenophon, presumed to recognize the seed of greatness in the child and then to trace the fruit of that seed in the charmed manhood of the hero.[19]

As a contributor to the development of biography, Xenophon had counterparts in the Aristotelian school. It is probable that biographical writing within the Peripatos was stimulated in part by its interest in individual writers. Treatises like *On Sappho* and *On Pindar* were historical exegeses of passages from the particular author's work, not biographies, but they used the technique of extracting information about the lives of writers from allusions in their works. Related to this process of biographical deduction was the interest of Peripatetics in the various competing philosophical schools, which resulted in collections of anecdotes about philosophers, like Dicaearchus' *Lives*.[20] Another important result of this fascination with fellow philosophical schools was the growth of a kind of biographical polemic against them. For example, in his work on the Socratics, Phainias of Eresus included stories about some of the philosophers that were clearly discreditable and that tended to cast a shadow on the school's reputation. Although, as Momigliano speculates, this kind of polemic was first written by Peripatetics, it soon became the "common patrimony" of Hellenistic literature.[21]

19. In *Die griechisch-römische Biographie*, pp. 89–90, Leo notes that Thucydides' portrayal of character was confined to the intellect, whereas in Xenophon's biographical writings there is a "determined turn toward the moral," an indication that men are important in themselves and not simply for the course of History writ large.

20. Ibid., pp. 99–101; Momigliano, *Development of Greek Biography*, pp. 69–72.

21. *Development of Greek Biography*, pp. 71–72. Examples from other schools are the hostile works "On the Socratics" by the Epicurean Idomeneus and "On the Stoics" by Philodemus.

The most outstanding biographer that the Aristotelian school produced united the various biographical impulses of Peripatetic literature to form full-fledged biographies. He was Aristoxenus of Tarentum, a Pythagorean convert to the Peripatos whose fame as a biographer is attested by Jerome's citation of him as one of Suetonius' predecessors.[22] Aristoxenus' *Lives*, which included biographies of Pythagoras, Socrates, and Plato, were, like Xenophon's biographies, marked by the use of legendary traditions, the invention of characteristic traits, and the use of anecdotes as a method for depicting character, though he seems to have been the first to make anecdotes a basic component of biography.[23] More important, however, is the fact that he capitalized upon the Hellenistic habit of composing derogatory books on rival philosophical schools by using biography for this purpose. Aristoxenus' abiding dislike was focused on the Socratic school. In the *Life of Plato*, his malice against the school's master was revealed in his insistent accusation that Plato had plagiarized "the fruit" of Pythagoras' doctrines.[24] Even more indicative of his hostility toward the Academy was his *Life of Socrates*. His characterization of Socrates was little short of scathing. Socrates is portrayed as an uneducated, undisciplined man whose temper was often uncontrollable.[25] He is accused of an excessive need for sexual pleasures, and rumors concerning pederasty with his teacher Archelaus and bigamy are related as fact.[26] This is not the rational, self-controlled Socrates that one would expect. It is difficult to avoid concluding that Aristoxenus was using Socrates as a scapegoat for the school of which he was the traditional founder, since Aristoxenus was born thirty years after the philosopher's death and so could have had no personal enmity against him. Evidence for this scapegoat function and the corresponding lack of personal spite as a motive for the biography is the fact that Aristoxenus' most serious

22. "apud Graecos Hermippus Peripateticus, Antigonus Carystius, Satyrus doctor vir et omnium longe doctissimus Aristoxenus Musicus." *De viris inlustribus*, pref. By way of noting the importance of the Aristotelians' contribution to biography, only one of these four, Antigonus, was not connected with the Peripatetic school.

23. Leo, *Die griechisch-römische Biographie*, pp. 102–103.

24. "*ta men karpima spheterisasthai*." See *Die Schule des Aristoteles*, ed. Fritz Wehrli, 10 vols. (Basel: Benno Schwabe and Co. Verlag, 1944–1959), vol. 2: *Aristoxenos* (1945), p. 27, fr. 68 (= Porphyry *Vita Pythagorae* 53).

25. "*apaideuton kai amathē kai akolaston*," Wehrli, *Aristoxenos*, p. 25, fr. 55; "*hōs phūsei gegogei trachus eis orgēn*," ibid., fr. 56.

26. Ibid., p. 24, fr. 52b (pederasty); pp. 24–25, fr. 57–58 (bigamy).

charge against Socrates, that of sexual licentiousness, was a stylized mode of defamation that had been applied to Pericles and a veritable host of others.[27]

Aristoxenus' *Life of Pythagoras* was perhaps meant to be a weapon in the same anti-Socratic battle. Pythagoras assumes the role of rational wise man and moralist credited with founding a society of virtuous sages. Aristoxenus' technique in this biography is the same as in the *Life of Socrates*: he presents only one aspect of the traditional lore surrounding the philosopher. His portrait of Socrates uses material that maligns Socrates' reputation and excludes favorable opinion, while his depiction of Pythagoras ignores or explicitly counters earlier traditions that cloaked Pythagoras in an aura of the supernatural and emphasizes instead his numerological and musical contributions to philosophy and his rational approach to the conduct of human affairs.[28] Also, just as the biography of Socrates was an indictment of the Socratic school, so the biography of Pythagoras commends the Pythagorean community as a whole with sympathetic descriptions of its lifestyle.[29]

Aristoxenus' biography of Pythagoras was highly regarded by later biographers. It formed the heart of the *Life of Pythagoras* by Nicomachus of Gerasa and is quoted frequently by Porphyry and Iamblichus in their biographies of Pythagoras.[30] Although the lineage of polemical biography cannot be traced from Aristoxenus' time to the Imperial era due to the loss of most of the biographical writing from the third to the first centuries, his school orientation must be credited as a milestone in the use of biography. His method of glorifying or condemning a philosophical school by creating a biographical caricature of a representative of that school was taken up by such authors as Philostratus, Porphyry, Eusebius, and Iamblichus in the

27. The accusation against Pericles is reported by Plutarch *Pericles* 13–14. See Stuart, *Epochs of Greek and Roman Biography*, p. 148, for further examples.

28. For earlier miracle traditions about Pythagoras, and Aristoxenus' criticism of them, see Isidore Lévy, *Recherches sur les sources de la légende de Pythagore* (Paris: Éditions Ernest Leroux, 1926), pp. 6–22, 46–48. For an example of Pythagoras' statesmanship according to Aristoxenus, see Wehrli, *Aristoxenos*, p. 12, fr. 17 (= Porphyry *Vita Pythagorae* 21–22), where Pythagoras is represented as bringing democracy and justice to cities in Italy and Sicily.

29. For Aristoxenus' good opinion of the Pythagorean community, see Wehrli, *Aristoxenos*, p. 16, fr. 30 (= Iamblichus *Vita Pythagorica* 197), which shows that Pythagoreans never act in anger, and ibid., pp. 16–17, fr. 31 (= Iamblichus *Vita Pythagorica* 233), which describes friendship within Pythagorean circles.

30. See the detailed source analysis of Porphyry's *Vita Pythagorae* and Iamblichus' *Vita Pythagorica* in Lévy, *Recherches sur les sources de la légende de Pythagore*, pp. 90–128.

battle between pagans and Christians in the third and fourth centuries. His biographies are good examples of how legend, history, and pure fabrication were combined in the production of biographical portraits. This stylized exaggeration of either virtues or vices was the essence of early Greek biography, and it continued to dominate the character of biography writing under the Empire.

Biography in the Imperial Age

By the beginning of the Imperial era, biography had gained currency as an established literary genre. The distinctiveness of the genre was made explicit by Plutarch, who used historiography as the standard against which to define biography much in the same way that classical writers had contrasted erudite monographs with history. According to Plutarch, the difference between history and biography lay not primarily in form but in content. Using the same basic categories that Xenophon had used, *praxeis* and *ēthos*, he stated that history depicts the *praxeis* of men whereas biography illustrates the *ēthos* of a man. In biography, a man's acts are recounted only to the extent that they shed light upon his character.[31] This theory of biographical composition explains why Plutarch pleads with his readers not to criticize the selective nature of his account of deeds and events in his biography of Alexander. For biography does not aim to give exhaustive historical reporting. It succeeds in its portrayal of character by a careful selection of whatever actions serve best to illustrate it.[32] This "pars pro toto" technique was well suited to the perpetuation of political and moral ideals.

31. Plutarch, *Pompey* 8. See also the prefaces to his biographies of Julius Caesar, Nicias, and Galba.

32. On selectivity in biography see Plutarch, *Alexander* 1.1–2: "For it is not histories that I am writing, but lives; and in the most illustrious deeds there is not always a manifestation of virtue or vice, nay a slight thing like a phrase or jest often makes a greater revelation of character than battles where thousands fall." That biography could be distinguished from history primarily by its concentration on character is illustrated by late Hellenistic literary theory, which viewed character portrayal as only one component of history. The subject matter for true history is defined by the first-century B.C. grammarian, Asclepiades of Myrleia: "*tēs de alēthous, tria palin merē: hē men gar esti peri ta prosōpa theōn kai hērōōn kai andrōn epiphanōn, hē de peri tous topous kai chronous, hē de peri tas praxeis.*" (Quoted in Richard Reitzenstein, *Hellenistische Wundererzählungen* [Leipzig: B. G. Teubner, 1906], pp. 90–91). It is obvious that at least in Plutarch's opinion, biography was concerned only with *ta prosōpa*

Like other biographers, Plutarch was not an unbiased observer of character. He maintained the standpoint of moral judge, and in this sense his biographies are pedagogical since they measure character against certain ideal virtues. Usually "men above the crowd," the individuals delineated by Plutarch became historical exempla of preconceived notions about the characteristics which men in certain societal niches should possess. The historical selectivity that Plutarch claimed for biography made the matching of the person with the ideal possible without tedious apology for actions that deviated from the model put forth. Plutarch did not, however, indulge in heavy-handed moralizing; rather, he presented the life of the hero from birth to death and inserted characterizations along the way—much in the manner of Isocrates—and he took care to note the early appearance of traits that influenced and guided the course of the entire life considered.[33]

Plutarch's interest in types of men was shared by his fellow biographer, Suetonius, whose *Lives of the Caesars* used the now-familiar *praxeis–ēthos* categories. But in the biographies of Suetonius, as in the *Agesilaus* of Xenophon, the narrative of events is little more than a framework for the discussion of character. Although, like Plutarch, Suetonius was interested in portraying ideal traits that statesmen should possess, he used biography as a vehicle to criticize as well as to extol. He did not refrain from constructing rather scurrilous profiles of those emperors who exemplified the dark side of his political ideal and thus evaluated the emperors on the basis of two models, one of virtue and one of vice. The individual personality was not entirely subsumed by the type since he personalized his portraits of the various emperors by reporting distinguishing traits and habits. However, it is indicative of the tendency of biography to stylize reports of character that

---

andrōn; matters of place, time, and action were introduced only to highlight character. Literary theorists were not unanimous in their definitions of history, however, and their confusion makes it difficult to discover a precise niche for biography within literary theory apart from what the biographers themselves say. Cicero, for example, supposed history to be no more than a collection of models to be studied for the purpose of "calling to our minds illustrious and courageous men and their deeds, not for any gain but for the honor that lies in praising their nobility by itself" (*De finibus* 1.10.36). This sounds very close to the ideals biography espoused. However, Quintilian *Oratorical Institutes* 10.1.31 and Polybius 12.25–28 both held to the Thucydidean style of history devoted to truth and the transmission of events. For detailed discussions see G. M. A. Grube, *The Greek and Roman Critics* (London: Methuen and Co., Ltd., 1965), pp. 157–58, 170–72; and Reitzenstein, *Hellenistische Wundererzählungen*, pp. 84–94.

33. Leo, *Die griechisch-römische Biographie*, pp. 179–85.

Suetonius followed closely the schemata contained in current handbooks of physiognomy.[34]

The physiognomists sought to reveal a man's virtuous or vicious nature by emphasizing certain aspects of the physique and linking these to specific character traits. Suetonius was the first biographer to connect the physical and moral portraits of a man in this way; and though it would be difficult to agree with one scholar's opinion that his biographies were scientific studies of personality,[35] given his overriding interest in ideal types, it is certain that he was an astute observer of human foibles and cleverly integrated his observations with physiognomic theory.

Suetonius' source for his physiognomical material was the handbook of Pseudo-Aristotle, *Physiognomy*,[36] which provided three principal methods of description. The first described the body with general phrases; the second described the effects of emotion on the face or body; and the third involved a photographic description of the entire body.[37] It was this third method that Suetonius used, and he applied it in the greatest detail when dealing with those emperors whose characters he regarded as extreme: monsters like Tiberius, Caligula, and Nero; heroes like Caesar and Augustus. One example of each extreme will be sufficient to show how this physiognomical artifice allowed Suetonius to propagandize for his political principles by creating ideal and demonic types for the Imperial character.

Suetonius' description of Augustus in *Augustus* 79 has exact parallels in the physiognomical literature. Augustus' "clear, bright eyes" signify energy and boldness (Pseudo-Aristotle 15; 68); his wavy golden hair denotes a well-endowed nature (Pseudo-Aristotle 69, 41; Polemo 39); his aquiline nose means greatness of soul (Pseudo-Aristotle 61; Polemo 34); and the

34. On the topic of ancient physiognomy, see Geneva Misener, "Iconistic Portraits," *Classical Philology* 19 (1924): 97–123; Elizabeth C. Evans, "The Study of Physiognomy in the 2nd century A.D.," *Transactions and Proceedings of the American Philological Association* 72 (1941): 96–108; idem, "Roman Descriptions of Personal Appearance in History and Biography," *Harvard Studies in Classical Philology* 46 (1935): 43–84.

35. Jean Coussin, "Suetone Physiognomiste dans les Vies des XII Césars," *Revue des études Latines* 31 (1953): 255.

36. It is possible that Suetonius also knew the work of his contemporary, Polemo of Laodicea, Sophist and friend of Hadrian, who wrote a treatise based on the *Physiognomonica*. On Polemo, see Philostratus *Vitae Sophistarum* 1.530–44. Texts of Pseudo-Aristotle and Polemo are in *Scriptores Physiognomonici*, ed. R. Förster, 2 vols. (Leipzig: B. G. Teubner, 1893).

37. Evans, "Roman Descriptions of Personal Appearance in History and Biography," pp. 44–45.

"fine proportion and symmetry" of his body are characteristic of an upright and brave man (Pseudo-Aristotle 13; Polemo 44). Similar parallels can be found in the portrait of Caligula, *Gaius Caligula* 50. Caligula's pale skin means cowardliness and a taste for inflicting harm (Pseudo-Aristotle 31); his "very thin neck" denotes a lack of energy, bad morals, and a dishonest spirit (Pseudo-Aristotle 59; Polemo 31); his hollow eyes and temples indicate folly and an agitated nature (Pseudo-Aristotle 63); his "broad and grim" forehead signifies bestiality, drunkenness, and avarice (Pseudo-Aristotle 64; Polemo 17).

Suetonius' physical descriptions of the emperors, which often bring to mind grotesque images, are not simply photographic impressions of the actual men. He had never even seen the earlier emperors; and in the case of Caligula, for example, statues and coins give an impression of physical beauty that hardly coheres with Suetonius' portrait—and this in an age when iconography was leaning more and more toward realism.[38] Suetonius' physical descriptions were not based solely on physical appearance, then, but were taken from physiognomic manuals that attached definite moral attitudes to specific bodily features. This method of typecasting was not so esoteric as it might seem, for physiognomical theory had captured the imagination of a broad spectrum of the Graeco-Roman literati.[39]

Suetonius' biographies are good examples of a major dynamic operative in biography writing: the molding of a man's character to a preconceived model. From its inception, biography was marked by its encomiastic tendencies to exaggerate a person's achievements and virtues, carefully selecting traits and deeds that lent themselves to idealization. Heroes were created by using historical detail as a backdrop to display nobility of character; the ideal would thus gain credence by having a base in historical reality. Certain literary and thematic devices aided the process of characterization: the use of legendary materials and rumor, the invention of character traits, the use of anecdotes and speeches, and the development of character from traits revealed in childhood. Equally important for the uniqueness of biog-

38. See, for example, the realistic sculpture of Vespasian and Titus in J. J. Bernoulli, *Römische Ikonographie*, 2 vols. (Stuttgart: W. Spemann, 1882–94), vol. 1, plate 7. Nero was also treated realistically: Bernoulli, vol. 2, plates 23–25.

39. The following writers, to name a few, all commented on physiognomical theory: Seneca *Ep.* 52.12; Tacitus *Ann.* 13.8, 15.53, 4.57; Pliny *NH* 11.143–46, 11.274; Clement of Alexandria *Paedagogus* 2.5, 46, *Protrepticus* 2.26; Origen *Contra Celsum* 1.33; Ammianus Marcellinus 15.8.16, 23.5.15.

raphy as a genre was its propagandistic, often polemical, mood. The biographies of Aristoxenus and Suetonius were often profound critiques of men who far from measuring up to an ideal exemplified its reverse. The philosophical, scholastic orientation of Aristoxenus was also a polemical device; he used biography as a weapon to further the cause of one school at the expense of others by making an individual philosopher the embodiment of the virtues, or vices, of his school. The conclusion that many of these biographies were written to sway, perhaps even create, opinion about certain political and philosophical principles is unavoidable.

The biographies to which we now turn exhibit the idealizing and propagandistic features of Graeco-Roman biography but with a crucial addition. They were involved in religious controversy and so attempted to sway not mere opinion but belief. We shall see that the nature of this struggle led to a new standard for biographical idealization, the "divine sage," a literary type that became a major influence on the portrayal of the character of philosophers in Late Antiquity.

CHAPTER TWO

Biography and Paradigms of the Divine Sage

Biographers of Late Antiquity thought divinity to be a distinguishing characteristic of the philosopher. This conviction can be viewed as an intensification of older philosophical notions of the extent to which men can be divine. Plato, for example, stated in *The Republic* that "the lover of wisdom, by keeping company with the divine and orderly, becomes himself divine and orderly in so far as it is possible for man," but he qualified this statement by adding that "there is much imbalance in all men." Any man who loves wisdom, then, is divine because his love places him in harmony with cosmic order; no man, however, is completely divine since we are all prey to human factiousness. Aristotle held a similar opinion. Writing about the life of contemplation, he remarked in the *Nicomachean Ethics* that consistent practice of such a life is beyond our mortal element: "for it is not in so far as he is man that he will live so, but in so far as something divine is present in him." Reason is divine, and the "activity of philosophic wisdom" is divine in comparison with ordinary human life.[1]

Six centuries later, the Neoplatonic philosopher Porphyry could speak of the philosopher as the "priest of the universal god."[2] Notions of what the philosophic life is, and who is capable of living it, had undergone a great change, such that the comments of Plato and Aristotle would have seemed gross understatements to their philosophical heirs, the intellectual elite of Porphyry's time. A more aristocratic idea had replaced their rather egalitarian thought that once apprised of the course of the truly virtuous life, all men could at least aspire toward philosophy, the one divine activity. For Porphyry's contemporaries, philosophy was a profession limited to a select

1. Plato *The Republic* 500c–d; Aristotle *Nicomachaean Ethics* 1177a–b.
2. Porphyry *De abstinentia* 2.49: "*ho tou epi pasin theou hiereus.*"

group, the teachers of the religious sects and of the philosophical circles, and dedicated to a single end, knowledge of god.

By the third century, there was no question that philosophy was an essentially religious endeavor. A passage from the Hermetic treatise *Asclepius* states the case succinctly: "Philosophy consists solely in learning to know the deity by habitual contemplation and pious devotion."[3] The practical, action-oriented life of the human community was denigrated: it was a "tragi-comedy," a "shadow of contemplation," an inferior mode of being.[4] Pagan and Christian alike subscribed to an ontological doctrine that defined the real as the degree of one's assimilation, through contemplation and other salvific acts, to the divine.[5] Though all men were thought to contain a divine spark—Sextus stated that to see God would be to see oneself[6]—only a few were sufficiently aware of it.[7] These latter were, of course, the sages, whose souls were "God's mirror."[8] As Porphyry remarked, the sage became divine by his likeness to God,[9] and his contemporaries looked to him as a spiritual doctor and moral guide.[10] The philosopher, then, was the man

3. *Asclepius* 12 (*Corpus Hermeticum* 2.312). See also Maximus of Tyre (*Diss.* 5.8) who states that philosophy is the only pure religion, and Apuleius (*De Dog. Plat.* 2.7) who identifies justice with holiness. Christians too considered philosophy to be identical to religion. Among the apologists, Melito of Sardis (in Eusebius *HE* 4.26), Athenagoras (*Supplicato pro Christianis* 2), and Justin (*Dialogue with Trypho* 2ff.) all regard Christianity as philosophy. Reading his own convictions into the past, Justin suggested that the vision of God was the true goal of Plato's philosophy, an opinion that came to be widely accepted among all philosophers, regardless of their sectarian affiliations (*Dialogue* 2.3–6). But the only true philosophy that alone could lead men back to God was, of course, Christianity (*Dialogue* 8.1, 2.1). Clement of Alexandria had a more complicated definition: on the one hand, true philosophy was the knowledge transmitted by Christ; on the other, Greek philosophy properly so called was simply a preparation for the perfection offered by life as a Christian (*Stromata* 1.18.90, 1.3.28). Eusebius used the term "philosophy" to mean both Christian doctrine and the ascetic life (*Praeparatio evangelica* 12.29). For further examples see Gustave Bardy, "'Philosophie' et 'philosophe' dans le vocabulaire chrétien des premiers siècles," *Revue d'ascétique et de mystique* 25 (April-December, 1949):97–108.

4. Porphyry *Ad Marcellam* 2; Plotinus *Enn.* 3.8.4.

5. See, for example, Plotinus *Enn.* 1.2.6; Clement of Alexandria *Stromata* 6.113.3: human life should be directed toward becoming a god (realizing fully one's divine potential).

6. Sextus 446. 7. Plotinus *Enn.* 1.6.8. 8. Sextus 450.

9. Porphyry *Ad Marcellam* 285.20.

10. See, for example, Clement of Alexandria, who held that the person who had gained mastery over his desires was able to see God; being raised above the body, that person would be filled with the spirit and possess insight into the imperceptible world. Those who reach this height, "friends of God," become the counsellors and spiritual leaders of others (*Stromata*

who had an assured share in the divine kingdom;[11] he was free to take what Plotinus, quoting Homer, called true advice: "'Let us fly to our dear country,'" the realm of the soul.[12]

But the philosopher was not simply a passive figure, content to occupy a saintly periphery in ancient society. He was a man with a mission, a mission that was central to life in Late Antiquity: to communicate the divine, and to protect from the demonic. By the first century A.D., the philosopher—whether he was a roving preacher, a magician-prophet, or an acknowledged leader of a particular school of thought—had become a holy man in the eyes of his fellows, and his prestige was such that admirers were able to make extravagant claims for his abilities.[13] Indeed the *idea* of the holy man became at least as important as the men themselves, for their existence (or, perhaps, their reputations) attested to the gods' concern for the welfare of humankind.

The idea of the philosopher as holy man had a dramatic effect on biographical portrayals of philosophers in the Imperial age. The sage was, of course, a time-honored, traditional paradigm; and we have seen how earlier biographers developed certain literary techniques and modes of presentation that allowed them to concentrate on the ideals suggested by the actual lives of their subjects. In later biographies by such authors as Philostratus, Porphyry, Eusebius, and Iamblichus, the great wisdom and noble character of the philosopher are augmented, and sometimes overshadowed, by specific qualities and talents linking him to divinity. These "holy" embellishments on the image of the philosopher represent more than a simple application of a divine veneer, however; they signify a major shift in cultural values. This shift had several aspects: the flowering of heroic asceticism; the

---

6.102.2, 7.13.1, 8.19.2, 6.106.2, 7.3.4). Damis' praise of Apollonius is instructive here: "for when I first met with Apollonius here, he at once struck me as full of wisdom and cleverness and sobriety and of true endurance; but when I saw that he also had a good memory, and that he was very learned and entirely devoted to love of learning, he became to me something superhuman; and I came to the conclusion that if I stuck to him I should be held a wise man instead of an ignoramus and a dullard, and an educated man instead of a savage." Philostratus *Vita Apollonii* 3.43.

11. Sextus 311. For a wealth of examples, see Karl Holl, "Die schriftstellerische Form des Griechischen Heiligenlebens," *Neue Jahrbücher für klassische Altertum* 29 (1912): 414–18.

12. Plotinus *Enn.* 1.6.8.

13. On the claims of holy men, see the comment of Dio Chrysostom 33.4: "It seems to me that one often hears about divine men [*theiōn anthrōpōn*] who say that they know all things and speak about all things."

conflation (and confusion) of several modes of "philosophic" activity, including miracle- and magic working, prophecy, and the more usual business of superior intellection; and the wholesale allegiance of both pagans and Christians to the new holy personality cult.

The appearance of the divine philosopher also represents major changes on the literary scene: the biographical genre came to be closely associated with holy sages—so closely, in fact, that Lucian of Samosata chose a biographical framework within which to satirize holy men; biography helped create and promote the myth of the holy man and was not simply a vehicle for reporting idealistic embroiderings on historical lives; biography became an important tool, along with apology, in the proselytizing of Christians and pagans; and, finally, the special techniques that biography traditionally used to portray character were refined and, in a sense, "institutionalized"—in other words, biography now included certain necessary ingredients.

In this chapter, we will examine the new divine image of the philosopher and the cultural significance of the emergence and popularity of this figure. The chapter that follows will document in detail how the idea of the divine philosopher transformed, and was transformed by, biography.

The Character of the Holy Philosopher

The idea that wise men were somehow divine was not simply a figment of the biographers' imagination; nor was the mantle of holiness forced upon philosophers. There is some evidence that philosophers were not unwitting recipients of this new honor. Apollonius of Tyana, for example, was fully aware that other men considered him a god, and he himself believed that he was "superior to most men."[14] Origen, the great biblical exegete, implied that he possessed the grace of the mind of Christ when he stated that accurate scriptural interpretation demanded that grace.[15] Although these "intimations of immortality" on the part of the philosophers themselves are pale reflections of the opinions that their biographers recorded, they illustrate

14. Apollonius *Ep.* 44: "Other men regard me as the equal of the gods [*isotheon*] and some of them even as a god. . . . I am superior to most men, both in my language and in my character." It is important to note that the authenticity of Apollonius' letters is disputed. See Eduard Norden, *Agnostos Theos: Untersuchungen zur Formengeschichte Religiöser Rede* (Leipzig: B. G. Teubner, 1913), pp. 49–56, 94, 337–46.

15. Origen *De principiis* 4.2.3.

nevertheless the important point that conceptions of divinity differed. For some the claim of actual godhood could be made, while others were thought to occupy a more modest god*like* status.

There was in fact a complex battery of characteristics of the holy man from which biographers were free to choose: Morton Smith has remarked upon the veritable "mob of divine or deified men" known to Graeco-Roman antiquity.[16] Stories that were circulated and written down about heroes, demigods, magicians, prophets, healers, and the like provided a copious depository of traits that might signify divinity. It should be noted, however, that in this period the idea that men could be divine did not include absolute identification with the supreme god, whether he be Zeus, the Neoplatonic One, or the Christian God.[17] Pagans and Christians agreed that the supreme god was incorporeal, unchanging, and incapable of mixing with the material realm. Identification with this god was certainly an ideal. Plotinus reportedly achieved union with (or illumination by) the divine source four times during his life, and Origen, whom E. R. Dodds called a "mystic manqué," stated that "often, God is my witness, I have felt that the Bridegroom was approaching me and he was, as far as may be, with me; then he suddenly vanished, and I could not find what I was seeking."[18]

This ideal of identification with God was not, however, the factor usually operative in the divinification of philosophers. Much more common was the concern to demonstrate the extent of a man's assimilation to God, or how he was godlike. The traits selected to depict the philosopher's divine status became literary motifs, and biographers used various combinations of these motifs, depending upon the degree of divinity being claimed for the specific philosopher. Two basic types of divine philosopher—those who were said to be gods or sons of gods, and those who were godlike—were current in biographies in Late Antiquity. Before distinguishing between these two types in detail, however, I will draw a brief composite image of the biographers' vision of the divine philosopher in order to show which traits among the many available ones came to typify his character.

Chief among these characteristics is wisdom. Generally he is shown to

16. Smith, "Prolegomena to a Discussion of Aretalogies, Divine Men, the Gospels, and Jesus," *JBL* 90 (June 1971): 184.

17. C. H. Talbert, "The Concept of Immortals in Mediterranean Antiquity," *JBL* 94 (September, 1975): 419–21; Dodds, *Pagan and Christian in an Age of Anxiety* (New York: W. W. Norton, 1970), pp. 118–19.

18. Porphyry *Vita Plotini* 23; see Plotinus *Enn.* 4.8.1. Origen *Hom. in Cant.* 1.7, quoted in Dodds, *Pagan and Christian in an Age of Anxiety*, p. 98.

possess superior gifts of perception and understanding from a very early age. Origen, for example, understood the profundities of allegorical exegesis of scriptural texts "while still a boy" and applied himself with that "excessive zeal"[19] that was later to earn him the nickname "Adamantius."[20] Similar was the child Apollonius, who "showed great strength of memory and power of application" and soon surpassed his teacher.[21] This idea that the greatness of the man must have been already evident in the child was a popular biographical convention, stemming back to Xenophon, who used childhood and education as important features in his portrayal of Agesilaus' character. In portraits of divine philosophers, however, there is more than simply a hint of future grandeur in the child; rather, his wisdom is already fully developed. This may explain why the accounts of the young philosopher's education, which follow the revelation of his youthful sagacity, seem somewhat superfluous. The point of his education seems primarily to be a kind of discipline, the fine tuning of an already overpowering intelligence.[22] The child is immersed in studies both sacred and secular that are the foundation of the mature sage's philosophy. Philostratus' statement about Apollonius illustrates this point of view: "Apollonius however was like the young eagles who, as long as they are not fully fledged, fly alongside their parents and are trained by them in flight, but who, as soon as they are able to rise in the air, outsoar the parent birds."[23] But another episode in Apollonius' life runs counter to this statement and shows instead the philosopher's freedom from the need for conventional education. As Apollonius is about to depart for Babylon, his pupil Damis offers himself as a guide, claiming that his facility with languages will ease the sage's way. To this Apollonius replies, "I understand all languages, though I never learned a single one."[24] This is surely an unqualified affirmation of the philosopher's superhuman intelligence and stands in stark contrast to passages indicating the wise child's educational needs. Whatever the biographer's intentions, these ambiguous stories of the philosopher's education really serve to highlight the two sides of the philosopher's nature, which are sometimes difficult to reconcile: his superiority to other men, which is due in part to his

19. Eusebius *HE* 6.2.7–9.

20. Ibid., 6.14.10; Jerome *De vir. ill.* 54 and *Ep.* 33.4.11; Epiphanius *Heresies* 64.1.1; Photius *Library* 118.

21. Philostratus *Vita Apollonii* 1.7.

22. Iamblichus *Vita Pythagorica* 2.11–12; Eusebius *HE* 6.2.7–10.

23. Philostratus *Vita Apollonii* 1.7.

24. Ibid., 1.19.

great wisdom, and his humanity, which suggests that he must have passed through the various stages of life like other men.

Another feature of the divine sage's wisdom is his extraordinary insight into human nature. Pythagoras, for example, scrutinized potential disciples by refining the methods of physiognomy and was thereby able to perceive the dispositions of the candidates' souls.[25] Plotinus' perception was so acute that he was able to turn the magical attacks of a secret enemy back on the perpetrator.[26] Porphyry attributes to him a "surpassing degree of penetration into character,"[27] a talent from which Porphyry himself benefited, since Plotinus had at one time perceived his student's increasing desire for death and advised a rest, thus saving him from suicide.[28] The emphasis that biographers place on their heroes' wondrous insight is intended to point to divinity: a priest of Asclepius replies to Apollonius' careful Socratic questioning that it is just at this point that the gods excel men, "for the latter, because of their frailty, do not understand their own concerns, whereas the gods have the privilege of understanding the affairs of both men and themselves."[29] It is not therefore surprising to find that divine philosophers possess this talent.

The philosopher does not, however, use his talent simply to judge lesser men. He is credited with a real sympathy and concern for the welfare of his fellows. Origen's philanthropy placed him in a particularly dangerous position, and that may account in part for the fame he received as a result. He gave comfort and encouragement to Christian martyrs caught in the Alexandrian persecutions of the early third century. Since several of the martyrs had apparently been converted by Origen, he no doubt felt responsible for bolstering their courage to witness for their new-found faith, and he risked the fury of "the heathen multitude" to do so.[30] Pythagoras also took a personal interest in his disciples. He devised medicines and melodies that soothed the soul and administered these in the evening to promote "pleasing dreams" and in the morning to free his students from "nocturnal torpor."[31] Porphyry reports an extraordinary kindness of Plotinus: he agreed to take in the children of "many men and women on the approach of death" and to oversee their education and manage their property. His home must

25. Porphyry *Vita Pythagorae* 13; Iamblichus *Vita Pythagorica* 17.71.

26. Porphyry *Vita Plotini* 10.

27. Ibid., 11. Note the similar example of unmasking an evil character by Apollonius in Philostratus *Vita Apollonii* 1.10.

28. Porphyry *Vita Plotini* 11.

29. Philostratus *Vita Apollonii* 1.11.

30. Eusebius *HE* 6.3.1–6.

31. Iamblichus *Vita Pythagorica* 15.64–65.

have been an orphanage of sorts, yet it would be incorrect to picture Plotinus as a harried social worker, for Porphyry notes that "though he shielded so many from the worries and cares of ordinary life, he never, while awake, relaxed his intent concentration upon the intellect."[32]

A final, perhaps more prosaic, indication of the philosopher's wisdom is his desire to communicate it. Philosophers are teachers; divine philosophers are proselytizers, and their teaching not only touches but changes the lives of their disciples. Origen converted the heathen by his teaching, and was reportedly so successful in one case that the student, Heraclas, became bishop of Alexandria.[33] Eventually Origen had so many students in his course of "divine studies" that he had to abandon his instruction of secular literature. Describing his popularity, Eusebius notes that his students "did not give him time to breathe, for one batch of pupils after another kept frequenting from morn to night his lecture room."[34] Plotinus' persuasiveness as a teacher was so great that he converted several members of Roman officialdom to philosophy,[35] but this feat was far surpassed by Pythagoras, who once captured "more than two thousand men" by a single lecture and not only converted politicians but took on the legislative role himself, handing down laws to several Italian cities.[36] Origen remarked in his *Against Celsus* that the real defense of the holy man lies in the lives of his genuine disciples.[37] Biographers agreed that one of the important measures of a philosopher's stature was the quality and quantity of his disciples. The philosopher's holiness might be described as effusive, and biographies of divine philosophers give considerable attention to worthy heirs and imitators of the philosophical masters. One of Iamblichus' hyperboles illustrates this point well. He asserts that as a result of the studies that Pythagoras instituted, "all Italy was filled with philosophers."[38]

The biographers' conception of the divine philosopher and his circle of

32. Porphyry *Vita Plotini* 9.
33. Eusebius *HE* 6.3.2.
34. Ibid., 6.3.8, 6.15. See also 6.8.6: Origen "devoted his whole time untiringly to the divine studies and his pupils."
35. Porphyry *Vita Plotini* 7.
36. Porphyry *Vita Pythagorae* 20–22.
37. Origen *Contra Celsum* praef. 2. This view is echoed by Eusebius in his *Contra Hieroclem* 4.
38. Iamblichus *Vita Pythagorica* 29.166. Iamblichus devotes at least half of his biography to discussions of how Pythagorean virtues lived on in his disciples. See A. Priessnig, "Die literarische Form der Spätantiken Philosophenromane," *Byzantinische Zeitschrift* 30 (1929): 26–27, for a detailed classification of topics. Eusebius also devotes large sections of *HE* 6 to episodes in the lives of some of Origen's pupils. See especially *HE* 6.4–5.

disciples resembles a universe in miniature, with the philosopher at the center radiating the light of wisdom in the form of faithful followers. This suggests that the philosopher wielded real power. His wisdom did not die with him but lived on in adherents to the ideal that he so successfully embodied. Unfathomable knowledge was not the sole component of the holy philosopher model, however; nor could this wisdom by itself qualify a man for that divine status. In fact there is a trait as basic to the holy philosopher's character as his wisdom and one that serves as the foundation of all he is able to accomplish. The trait that complements the philosopher's wisdom is his devotion to an ascetic lifestyle.

From a perusal of biographies about holy philosophers, it is apparent that the men described have static personalities at best; holy philosophers never change. Apart from the biographers' interest in types of men rather than in individuals as such,[39] what accounts for the philosopher's constant espousal of the whole company of virtues? How is he sustained in his perfection?

Philostratus gives us a clue when, reflecting on the fact that Apollonius was true to his mission in such far-flung places as Ethiopia and Achaia, he says, "hard as it is to know oneself, I myself consider it still harder for the sage to remain always himself; for he cannot ever reform evil natures and improve them, unless he has first trained himself never to alter in his own person. . . . a man who is really a man will never alter his nature."[40] The wellspring of the sage's perfect self-knowledge, which enables him never to change, is his asceticism, which in Late Antiquity connotes not mere "training" but a renunciation of worldly values and bodily deprivation, if not actual abuse.

By the late first century A.D., the profession of philosophy and an ascetic mode of living were firmly linked in the popular mind and in the thinking of the intelligentsia as well.[41] Epictetus, for example, found it necessary to chide both those who indulged in extreme forms of self-discipline and those who encouraged the practice by admiring it.[42] Philosophers themselves advised philosophical seekers to follow an ascetic discipline: Sextus asserted

39. See Bieler, *ΘΕΙΟΣ ΑΝΗΡ*, 2 vols. (Vienna: Buchhandlung Oskar Höfels, 1935–36) 1:21–22, who notes that popular tradition is preserved in the remembering of historical personalities, which are subjected to a kind of "homogenizing" process when they are made to conform to a type.

40. Philostratus *Vita Apollonii* 6.35.

41. For general discussions of asceticism see Bieler, *ΘΕΙΟΣ ΑΝΗΡ*, 1:60–73, and Dodds, *Pagan and Christian in an Age of Anxiety*, pp. 1–36.

42. Epictetus *Diss*. 3.12.

that true piety was founded on self-control; Maximus of Tyre's advice was to shun worldly preoccupation if one wanted to find the good; and in the *Hermetica*, knowledge of the good can come only with the inhibition of all the senses.[43] Philostratus, supporting the kind of thinking that Epictetus had earlier deplored, stated admiringly that Peregrinus Proteus was "one of those who have the courage of their philosophy, so much so that he threw himself into a bonfire at Olympia."[44] In his biography of Peregrinus Proteus, Lucian provides ample evidence of the popular admiration, even veneration, that this kind of "ascetic" display provoked. It is probable that a major purpose of his biography was to expose the pretentious and vainglorious origins of the cult and oracle established in Peregrinus' name after his death and to ridicule the "fools and dullards" so "wonderstruck" that they were willing to deify a charlatan on the illegitimate basis of a spectacular ascetic feat.[45]

Lucian's withering jibes at the showy asceticism of the simpleminded or unscrupulous philosopher provide the best testimony to the boom in a type of ascetic philosopher that his era experienced.[46] Ramsay MacMullen's description of the type is a good distillation of Lucian's view: "identified by their long hair, beards, bare feet, grimy rags, staffs and knapsacks; by their supercilious bearing, paraded morals, scowling abuse against all men and

43. *Sextus* 86a; *Corpus Hermeticum* 10.5.

44. Philostratus *Vitae Sophistarum* 563. In "The Volatilization of Peregrinus Proteus," *American Journal of Philology* 67 (1946): 334–45, Roger Pack suggests that Peregrinus' "volatilization" was not simply for notoriety, as Lucian thinks (*De morte Peregrini* 42), but may have been based on certain Neoplatonic doctrines on the soul. The notion of being "commingled with ether" (*De morte Peregrini* 33) may be based on the Heraclitean fragment that Porphyry preserves to the effect that "the dry soul is wisest" (Heraclitus fr. 118 Diels-Kranz, in Porphyry *De antro nympharum* 11). The idea of riding "upon the wings of fire" (*De morte Peregrini* 6) suggests "the Neoplatonic doctrine of *ochēma*, a kind of fiery envelope which enclosed the soul, protected it, and served as a vehicle for ascent." For further discussion of these doctrines, see E. R. Dodds, ed. and trans., *Proclus: The Elements of Theology*, 2nd ed. (Oxford: Clarendon Press, 1963), p. 304 and Appendix II. Even if Peregrinus' self-immolation did have philosophical justification, it is certainly the most extreme form of ascetic witness to one's philosophical integrity.

45. Lucian *De morte Peregrini* 39–40. For a discussion of Lucian's motives, see Marcel Caster, *Lucien et la pensée religieuse de son temps* (Paris: Société d'Édition "*Les Belles Lettres*," 1937), pp. 237–46.

46. See Lucian *The Cynic*, esp. 1, 14, 17, 19; *Alexander*; *De morte Peregrini*; compare Lucian's *Philosophies for Sale* with the witness of several men to their own agonized searches for the "true" philosophy: Justin *Dialogue with Trypho*; Plotinus as reported by Porphyry *Vita Plotini* 3; Clement in *Clementine Homilies*; and the Cynic hero in Lucian's *Menippus*.

classes; they seemed shameless, and half-educated, vulgar, jesting; beggars for money, beggars for attention, parasites on patrons or petitioners at the door, clustered at temples or on street corners in cities; loudmouthed shouters of moral saws driven to a life of sham by poverty."[47] Much in the biographers' portraits of the holy philosopher's asceticism accords with Lucian's picture, although of course theirs are refined portrayals, divested of the sarcasm and satirical pungence of Lucian's

The divine philosopher's asceticism has two aspects. The first is an exterior one, which enables him to be identified publicly. Eusebius says that Origen persevered "in the most philosophic manner of life," and this is what his discipline consisted in: fasting; limiting sleep, which he took not on a couch but on the floor; going barefoot; living "in cold and nakedness" (i.e., extreme poverty); refusing the "numbers" of admirers who sought to share their goods with him; and eating a scanty diet, which actually injured his health. These feats were accompanied by Origen's avoidance of "everything that might lead to youthful lusts"; he spent his entire day teaching (" labors of no light character"), and for most of the night he engaged in his studies of scripture.[48] The picture Porphyry gives of Plotinus is much the same: he disapproved of eating animal flesh and took very little food, "often not even a piece of bread," and neglected sleep in order not to interrupt his contemplations.[49] Plotinus was actually ashamed of his body, considering it something "not worth looking at," and refused medical treatment for his illnesses.[50] That Plotinus practised what he preached is confirmed by his treatise "On Well-Being." Here he states that the good man is not a mixture of body and soul, nor is well-being measured by bodily health or beauty. "It is absurd to maintain that well-being extends as far as the living body, since well-being is the good life, which is concerned with the soul and is an activity of the soul." In order to make clear the fact that the real man reposes in the soul, Plotinus actually advises "a sort of counterpoise on the other side." One should make the body worse, to highlight the soul.[51] With

47. Ramsay MacMullen, *Enemies of the Roman Order* (Cambridge: Harvard University Press, 1966), p. 59.

48. Eusebius *HE* 6.3.9–12. 49. Porphyry *Vita Plotini* 2, 8. 50. Ibid., 1–2.

51. Plotinus *Enn.* 1.4.14. Note that at the end of this treatise, Plotinus softens his language by adopting the metaphor of a musician playing a lyre: the wise man "will care for and bear with that which is joined to him [the body] as long as he can, like a musician with his lyre, as long as he can use it; if he cannot use it he will change to another, or give up using the lyre and abandon the activities directed to it. Then he will have something else to do which does not need the lyre, and will let it lie unregarded beside him while he sings without an

respect to actual physical deprivation and injury, Origen and Plotinus are exemplars of an extreme ascetic ideal not characteristic of Pythagoras and Apollonius, though these latter are similar in respect to the other physical manifestations of the holy sage's ascetic style of life.[52]

One scholar has characterized the ascetic attempt to master the body a "flagrant antithesis to the norms of civilized life in the Mediterranean."[53] What is the point of it all? The most obvious reason is for identification. As Lucian's Cynic notes, his style of dress enables him to keep the kind of company he chooses, and to live the quiet philosophical life. Ignorant men and "fops," not understanding what his dress and appearance mean, will shun him, which is all the better.[54] The sage's style of life identifies him to those who know and desire what the philosophic life is, and it excites admiration for him.

Both Eusebius and Philostratus make a direct connection between the sage's ascetic lifestyle and the admiration for him which his followers express.[55] Asceticism places the philosopher in the public eye and advertises the value of his profession. But the sage's physical withdrawal from the ways of the world is not just for the purpose of public relations; it is also a sign of his freedom. The more he retreats from the society around him, the freer he is from the passions that bog down and befuddle lesser minds. His spirit is liberated, and this gives him the rare ability to exercise his wisdom in communication with the gods.[56] This idea points to the other, interior or spiritual, aspect of the divine sage's asceticism, because the sage's physical withdrawal is simply the outer manifestation of certain philosophical convictions.

The abstention from eating meat is a widely attested ascetic practice,

---

instrument. Yet the instrument was not given him at the beginning without good reason. He has used it often up till now" (*Enn.* 1.4.16).

52. See Philostratus *Vita Apollonii* 1.8: "he declined to live upon a flesh diet, on the ground that it was unclean, and also that it made the mind gross; so he partook only of dried fruits and vegetables. . . . he took to walking without shoes by way of adornment and clad himself in linen raiment . . . and he let his hair grow long and lived in the Temple." See also Porphyry *Vita Pythagorae* 7, 34–35.

53. Peter Brown, *The World of Late Antiquity* (London: Thames and Hudson, 1971), pp. 97–98. Note that Brown applies this statement to the Christian holy men; it is true of the pagan sages as well.

54. Lucian *The Cynic* 19.

55. Philostratus *Vita Apollonii* 1.8; Eusebius *HE* 6.3.13.

56. See the discussion by A. J. Festugière, "Sur une nouvelle édition du 'De Vita Pythagorica' de Jamblique," *Rev. Ét. Grec.* 50 (1937):492–94.

characteristic of all the holy philosophers under discussion. The philosophical basis for this abstention is expressed explicitly by Porphyry, who thought that meat-eating bound the soul more closely to the body. The soul, originally a spiritual being, now exists, through some fault, in a corporeal prison. By denying it corporeal sustenance, it is brought closer to its former spiritual self.[57] Abstention from meat, then, is a rite of purity; as Apollonius notes, one should avoid meat because it is "unclean" and dulls the mind.[58]

A clear picture of ascetic dietary practices in general is given in the biographies of Pythagoras. Porphyry describes Pythagoras' vegetarian diet in detail and remarks that, as a consequence, his health was consistently good. He did not fluctuate between good health and disease, and his soul "always revealed through his appearance the same disposition."[59] The point is that Pythagoras, because of his ascetic discipline, was not subject to passions of the body and thus was not prevented from "familiarity with the gods."[60]

The Pythagorean view of dietary asceticism, which nourishes the body for the good of a correspondingly harmonious soul, is in contradiction to the kind of ascetic self-torture Origen and Plotinus were said to engage in, which led to actual physical injury. Eusebius' portrait may be simply a stylized effort to show Origen going one step further than even the most famous ascetics, but Porphyry's picture is so detailed that it seems to be an actual (historical) description. Plotinus himself states that when the sage finds himself in pain, "he will oppose to it the power which he has been given for the purpose."[61] Perhaps he exemplifies that hostility to the material world which manifests itself in abuse of the body; in this respect he is akin more to the desert fathers than to his philosophical contemporaries.[62]

The whole course of ascetic practices is based on the idea that only by

57. Porphyry *De abstinentia* 1.30, discussed by Anthony Meredith, "Asceticism—Christian and Greek," *JTS*, N.S., vol. 27, pt. 2 (October, 1976), p. 319 and n. 1. Iamblichus agreed that "certain foods are hostile to the reasoning power, and impede its true energy," *Vita Pythagorica* 6.68. See also Porphyry *Vita Pythagorae* 46.

58. Philostratus *Vita Apollonii* 1.8. See also Bieler, *ΘΕΙΟΣ ΑΝΗΡ*, 1:63–64.

59. Porphyry *Vita Pythagorae* 34–35.

60. Iamblichus *Vita Pythagorica* 24.106.

61. Plotinus *Enn.* 1.4.14.

62. Dodds, *Pagan and Christian in an Age of Anxiety*, pp. 27–30. Dodds gives the following rather gloomy examples of his thesis that hostility against the material world was introjected, taking the form of bodily abuse: *Gospel of Thomas* 110: "Woe to the flesh that hangs upon the soul! Woe to the soul that hangs upon the flesh!"; *Corpus hermeticum* 7.2: the body is "the dark gaol, the living death, the corpse revealed, the tomb we carry about with us."

withdrawal from the world of the senses can the soul commune with the spiritual realm, which Numenius described as "a kind of divine desolation."[63] Asceticism was, in effect, a salvation from the body. The holy philosopher's great wisdom will bring him no benefit unless he is first purified. The genuine philosopher is united to God by his abstinence; it is on the basis of this union that his other virtues are nourished.[64]

We have seen that the holy philosopher was typically wise and typically ascetic. His wisdom was revealed not only in his communion with the gods, but also in his communion with men. He was the teacher par excellence whose instruction shaped the lives it touched, and he was the good shepherd, taking responsibility for the well-being of his disciples. His asceticism was based on the conviction that a body purified of material dross freed the soul to engage in divine contemplations. This inner purity had superficial connotations as well since holy sages adopted habits of dress, eating, and uncommonly heavy work schedules, all of which identified their station in society. These traits came together in biographies to form a pattern, a blueprint for the type of the divine philosopher. It is an ideal type, a picture of perfection, and it is difficult, if not impossible, to discern either the extent to which the biographers have molded their heroes to fit the type or the extent to which the heroes themselves actually imitated the ideal. Nevertheless, the image of the divine philosopher presented in biographies is a coherent one, at least with respect to the traits just discussed. However, there were other traits that were not held in common. Study of these traits shows that there were actually two major types, or paradigms, subsisting under the general appelation of holy sage.

Biographical Paradigms of the Divine Philosopher

In *The Charismatic Figure as Miracle Worker*, David Tiede asserts that the traditions about divine wise men fall into two categories: those describing the rational, philosophical figure and those describing the miracle worker. He maintains that the origins of these two traditions are "discrete," that early in the Hellenistic period there were two "competing conceptions of

63. Numenius as quoted by Eusebius *Praeparatio Evangelica* 11.22.

64. Porphyry *De Abstinentia* 2.49. See Meredith, "Asceticism—Christian and Greek," pp. 320–21.

divine presence": one highlighting the charismatic, miracle-working figure, the "pre-Socratic shaman type"; the other emphasizing the moral and intellectual virtues of the philosophical type, which "resists the admixture of teratological accounts."[65] He states further:

> This discrimination between differing notions of divine presence and their corresponding semi-literary forms is basic to this study. In order to create the complete aggregate portrait of the "divine man," it was necessary for Hellenistic authors like Philostratus and Porphyry to superimpose these contrasting images and to mix the forms in a way similar to the editorial work of the authors of the gospels of Mark and John. Largely because of the continuing vitality of the Platonic image of Socrates, authors like Plutarch, Lucian, and Celsus are able to resist such syncretism.[66]

This view of the origin and development of literary images of the holy man is difficult to accept for several reasons. The first concerns Tiede's use of sources to document the two contrasting images of the holy man. At times he appears to refer to holy men in a wide variety of sources; at other times he plainly means to discuss biographies of holy men, which are clearly formulated literary works marked by an intentionality, a conscious creative purpose not found in random reporting of tidbits about assorted "holy" characters. He notes the existence of "semi-literary" forms but does not say what they may have been, nor how they might have influenced the formation of images of the holy man. In either case, however, whether one considers the "traditions" or the biographies in which the images were given coherent literary expression, his notion that two images of the holy man—one a philosopher, the other a magician or miracle worker—developed separately and merged only as a result of "syncretism" at a much later time (the second century A.D.) is incorrect. In fact, Tiede's own analysis of the first two holy men he chooses to discuss, Pythagoras and Empedocles, contradicts his opening assertions.

In the case of Empedocles, Tiede admits that it seems likely that he actually did "unite the roles of shaman and scientist in his own person,"[67] and quotes with approval E. R. Dodds' statement in *The Greeks and the Irrational* (p. 146) that "Empedocles represents not a new but a very old type

65. David Tiede, *The Charismatic Figure as Miracle Worker*, SBL Dissertation Series 1 (Missoula, Montana: Society of Biblical Literature, 1972), pp. 5, 29, 22, 60.
66. Ibid., pp. 41–42.
67. Ibid., p. 20.

of personality, the shaman who combines the still undifferentiated functions of magician and naturalist, poet and philosopher, preacher, healer, and public counsellor."[68] According to Tiede, however, the likelihood that Empedocles was both philosopher and magician does not contradict his thesis because Empedocles' combination of these roles was "personal." He goes on to state that the source for Diogenes Laertius' portrait of Empedocles was apparently Heraclides' collection of legends, which gave a shamanistic interpretation of Empedocles, and adds that there are "less paradoxographical" options for understanding Empedocles. Aristotle, Satyrus, and Lucretius all praise his more "rational" gifts and treat him as a philosopher.[69] But what does this prove? It is not really too surprising to find a person like Heraclides, known to be a "collector of absurdities," emphasizing the miraculous or fantastic aspects of an unusual individual like Empedocles, nor is it surprising to find philosophers praising philosophical virtues. The fact that the personal biases of Empedocles' interpreters are reflected in the way they chose to remember him says nothing about the original differentiation between the philosopher and the miracle worker. The most one can say on the basis of such evidence is that divinity lies in the eye of the beholder. And, despite what later interpreters thought, Empedocles' assertions about himself in his poems suggest that in fact he and other early holy men were omnicompetent, and that philosophy and magic were not competing but complementary characteristics.[70]

The case for Pythagoras is much the same. He was pictured as both a philosopher and a miracle worker as early as the fourth century B.C.,[71] a fact that disproves the notion that a synthetic or syncretistic portrait of Pythagoras did not appear until the work of Apollonius. Tiede is correct in pointing to disagreements about Pythagoras' integrity.[72] Hermippus characterized his wonderworking as a charlatan's tricks, whereas Callimachus defended both his miraculous abilities as well as his superior intellect.[73] It is not correct, however, to suggest that the more rational picture of Pythago-

68. Ibid.

69. Ibid., p. 21.

70. See E. R. Dodds, *The Greeks and the Irrational* (Berkeley: University of California Press, 1951), pp. 145–46. For the fragments of Empedocles, see H. Diels, *Fragmente der Vorsokratiker* (Berlin, 1934), I:276–375.

71. Isidore Lévy, *Recherches sur les sources de la légende de Pythagore* (Paris: Éditions Ernest Leroux, 1926), pp. 22–36.

72. Tiede, *The Charismatic Figure*, pp. 14–23.

73. Lévy, *Recherches sur les sources de la légende de Pythagore*, pp. 36–42.

ras the philosopher was eroded or corrupted by the image of the miracle worker.[74] The earliest testimonies we have show that Pythagoras' reputation was established first on the basis of his miracles; in his case, the image of the miracle worker was later combined with the philosophical image.[75]

A further point against the untenable suggestion that conceptions of wise man and miracle man were in constant competition concerns evaluations of Socrates after his death. Tiede asserts that the "moral and rational image" of Socrates that Plato created provided the criterion by which other interpretations of Socrates were judged "incorrect."[76] Yet Plato himself attributed part of Socrates' status as a wise man to "irrational" sources: Socrates pursued his quest for truth at the behest of the god and through oracles and dreams; his daimon was "divine and spiritual" and "the signal of God."[77] Subsequent portraits of Socrates emphasize this aspect even more heavily so that the voice becomes an actual divine being.[78] What, then, of the rational image that shows the miraculous aspect to be incorrect? Tiede's documentation of the continuing influence of the rational Socratic image on succeeding holy man portraits is insufficient, and it does not help to explain why, for example, the mantic and wise figure of Pythagoras, not Socrates, came to hold the position of honor among Neoplatonists; nor is his thesis aided by the critique of Plato himself found in the Pythagoras biographies.[79]

Clearly, Tiede's argument that the divine philosopher of Graeco-Roman biographies is simply an aggregate of two distinct ancestors, one revered for his intellect, the other for his magical talents, does not provide an adequate basis for precise evaluation of the image of the divine philosopher. We have seen that in all biographies of divine philosophers, the heroes hold some characteristics in common. However, there are also important differences.

74. Tiede, *The Charismatic Figure*, p. 22.

75. Lévy, *Recherches sur les sources de la légende de Pythagore*, pp. 1–22.

76. Tiede, *The Charismatic Figure*, p. 60.

77. Plato *Apology* 33C, 31C, 40A–B.

78. See Plutarch *De genio Socratis* 580–82, and Apuleius *De deo Socratis* 157–67. For a discussion of Apuleius' treatment of Socrates' daemon see Jean Beaujeu, ed. and trans., *Apulée: opuscules philosophiques* (Paris: Société d'Édition "Les Belles Lettres," 1973), pp. 239–44.

79. See Porphyry *Vita Pythagorae* 54: Plato and his followers "took as their own the fruitful elements" of Pythagoras' philosophy; Iamblichus *Vita Pythagorica* 27.131: Plato plagiarized Pythagoras' political theory, and 30.167: Plato learned the principle of justice from Pythagoreans.

As we will see, the biographers of Late Antiquity presented two distinct paradigms of the divine philosopher, and a dichotomy between "miracle" and "intellect" does not distinguish them sufficiently.

The two paradigms are best differentiated by the degree of divinity attributed to the specific philosopher. One paradigm, followed by Philostratus (*Life of Apollonius*), Porphyry (*Life of Pythagoras*), and Iamblichus (*Pythagorean Life*), characterizes the divine philosopher as a son of god. The other, followed by Porphyry (*Life of Plotinus*) and Eusebius ("Life of Origen"), attributes only a godlike status to the divine philosopher.[80] The essential decision as to whether the philosopher is a son of god or simply godlike determines the specifics of the biographical characterization.[81] Tiede would make miracle working or trafficking in magic the basic differentiation among holy men, but we shall see that the attribution of miracle- or magic working is a characteristic secondary to the more basic category "son of god."

In biographies, philosophers who are sons of god are distinguished from their godlike fellows by their birth stories, which provide them with divine parentage. Just before the child was born, Apollonius' mother was visited by the god Proteus in the form of an Egyptian daemon who claimed that she would bear Proteus, although another story, also reported by Philostratus, states that Apollonius' countrymen believed him to be a son of Zeus. Apollonius' birth was attended by swans or, according to the story that Philostratus prefers, by a thunderbolt, whose descent and ascent signified "the great distinction to which the sage was to attain . . . and how he should transcend all things upon earth and approach the gods."[82] The wonders accompanying his birth lend credence, in the opinion of Philostratus, to traditions acclaiming Apollonius as a true son of god.

Porphyry begins his biography of Pythagoras with accounts of various

80. In "The Concept of Immortals in Mediterranean Antiquity," Talbert makes a similar distinction between "immortals" and *theioi andres*, based primarily on the divine birth and final assumption of the former. In biographies, the distinctions between the two models are more complex.

81. That there were "degrees" of divinity a human being might attain, or a "scale" of divinity along which a given man might be located, was a popular idea, especially in early Neoplatonic circles. In *De defectu oraculorum* 415B–C, Plutarch even imagines that one could slide up and down on the scale, "a continual promotion and demotion," as John Dillon has remarked in *The Middle Platonists* (Ithaca: Cornell University Press, 1977), p. 219. Biographers, however, were not concerned to slide their heroes up and down but rather to establish precise ranking on the scale.

82. Philostratus *Vita Apollonii* 1.5–6.

historians concerning the historical identity of Pythagoras' father Mnesarchus, but ends his discussion of Pythagoras' patrimony by remarking that Apollonius' biography shows Pythagoras to be the son of Apollo and only nominally the son of Mnesarchus.[83] Porphyry himself has found, and quotes, confirmation of this in "one of the Samian poets," and adds further support to the connection with Apollo by relating the story linking Pythagoras with Abaris, priest of the Hyperborean Apollo. Abaris guesses Pythagoras to be the Hyperborean Apollo incarnate, and Pythagoras confirms his guess by showing him his golden thigh.[84] Porphyry's account of Pythagoras' divine lineage is magnified by Iamblichus. In his *Pythagorean Life*, a brief genealogy is developed, in which Pythagoras' line is traced back to Ancaeus of Samos, said to be a son of Zeus, though Iamblichus is not sure whether this descent was credited to him because of his virtue or "a certain greatness of soul."[85] Iamblichus explains that reports about Pythagoras' noble birth were due to his descent from Ancaeus, and he implies that these reports were eventually mythologized, so that Pythagoras came to be considered a son of Apollo.[86] This is how he accounts for the quotation from the Samian poet to which Porphyry had also referred.

Although Iamblichus seems unwilling to give historical credence to the idea of a god uniting with a human woman, he does not want to relinquish Pythagoras' divine status. He concludes that "no one disputes the fact that the soul of Pythagoras was sent down to men on the authority of Apollo, Pythagoras being either a companion of the god or related to this god in a more intimate (familial) way."[87] Iamblichus' opinion about Pythagoras' status becomes clearer in his version of the Abaris story. As in Porphyry's

83. Porphyry *Vita Pythagorae* 1–2. Further support for the nominal fatherhood of Mnesarchus *may* be found in the divine child legend in *Vita Pythagorae* 10. This story, which Porphyry has taken from Antonius Diogenes, *The Wonderful Things Beyond Thule*, is about a wondrous child whom Mnesarchus finds during his travels and adopts as his son. As Porphyry relates the story, Mnesarchus names this child Astraeus and raises him along with his other sons, one of whom is Pythagoras, who later adopts Astraeus as *his* son. The story seems confused. Was it originally intended to explain how Mnesarchus came to be Pythagoras' father, and was the child at first identified as Pythagoras himself? The name Astraeus (starry) would seem to fit well with later conceptions of Pythagoras' astrological discoveries.

84. Porphyry *Vita Pythagorae* 28.

85. Iamblichus *Vita Pythagorica* 2.3.

86. Iamblichus *Vita Pythagorica* 2.4–5. The poetic passage states that Pythagoras was the offspring of Pythais and Apollo: "Pythais, the most beautiful of the Samians, brought forth Pythagoras for Apollo, friend of Zeus."

87. Ibid., 2.8–9.

version, the revelation of the golden thigh confirms Abaris' conjecture that Pythagoras was Apollo. But Iamblichus appends to this a passage that sounds very much like a "christological" interpretation of Pythagoras: Pythagoras tells Abaris that he has come into the world for the care and well-being of men, and that he took on a human form (*anthrōpomorphos*) so that men would not be so astonished and unsettled by his "surpassing excellence" (*to hūperechon*) that they avoided his teaching.[88] Thus in Iamblichus' biography Pythagoras is at the very least a soul sent from Apollo's realm, and at most a god descended from Apollo.

In all three of these biographies of a son of god, the authors throw some doubt on the idea of the actual physical generation of the philosopher from a god, perhaps to be fair to historical sources (which obviously preserved differing views of each hero's divinity), perhaps to retain the hero's humanity and to avoid the notion of a corporeal god so repugnant to pagans. However, the fact remains that the miraculous birth stories are reported and later confirmed by other evidence of divine origins. It is instructive to note that Porphyry's presentation of a divine Pythagoras, although qualified by a profusion of conflicting reports of parentage, was clearly perceived and magnified by Iamblichus. And the point of Philostratus' portrayal of Apollonius was discerned much later by the biographer Eunapius, who remarked that Philostratus should have titled his work not *The Life of Apollonius* but *The Visit of God to Mankind*.[89]

The biographies using the godlike paradigm for the divine philosopher do not present miraculous birth stories; nor is there even a hint of his generation from a god. Origen's life story begins with his childhood. Except for one anecdote from his youth, we do not meet Plotinus until he is a young man engaged in an agonized search for the true philosophy. Why this difference? Plotinus and Origen's lack of divine origins can be explained by certain philosophical convictions of the philosophers themselves. A statement in Porphyry's biography of Plotinus gives us an intriguing clue: no one knew when Plotinus was born because he refused to celebrate his birthday. This refusal stemmed from his rather gnostic shame of being in a body, which also led him to avoid discussing his parents and place of birth.[90] Similar feelings were expressed by Origen. In his *Commentary on Matthew*, he states: "A certain author has observed before us what has been recorded in

88. Ibid., 19.92.
89. Eunapius *Lives of the Philosophers and Sophists* 454.
90. Porphyry *Vita Plotini* 1–2.

Genesis about the birthday of Pharaoh, and has explained that the common man, being fond of the circumstances of his birth, celebrates his birthday. But in no writing do we find a birthday being celebrated by a righteous man."[91] Elsewhere he treats birth in an even more derogatory manner, asserting that the saints not only do not celebrate their birthdays; they curse the day they were born.[92] This is a telling example of the alienated feeling that was one of the justifications for the ascetic lifestyle discussed earlier. Clearly if the body is a jail for the soul, one would not want to celebrate the anniversary of the imprisonment. If Eusebius was a faithful follower of his mentor's strictures, he could not give a glamorous account of Origen's birth in his biography, for by Origen's own admission that would place him in the company of sinners, and that is the last thing Eusebius wants to do. The same can be said of Porphyry. The philosophical bias against birthdays, symbols of human corporeality, could have prevented the fabrication of marvelous birth stories for these two philosophers.

This is, however, only a partial explanation and not wholly convincing when the dynamics of biography writing are considered. The biographical process of creating an ideal character out of the historical data of a man's life suggests that it is the philosophical and historical stance of the biographer, rather than of the subject himself, that dominates the composition of the biography. As Aristoxenus' scurrilous biography of Socrates illustrates, there was no biographical "ethic" that might have prevented the creation of stories about Origen and Plotinus for the purpose of highlighting or bringing into focus certain facets of their characters. In other words, there was nothing to prevent either Porphyry or Eusebius from initiating a myth; after all, the mythologizing process has to start somewhere. Although the origin of a myth is difficult to trace, we have seen a good example of how a myth grows in Iamblichus' elaboration of Porphyry's version of Pythagoras' divine birth. It is possible, of course, that since Porphyry and Eusebius considered themselves heirs in a philosophical sense to Plotinus' and Origen's work, their biographies reflect a continuity from mentor to student that made their characterizations more straightforward, less mythological. However, the fact that Porphyry wrote two biographies of divine philosophers that use very different standards for assessing and portraying character was not an historical accident or a slip of the biographical pen. It is most probable that in their biographies of Plotinus and Origen, Porphyry and

91. Origen *Commentary on Matthew* 10.22.
92. Origen *Homilies on Leviticus* 8.3.

Eusebius are portraying a type of the divine philosopher that differs from the numinous, savior-like posture of Pythagoras or Apollonius.

Another difference between these two paradigms concerns the extent to which the divine philosopher can be known and identified. As Jonathan Smith has pointed out, what is most characteristic of the philosopher who is considered to be a son of god is that he is *sui generis*, in a class by himself. Because he occupies this special, sacred territory, which is inaccessible to others, he is misunderstood and wrongly classified by both enemies and disciples alike.[93] Philostratus' *Life of Apollonius* provides good examples of both the elusive identity and the misconceptions of the sage who is a son of god. Philostratus begins his biography with a brief paean of praise to Pythagoras, emphasizing his contact with, and good favor among, the Olympian gods. The reader learns from later passages that Apollonius considered himself to be a votary of Pythagoras, had vowed to live the Pythagorean life, and called Pythagoras his "spiritual ancestor."[94] In spite of this apparent identification of Apollonius with Pythagoras, however, Philostratus does not intend this little introduction to be an indirect eulogy to Apollonius through praise of the figure he emulated. It is intended rather to define in a positive way what Apollonius was not, for we read in the following chapter that Apollonius was in fact more divine than his "spiritual ancestor."[95] Apollonius, then, was greater than Pythagoras. What does this tell us about him? Philostratus does not say but continues instead with comments on what Apollonius was not: he was not a magician, nor a "sage of an illegitimate kind," nor a false prophet. Similar misconceptions obscured the identity of Pythagoras. Iamblichus notes that "some celebrated him as the Pythian, but others as the Hyperborean Apollo, some again considered him as Paeon, others as one of the daemons that inhabit the moon, and others as one of the Olympian gods who sometimes appear in human form."[96]

As elusive as the conflicting views of outsiders (who remain largely anonymous) are the self-revelations of the sons of god themselves and the re-

93. Jonathan Z. Smith, "Good News Is No News: Aretalogy and Gospel," *Christianity, Judaism, and Other Greco-Roman Cults*, ed. Jacob Neusner, 4 vols. (Leiden: E. J. Brill, 1975), vol. 1: *New Testament*, pp. 24–27.

94. Philostratus *Vita Apollonii* 1.7; 4.16.

95. Philostratus *Vita Apollonii* 1.2: "more divinely than Pythagoras he wooed wisdom and soared above tyrants."

96. Iamblichus *Vita Pythagorica* 6.30.

sponses of their disciples. In Apollonius' case, as Smith has observed, the sage's favorite form of self-identification is an "I am" (*egō eimi*) pronouncement: he is, simply, Apollonius.[97] Tantalizing clues of what this might mean are scattered throughout the biography. His pupil and traveling companion Damis at first regards Apollonius as a daemon, but later finally understands Apollonius to be divine and superhuman—although even after this supposed realization he continues to be amazed by Apollonius' freedom from human convention.[98] Apollonius himself speaks in riddles and parables,[99] although he was able to communicate effectively even while keeping the ritual five-year Pythagorean silence,[100] and is fond of making enigmatic statements about himself.[101] He is fundamentally a free spirit, able to command respect among the most diverse groups and to break through the usual human boundaries of language and custom. Most of all, Apollonius possesses power, as even the most formidable of Roman officials are forced to admit.[102] In spite of Philostratus' long, rambling narrative, Apollonius' true nature is never really classified adequately. He is the changeling, as his early identification with Proteus suggested. His life is simply a series of episodes, from which the reader receives momentary glimpses of Apollonius' effect on other men. The only lasting impression is one of superhuman power, and perhaps this, more than any of his marvelous acts, is what defines Apollonius' character.

Pythagoras' special position in the cosmic scheme of things is stated more explicitly. Iamblichus relates one of the Pythagoreans' greatest secrets, preserved by Aristotle in his work on Pythagorean philosophy: three kinds of rational, living beings exist—gods, men, and beings like Pythagoras.[103] Pythagoras is thus in a class by himself, and tags like "child (son) of god" (*ho*

97. Jonathan Z. Smith, "Good News Is No News: Aretalogy and Gospel," p. 28. See Philostratus *Vita Apollonii* 1.21; 6.9.

98. Philostratus *Vita Apollonii* 1.19; 7.38; 7.41.

99. Ibid., 1.20, 4.9, 6.11.

100. Ibid., 1.15.

101. Ibid., 1.21: In an interview, a Babylonian satrap asks Apollonius, "Whence do you come to us, and who sent you?" as if he was asking questions of a spirit. And Apollonius replied: 'I have sent myself, to see whether I can make men of you, whether you like it or not.' He asked a second time who he was to come trespassing like that into the king's country, and Apollonius said: 'All the earth is mine, and I have a right to go all over it and through it.'"

102. Ibid., 4.44, the statement by Tigellinus, "you are too powerful to be controlled by me."

103. Iamblichus *Vita Pythagorica* 6.31.

theou pais) and "divine daemon" (*daimōn theios*) are really inadequate means of pinpointing his character.[104] As in Apollonius' case, the reader is presented with a catalog of acts and sayings that illustrate but do not exhaust the figure's richness. One can document Pythagoras' oracular speech, his knowledge of the odyssey of his own soul, and his unique understanding of the "heavenly harmonies of the cosmos,"[105] but eventually one can only say, with Porphyry, that "ten thousand other things yet more marvelous and more divine are told about the man. . . . To put it bluntly, about no one else have greater and more extraordinary things been believed."[106] Once again, what remains is a potent impression of an "unspeakable, unfathomable divine nature" that hovers just beyond the reach of mortal comprehension.[107]

By contrast, the godlike philosopher is not shrouded in such deep mystery. Origen and Plotinus are not pictured as phenomena in spiritual, moral, and intellectual worlds of their own creation. They are rather squarely placed in philosophical traditions that validate and help to identify them. In a later chapter I will discuss whether the "schools" to which they belonged were really as cohesive as the biographers suggest, but it is sufficient here to point out that Eusebius and Porphyry have described a *diadochē*, a philosophical chain of succession from teacher to student, within which Origen and Plotinus are placed and thereby identified. It is true, of course, that Apollonius' and Pythagoras' teachers are also enumerated; but they constitute a diverse, largely anonymous group ("the Chaldeans," "the Magi," "the Egyptian priests") and they certainly do not form a scholastic tradition. In Apollonius and Pythagoras' case the educational background serves more as a *praeparatio*, a demonstration of the sage's intellectual flexibility, and proof of his comprehensive grasp of sacred knowledge. Origen and Plotinus, however, are not portrayed as philosophical eclectics. They are located in specific traditional positions, albeit special ones, for they are the figures who have given their respective schools focus and fame.

Plotinus, pupil of the middle Platonist Ammonius, is shown to be the heir, ultimately, of Socrates and Plato. Porphyry says that Plotinus celebrated the traditional anniversaries of their birthdates, and made plans to found a city of philosophers, called Platonopolis, governed by Plato's *Laws*.[108] More important, however, was his study of the commentaries of his

104. Ibid., 2.10, 3.16. 105. Ibid., 7.34, 14.63, 15.65.

106. Porphyry *Vita Pythagorae* 28–29. 107. Iamblichus *Vita Pythagorica* 15.65.

108. Porphyry *Vita Plotini* 2, 12. On birthday celebrations in the Academy for Socrates and

Platonic predecessors, which formed a basic component of the sessions of Plotinus' school.[109] His fame as a vital and prominent link in the succession of Platonic philosophers is suggested by his enemies' charge that he simply plagiarized Numenius, one of the giants of second-century Platonic and Neopythagorean philosophy.[110] But it is best attested by his writings, which are given conspicuous attention in Porphyry's biography.[111]

Origen, too, is shown as a schoolman. Eusebius pictures him as successor to Clement of Alexandria and Pantaenus in the leadership of the Alexandrian catechetical school and, later, as founder of the Caesarean school in which Eusebius himself had studied.[112] Like Porphyry, Eusebius shows his hero as safeguard and brilliant interpreter of his inherited philosophical tradition, and he also devotes a large part of his biography to lists and brief discussions of the philosopher's writings.[113] For the question of the philosopher's identity, it is important to note that not only are Origen and Plotinus located in specific scholastic traditions but also that their lasting, personal contributions in the form of treatises and students are clearly emphasized. Both Eusebius and Porphyry are careful to identify the students and successors of each philosopher;[114] they leave no doubt about the striking personal impact of the philosopher's teaching and the scholastic continuity it ensured.

There is no such clarity concerning the effect of Apollonius and Pythagoras. Their impact is universal but vague,[115] and the content of their public teaching consists of bland, commonplace ethical and metaphysical doctrines.[116] However, the popular morality that they preach to the world is really a mask, for hidden from general view are their private mysteries into which only an inner circle of disciples is initiated.[117] There is no such

Plato, see Plutarch *Quaest. conv.* 717B. It was a practice of philosophical schools in general to honor birthdays of founders and appearances of guardian daemons. See *PW* 13, cols. 1135–1149, s.v. *Genethlios hēmera*, by W. Schmidt.

109. Porphyry *Vita Plotini* 14.

110. Ibid., 17–18, 21.

111. Ibid., 4–6, 24–26.

112. Eusebius *HE* 6.3.3, 6.6.1, 6.26.

113. Ibid., 6.19, 6.3.9–11; lists of works: 6.16, 6.24–25, 6.28, 6.32, 6.36, 6.38.

114. Ibid., 6.4–5, 6.30, 6.40–42, 44–46 (Dionysius); 6.3.1–2, 6.15 (Heraclas). Porphyry *Vita Plotini* 4–5, 7, 9, 16–17.

115. For example, all Greece "flocks" to hear Apollonius (Philostratus *Vita Apollinii* 8.15), and Pythagoras is able to convert and reform entire cities (Porphyry *Vita Pythagorae* 2–22).

116. Note the long sections in Iamblichus' *Vita Pythagorica* devoted to such topics as piety (28.134–56), justice (30.167–86), courage (32.214–28), and friendship (33.229–40).

117. Philostratus *Vita Apollonii* 1.16: "At sunrise he performed certain rites by himself, rites

dichotomy in the teaching of Plotinus and Origen, who are portrayed throughout their biographies as exponents of a particular philosophy to a particular group. Nor are their profound philosophical discoveries obscured by "arcane symbols" in the Pythagorean manner, since their thoughts were recorded in writing. In short, the *philosophical* characterizations of godlike sages do not deal in enigma and allusion; in this respect the character of godlike philosophers is subject to rational scrutiny.

In the same way that Origen and Plotinus are not elusive in the intellectual realm, they are also not part of an ontological category that excludes other men. They are not members of that mysterious middle category of beings neither god nor man. They are men, but they are special men. Porphyry begins his account of the revelation of Plotinus' special nature with the statement that "Plotinus certainly possessed by birth something more than other men."[118] The story concerns Plotinus' encounter with an Egyptian priest who wanted to evoke Plotinus' "companion spirit" (*oikeios daimōn*). "When the spirit [*ton daimona*] was summoned to appear a god [*theon*] came and not a being of the spirit order, and the Egyptian said, 'Blessed are you, who have a god for your spirit and not a companion of the subordinate order.'"[119] The idea of a companion spirit or indwelling daemon was not, of course, a startling one; it appears as early as Hesiod and was made "morally and philosophically respectable," as E. R. Dodds remarks, by Plato, for whom the daemon was the rational "spirit-guide" in men.[120] That Plotinus' daemon turned out to be "of the more godlike kind" (*tōn theioterōn daimonōn*), as Porphyry describes it, was unusual; his spirit was in the highest rank possible for a human being.[121]

Origen, too, was specially blessed. Time and time again, he is protected by "divine and heavenly providence" and deemed worthy of divine aid and grace that save his life—Eusebius says "it is impossible to say how often"—so that he might continue in his "excessive zeal and boldness for the word of Christ."[122] Even more revealing of his stature is the divine spirit (*theion pneuma*) that dwelt in his breast.[123] Clearly, like Plotinus, Origen was pos-

---

which he only communicated to those who had disciplined themselves by a four years' spell of silence."

118. Porphyry *Vita Plotini* 10.

119. Ibid., 10.

120. Dodds, *The Greeks and the Irrational*, pp. 42–43.

121. Ibid., Appendix III, pp. 289–91.

122. Eusebius *HE* 6.2.4, 6.3.5, 6.3.7, 6.2.13.

123. Ibid., 6.2.11.

sessed of a spirit of high order, but what distinguishes them so sharply from Pythagoras and Apollonius is that they are never elevated beyond the confines of mortality. Certainly they are "first among men," but never more than that; they do not ascend to the same height of divinity as the philosophers who are characterized as sons of god.

A final distinction remains to be made between our two models of the divine philosopher. Sons of god work miracles; the godlike types do not. We have seen that miracle working is not the primary distinguishing factor between these two types; that factor is rather the mode of presentation. One type remains essentially incomprehensible throughout the biographical characterization and is not really contained within the historical era with which he is associated. The power of his presence transcends the particularities of history. The other type is more closely associated with the human community; he is a man, although a remarkable one, and is more easily understood because his activities can be placed within definite historical frameworks. Miracle working is one more instance of the son of god's supernatural abilities: just as he is able to dominate men, so also is he able to dominate nature. This dominion takes two forms: the manipulation of natural phenomena, and the healing of mental and physical disease. Pythagoras, for example, is able to communicate with bears, oxen, birds, and rivers, quell violent weather, and appear in far-distant places on the same day.[124] Apollonius heals plague-stricken people, raises a woman from the dead, exorcizes demons, and so on.[125] Miracle stories like these are able to convey in a dramatic, colorful way the overwhelming power of the particular figure. This may be why ancient and modern scholars alike have seized upon them as demonstrations of the numinous. They give power an almost tangible reality. Biographers using the model of the son of god did not, however, emphasize miracle stories to the extent that some modern scholarship might lead one to believe.[126] They are simply part of the total range of characteristics marshaled in the attempt to define the nature of the son of god.

In this chapter we have seen that by the second century A.D., the philosopher had come to be considered a holy figure with spiritual and intellectual powers that far surpassed those of ordinary men. He was a figure for whom

124. Porphyry *Vita Pythagorae* 23–25, 27, 29.

125. Philostratus *Vita Apollonii* 4.10, 4.45, 4.20.

126. See Smith's discussion in "Prolegomena to a Discussion of Aretalogies, Divine Men, the Gospels, and Jesus," pp. 188–98.

the term "divine" was appropriate. But "divine" was a much-abused term. Comparison of the biographies devoted to these divine philosophers shows that there were two major types of divinity ascribed to philosophers. To call Pythagoras or Apollonius divine was to suggest that he was a son of god, possessed of miraculous, prophetic, and intellectual powers far beyond human capacity. To call Origen or Plotinus divine was to suggest that he was an especially gifted man, blessed by God, whose status was achieved by the purity and steadfastness of his devotion to philosophical tradition and to the reasoning faculty. It is apparent that there were two very different conceptions of a philosopher's holiness, and when these conceptions were applied in biographies, two different kinds of characterizations emerged. In biographies of sons of god, we have not an idealized account of the life of an historical personality, but impressions of a powerful, personal presence remembered and amplified through time. In biographies of godlike philosophers, in contrast, we have idealized accounts of men whose historical identity was at least partially protected by the survival of their written works in the very scholastic circles of which their biographers were a part.

CHAPTER THREE

Literary Aspects of Biography

Biographies of holy philosophers were creative historical works, promoting models of philosophical divinity and imposing them on historical figures thought to be worthy of such idealization. The stereotypical traits that the biographies used to develop the models—in other words, the contents of the texts—were discussed in the preceding chapter, but an adequate understanding of these texts calls for an explication of their literary form also. Scholarship devoted to a literary analysis of biographies of Graeco-Roman holy men has focused primarily on attempts to define a genre that these biographies represent.[1] Unfortunately, the literary heritage bequeathed to Graeco-Roman authors by classical and Hellenistic authors has been largely neglected in this search for genre, since the search has concentrated on later biographies primarily to determine whether they are later representatives of a genre within which the gospels might be placed. For the most part, these discussions of genre have dealt with content, that is, with recurring details in biographies of divine men, and the question of form has been either neglected or assumed to be identical with content. Clearly form and content are closely connected, and neither can be discussed fruitfully in isolation. However, scholars have been so preoccupied with determining the provenance of materials about the divine man and with tracing the amazing proliferation of traditions that they have attempted to impose organizing patterns on the traditions concerning the *theios anēr* (holy man) without really considering the structural elements of the supposed literary form itself. If the question of literary form, and its function, is to be addressed

1. Older studies include Richard Reitzenstein, *Hellenistische Wundererzählungen* (Leipzig: B. G. Teubner, 1906); A. Priessnig, "Die biographische Form der Plotinvita des Porphyrios und das Antoniosleben des Athanasios," *Byz. Zeitschr.* 64 (1971): 1–5; and idem, "Die literarische Form der Spätantiken Philosophenromane," *Byz. Zeitschr.* 30 (1929): 23–30. For a list of more recent studies see ch. 1, n. 1.

seriously, a referent more stable than fluctuating details of content must be established. Scholars will undoubtedly produce more and more verifying examples to increase the number and complexity of Morton Smith's "mob" of divine or deified men.[2] What is needed, however, to clarify the genre discussions is not simple verification of the "divine man" phenomenon but a consideration of the ordering principles that governed the use of these traditions in full-fledged biographies.

Much of the recent scholarship devoted to generic discussions of such Graeco-Roman biographies represents a revival of the early twentieth-century search for literary precedents to the gospels.[3] Both the old and the new quests have looked for a Hellenistic genre that would elucidate the form (and to a great extent the contents) of the gospels. Briefly stated, the focus of scholars engaged in this quest has been on ancient collections of miracles, which they have hypothesized into a literary genre termed *aretalogy*. This supposed genre has been extended to include any story of a man to whom marvelous activities or capacities were attributed. The basic problem in aretalogy research is the attempt to substantiate the claim for the existence early in the Hellenistic period of a literary form that follows a fixed pattern for the life of a holy or supernaturally gifted man.

The use of the term aretalogy to describe lives of holy men written in the Imperial era is derived ultimately from the work of Salomon Reinach,[4] whose aim was to provide a corrective to the usual definition by lexicographers of *aretalogos* as a buffoon or joking philosopher who told quasi-intellectual or fabulous stories at banquets of the rich.[5] This conception of how the *aretalogos* functioned in antiquity was derived from its use by Suetonius *Augustus* 74, where dinner guests are entertained by such a person, and by Juvenal *Satires* 15.13ff., where Odysseus is described as a "lying *aretalogus*" presumably because of the tall-tale quality of his accounts of his adventures. The importance of Reinach's study was his discussion of an inscription found at Delos that linked the *aretalogos* with the oneirokritēs, an interpreter of dreams.[6] Reinach suggested that the *aretalogos* was, like

2. Smith, "Prolegomena to a Discussion of Aretalogies, Divine Men, the Gospels, and Jesus," *JBL* 90 (June 1971): 184.

3. Representatives of the earlier search are listed and discussed in ibid., pp. 188–92.

4. Salomon Reinach, "Les Arétalogues dans l'Antiquité," *Bulletin de correspondence hellénique* 9 (1885): 257–65.

5. Ibid., p. 258. See also Kee, "Aretalogy and Gospel," *JBL* 92 (September 1973): 403.

6. Reinach, "Les Arétalogues dans l'Antiquité," p. 260.

the dream interpreter, a functionary associated with temple cults who recited or interpreted the acts of a god.[7] This suggestion was strengthened by Reinach's complex semantic discussion that proved that *aretē*, virtue, could also mean "miracle" if it referred to the beneficent acts of a divinity toward mankind.[8] The *aretalogos* could thus be defined as one who interpreted or recited the miraculous deeds of a god, and his recitation, the *aretalogia*, could be defined as the narration of these divine acts.[9] Reinach's conclusions have been accepted by modern scholars, but the definition of the *aretalogia* has been vastly extended. Aretalogies properly so called, like the Isis aretalogy,[10] were recitations of the virtuous and miraculous acts of a divinity, but the term was used as early as the work of Reitzenstein in *Hellenistische Wundererzählungen* (1906) to include biographies of holy men written in late Roman antiquity.

This extension of the term aretalogy to include biographies of men whose lives are characterized by marvelous deeds and superhuman qualities is problematic for several reasons. First, there is no suggestion in any ancient source that an aretalogy was ever written to divinize a human being. Aretalogies were simply catalogs of the *aretai* of a specific god.[11] Second, even if the notion of aretalogy is broadened to include lives of divine men, it is impossible to define a stable pattern that the life of the holy man follows. In his essay, Moses Hadas offers this definition of aretalogy: "a formal account of the remarkable career of an impressive teacher that was used as a basis for moral instruction. The preternatural gifts of the teacher often included power to work wonders; often his teaching brought him the hostility of a tyrant, whom he confronted with courage and at whose hands he suffered martyrdom. Often circumstances of his birth or his death involve elements of the miraculous."[12] Hadas admits that none of the first aretalogies have survived, but he asserts that Plato's *Apology* for Socrates was both a "catalyst" and a "paradigm" for aretalogy, and he thinks its form is implicit in the parody of the *theios anēr*, *Alexander the False Prophet*, written

7. Ibid., pp. 260–61.

8. Ibid., pp. 261–64.

9. Ibid., p. 264. See also Kee, "Aretalogy and Gospel," pp. 403–404.

10. See the discussion by Smith, "Prolegomena to a Discussion of Aretalogies, Divine Men, the Gospels, and Jesus," p. 175 and n. 10 for bibliography.

11. Kee, "Aretalogy and Gospel," pp. 402–404.

12. Moses Hadas and Morton Smith, *Heroes and Gods: Spiritual Biographies in Antiquity* (New York: Harper and Row, 1965), p. 3.

by Lucian of Samosata in the second century A.D.[13] Though he attempts to find a literary analogy in martyr literature, Hadas does not really specify the literary elements of the "form" of aretalogy. Rather, his argument shifts its focus to the hero on whom aretalogy concentrates, and he cites Philostratus' *Life of Apollonius* as the only example of "the pattern in all its details."[14] However, a comparison of this *Life* to the pattern Hadas defines ("towering intellect," "wonderful works," "persecution by a tyrant," and "glorious martyrdom") shows that even his prime example does not quite fit: there is no martyrdom of Apollonius.

In his "Prolegomena" article, Morton Smith attempts a modified definition of aretalogy: "it is a literary form which has no precise formal definition but is determined by its content; it must have a hero whom it celebrates, by reporting one or more of his miraculous deeds."[15] Smith recognizes that the characteristics of the *theios anēr* were often identical to those of Graeco-Roman gods, and remarks on the difficulty of establishing "specific influences and relationships between stories of different holy men, since similar elements may always have come, not from another example of the pattern but from the general religious and intellectual milieu."[16] Yet he still attempts to use miracles as signals to identify both the form and the content.[17] If, as Smith notes, "Graeco-Roman antiquity knew many holy men of many different patterns," thus confronting us with a "mob of divine or deified men of many varieties,"[18] how are we to account for these biographies of divine men, from the gospels to later pagan and Christian *Lives*?

First, that older traditions on miracles existed does not tell us anything about the biographies into which they were incorporated; nor can the motif of the miraculous be equated with the concept of the divine man. As Kee points out in his critique of the aretalogy thesis, "the aim of a miracle story is a function of the use to which the story is put rather than something that

13. Ibid., pp. 17, 58, 63.

14. Ibid., pp. 71–72, 94.

15. Smith, "Prolegomena to a Discussion of Aretalogies, Divine Men, the Gospels, and Jesus," p. 196.

16. Ibid., pp. 186–87.

17. See the similar argument by Helmut Koester, "One Jesus," *Harvard Theological Review* 61 (1968): 231, who also presupposes the existence of aretalogy prior to the gospels. The miracle stories are important because in them "Jesus appears as a man endowed with divine power who performs miracles to prove his divine quality and character."

18. Smith, "Prolegomena to a Discussion of Aretalogies, Divine Men, the Gospels, and Jesus," pp. 181, 184.

inheres in the miracle story as such."[19] Nor can any of the other common motifs, such as the conflict with established authority, be singled out as the organizing concept in biographies of the divine man. There are many motifs, and the authors of the biographies have used them selectively. Further, these biographies often use formally similar material to serve very different purposes. Different authors have adapted related motifs and styles for their own philosophical or theological ends.[20] One cannot isolate a single set of motifs, as proponents of aretalogy have done with miracle stories, and assume that this set defines the structure of texts that happen to include some of those motifs. In fact we have seen in the previous chapter that a biography of a holy man does not even need miracles to qualify as a member of the genre. It is simply not possible to define a stable literary pattern that such biographies follow if features of the textual content are taken as the organizing or ordering principles. The idea of an aretalogical form based on a textual motif creates a distorted view of the divine philosopher, a figure that cannot be defined by only one character trait; further, it ignores the question of true generic form by focusing only on the texts' descriptive contents.

While the most recent scholars concerned with aretalogy have pointed to the miracle story as the heart of Graeco-Roman biographies of holy men, an older generation of scholars adopted a much broader working definition of aretalogy. Reitzenstein found that biographies of holy men were organized around series of *praxeis*, collections of the hero's activities and sayings, that had no inner connection in the biography apart from the narrative setting provided by the author.[21] From his discussions of several biographies, it appears that Reitzenstein conceived of an aretalogy as a thematic assemblage of a man's deeds and speeches, always with an accent on the extraordinary or the supernatural. Thus he surmised that Apollonius' *Life of Pythagoras* (as reconstructed from Porphyry's and Iamblichus' *Lives*) was composed of material taken from a prophet aretalogy, a miracle aretalogy, and a voyage aretalogy.[22] Similarly, Philostratus' *Life of Apollonius* was built up from a collection of the public works of Apollonius, which had been combined with travel and miracle aretalogies.[23]

19. Kee, "Aretalogy and Gospel," p. 412.
20. Examples are given by ibid., pp. 412–16.
21. Reitzenstein, *Hellenistische Wundererzählungen*, p. 97.
22. Ibid., p. 39.
23. Ibid., pp. 40–41.

Reitzenstein's source-critical use of the concept of aretalogy was developed in greater detail by Anton Priessnig.[24] He agreed with Reitzenstein that the only real limit in biography writing was the biographer's imagination, but he found that the author's literary art was usually not successful in erasing traces of his sources.[25] Again like Reitzenstein, Priessnig conceived of the sources as collections of legends or popular stories, which he called aretalogies because of the exaggerated quality of the individual tales. Analyzing Philostratus' *Life of Apollonius*, he isolated three major types of aretalogy: the voyage aretalogy, which provided material for the numerous travel stories and which accounts for the formal structure of the biography; the miracle aretalogy, which Priessnig called an "unvaried mass" of miracles that included prophecies, healings, exorcisms, oracles, and revelations; the sermon aretalogy, which accounts for the discourses ("formal aretalogical excurses") that do less to characterize the hero than to provide information about such varied fields as aesthetics, natural history, and mythology. When these three kinds of aretalogy are combined in a single biography, the result is what Priessnig has variously called a mission aretalogy or a philosophical-religious instruction biography ("eine philosophisch-religiöse Belehrungsbiographie").[26] Other biographies from Late Antiquity are analyzed according to the same schema.[27] They are all, for Priessnig, biographies of philosophical-religious instruction, and his aretalogical classifications are intended as proof of his thesis that in biographies of this type the life history of the hero is simply a device, "a form of literary clothing," that facilitates explanations of particular philosophical world views.[28]

It is clear that Reitzenstein's and Priessnig's idea of aretalogy is more inclusive than the miracle-oriented conception of more recent scholars, but their discussions have only a limited usefulness for the questions of genre and literary form. Their value lies in their demonstration that several kinds of stories were basic to the makeup of Graeco-Roman biographies of holy men, and that it was the biographers' literary art and philosophical bias,

24. Priessnig, "Die literarische Form der Spätantiken Philosophenromane," pp. 23–30; idem, "Die biographische Form der Plotinvita des Porphyrios und das Antoniosleben des Athanasios," pp. 1–5.

25. Priessnig, "Die literarische Form der Spätantiken Philosophenromane," p. 25.

26. Ibid.

27. Ibid., pp. 26–27, Iamblichus' *Vita Pythagorica*; p. 28, Porphyry's *Vita Pythagorae*; idem, "Die biographische Form der Plotinvita," pp. 1–2, Porphyry's *Vita Plotini*.

28. Priessnig, "Die literarische Form der Spätantiken Philosophenromane," pp. 26–27.

rather than the literary elements themselves, that accounted for the finished literary product. Like recent scholarly work on biography, however, Reitzenstein's and Priessnig's analyses were really directed toward discovery of sources rather than to a consideration of the structure of the literary form. For example, Priessnig's description of the inner movement of Philostratus' *Life of Apollonius* as dependent upon the voyage motif[29] is not a sufficient comment on literary form; it does not do justice to the biography as a carefully crafted literary work. Also, the notion of aretalogy, even when expanded, has again led to concentration on the texts' contents rather than on their form—even though Priessnig claims to be discussing form.

Priessnig's remarks are more pertinent to literary form when he applies the structural theories of Friedrich Leo to biographies of holy men. Leo had arranged biographies into two types. The first, represented by Plutarch, was a chronological narration of those deeds and events that most clearly shaped and illustrated a man's character. The second, represented by Suetonius, was divided into two parts: a brief historical resumé, followed by a topical study consisting largely of systematic characterizations, each of which could range over the whole career to the neglect of chronological development. In Leo's view, the Plutarchian form was more subtle, since it drew the reader to make judgments about character based on the orderly narration of the hero's deeds. The Suetonian form, however, was more revealing of the biographer's own judgment on his subject, since the assessment of personality could come independently of, or in spite of, the character's actions.[30] As presented by Leo and adopted by Priessnig, this method of distinguishing between different biographical structures is very neat—so neat, in fact, that it breaks down immediately when Priessnig attempts to apply it to biographies of holy men.

Leo's clear distinctions seem to have suggested to Priessnig that there was such a thing as a "pure" *Life* which depicted only the hero's "Lebensgeschicke."[31] Thus he finds again and again that the Suetonian or the Plu-

29. Ibid., p. 25. He was not alone in this assumption. See Kee, "Aretalogy and Gospel," p. 406: "The *Life* [of Apollonius] reads like a combination of a travelogue and a compendium of popular philosophy." Ibid., p. 407: "The form of the *Life* is loose and unstructured, however, and reads like a cross between a Fodor travel guide and an extended version of a *Reader's Digest* 'Unforgettable Character' essay."

30. Leo, *Die Griechisch-Römische Biographie nach ihrer literarischen Form* (Leipzig: B. G. Teubner, 1901), pp. 147–48, 179–85 on Plutarch; pp. 131–44, 179, 187 on Suetonius.

31. Priessnig, "Die literarische Form der Spätantiken Philosophenromane," p. 26.

tarchian structures have been cluttered or obscured by the addition of "panegyrical schemas" and philosophical propaganda. Philostratus' *Life of Apollonius*, for example, had a "formal" (structural) organization whose "model was the peripatetic-Plutarchian schema with a chronological arrangement of acts and numerous short, characterizing remarks." But the model has been corrupted by the addition of frequent learned discourses that, according to Priessnig, have little to do with the process of biographical characterization.[32] The Pythagoras biographies by Porphyry and Iamblichus both follow a Suetonian model, but in both, the form has been interrupted by the addition of philosophical passages having more to do with Porphyry and Iamblichus than with Pythagoras. This is especially true of Iamblichus' biography, in which nearly half the total length is devoted to the virtues of Pythagoras' students.[33]

There is something to be said for the distinctions that Priessnig draws with respect to Porphyry's biography of Pythagoras, which does have fairly distinct sections, one dealing with events in the life and the other with topical treatments of virtues, daily life in the Pythagorean community, and so on.[34] But there are no such clear-cut sections in Iamblichus' biography, which freely intersperses sections on Pythagoras' life with sections on his philosophy and virtues. And Philostratus' *Life of Apollonius* is hardly what one would expect in a Plutarchian structure, for the chronological order is vague and the reader, far from being allowed to judge character from an orderly presentation of the hero's deeds, is informed in the very beginning of the narrative that the point of the biography is to demonstrate both the hero's practice of true wisdom and his divine nature.[35]

The impetus for Priessnig's determination to find the Suetonian form still flourishing in the Pythagorean *Lives* of Late Antiquity becomes clear in his second article,[36] which is based on his earlier study. Here he discusses Athanasius' *Life of Antony* in connection with the biographies of Pythagoras

32. Ibid., p. 25.

33. Ibid., pp. 26–28.

34. Porphyry's *Vita Pythagorae* deals with events (though not in any recognizable chronological order) of Pythagoras' life in sections 1–29. Beginning with section 30, there are topical treatments of Pythagoras' interaction with his disciples, accounts of his daily life, and long sections describing the Pythagorean symbolic teachings. The *vita* ends (54–59) with an account of the plot that dispersed the community and led to Pythagoras' death.

35. Philostratus *Vita Apollonii* 1.2.

36. Priessnig, "Die biographische Form der Plotinvita," pp. 1–4.

and Porphyry's *Life of Plotinus* (also Suetonian in form) and finds that Athanasius' work, like its predecessors, has by its use of the form been able to depict the life of the hero as a step-by-step ascent to full virtue. The historical section chronicles the ascent, and the topical section illustrates the glory achieved by the hero.[37] Athanasius' biography is, however, superior to the others in form because it is not interrupted by long philosophical sections but concentrates entirely on the personal development of Anthony. Priessnig's point is that Christian hagiography had its roots in pagan, especially Neopythagorean, biography, taking from it the *praxeis* (history)/*ēthos* (virtue) structure and using it in a more concise manner to depict spiritual development.[38] While I agree that Athanasius may very well have been influenced by earlier biographies in his own writing and that his *Life of Antony* is divided into two distinct sections,[39] I cannot agree with Priessnig's treatment of earlier biographies. On the one hand, the form he imposes on those biographies doesn't quite fit, and the idea of "ascent" is certainly erroneous. As we have seen in the previous chapter, the heroes of biographies of holy men do not change in any way as their stories unfold. That they have reached the pinnacle of glory is evident from the beginning of their biographies, and the stories in the narrative serve to document their multifaceted perfection. To claim that these biographies show development of character is to miss one of the major dynamics involved in their composition, the portrayal of a man's character according to a preconceived ideal. On the other hand, comparison of Athanasius' *Life of Antony* with earlier biographies fails to take into account the social and religious conditions that

37. Ibid., pp. 3–4.

38. Ibid., p. 4.

39. A. J. Festugière, "Sur une nouvelle édition du *De Vita Pythagorica* de Iamblique," *Rev. Ét. Grec.* 50 (1937): 472, and Richard Reitzenstein, "Des Athanasius Werk über das Leben Antonius," *Sitzungsberichte der Heidelberger Akademie der Wissenschaften* 8 (1914): 26–27, both emphasize the *praxeis–ēthos* form, which, according to Festugière, became the "classic model of hagiographical composition." But Festugière (p. 471) and Reitzenstein (*Hellenistische Wundererzählungen*, p. 97) claim that in earlier biographies there is no "inner" or spiritual development of the hero. For them the earlier biographies—aretalogies—are simply series of acts in the hero's life, from birth to death, which, far from forming a picture of character development or spiritual ascent,are connected only by formal transitions ("one day," "another source reports," etc.). See, however, Karl Holl, "Die schriftstellerische Form des griechischen Heiligenlebens," *Neue Jahrbucher für Klassische Altertum* 29 (1912): 413, 424–26, who states like Priessnig that aretalogies do show character development. But he was also arguing backwards from his convictions about Athanasius' *Vita Antonii*.

developed after Christianity's official Imperial recognition. Unlike Porphyry, Iamblichus, and Eusebius, Athanasius had no need to adopt an ideal of character whose appeal extended beyond sectarian boundaries. His biography, written for the Christian community, was a "sinner-to-saint" tale devoted precisely to a demonstration that development, spiritual ascent, was possible—possible, in fact, for "everyman."[40] Priessnig was correct to point to the motif of ascent in the *Life of Antony*, but his eagerness to find Athanasius' antecedents in earlier biographies led him to an incorrect view of their structure and aim.

The foregoing studies of biographies of holy philosophers shared a single approach. Both were interested in those biographies as stepping stones to, or models of, other literary phenomena. One type of study had a definition of the genre of the gospels as its goal; the other aimed at unearthing the antecedents of Christian hagiography. An alternative to those studies is one that considers the biography of the holy man as a literary phenomenon in its own right, although this does not mean that it should be discussed in isolated fashion. This type of biography should be treated as a stage in the history of Graeco-Roman biography, sharing certain features of that genre but also containing new ones that mark it as a unique part of the biographical tradition.

As the discussion of Priessnig's articles showed, the structures that Leo developed to characterize Suetonian and Plutarchian biography do not apply to our group of biographies. The composition of the latter does not lend itself to that kind of schematic analysis, which did not develop a conception of genre sufficient to account both for the continuity and the flexibility of the biographical medium. In order to define the genre of Graeco-Roman biography, we must abandon the notion that an intricate, standard biographical form was developed and passed on through the centuries. Attempts to discern a formal biographical pattern have failed because the biographies do not fit the abstract formulations. Analysis along formal

40. Note that in the monastic context of Athanasius' *Vita Antonii*, "everyman" appears to be first of all the monk. In section 94, he says, "Read these words to the brethren that they may learn what the life of the monks ought to be. . . ." A few sentences later, perhaps as an apologetic afterthought, he adds, "And if need be, read this among the heathen. . . ." For a discussion of the essentially Christian context of Athanasius' biography of Anthony, see Robert Gregg and Dennis Groh, *Early Arianism—A View of Salvation* (Philadelphia: Fortress Press, 1981).

structural lines would eventuate in a "genre" for each biography, certainly a defeat of the effort to reach an encompassing definition. In fact, the only structural statement one can make to characterize the genre as a whole is a very simple one: the Graeco-Roman biography of the holy man is a narrative that relates incidents in the life of its subject from birth or youth to death. The hero's activities provide points of reference for the insertion of material not always related in an obvious way to the narrative's presumed biographical purpose.

This structural definition provides at best only a skeletal sketch of the genre, although it is broad enough to provide a basis for associating several literary works while allowing for individual variations. But form, or structure, is only one aspect of genre, and thus should not be equated with it. Genre is a broader concept, best defined as an association of qualities that are standard features of the works under consideration.[41] In other words, genre is a "cluster of defining traits" that both shapes and distinguishes one group of literary works from another.[42] These traits, or qualities, include structure, formal literary units, sources, types of characterization and motifs, as well as social setting and the author's attitude and intention.[43]

The structural framework of ancient biography was, as we have seen, quite uncomplicated, resting simply on an account of events in a man's life. In our group of biographies of holy men, chronology did not play a very important part in determining the placement of events. Although the authors did give some indication of times for the births and deaths of their subjects,[44] they relied on only the vaguest chronological notices to provide narrative transitions from one event to the next. Such transitional devices as "once," "when," "after this," "it is reported that," and the like, abound in

41. R. S. Crane, *Critical and Historical Principles of Literary History* (Chicago: University of Chicago Press, 1971), p. 8, and Alastair Fowler, "The Life and Death of Literary Forms," *New Literary History* 2 (1971): 202, both discussed by William Doty, "The Concept of Genre in Literary Analysis," in *Working Papers of the Task-Group on the Genre of the Gospels* (Missoula, Montana: Society of Biblical Literature, 1972), pp. 34–35.

42. Doty, "Concept of the Genre," p. 37.

43. Ibid., pp. 36, 55–56.

44. For example, in *Vita Pythagorae* 1–2, Porphyry does not give an exact date for the birth of Pythagoras, but at least an "era," if not a specific year, could be inferred from his discussion of patrimony. Similarly, the date of his death could be inferred from Porphyry's discussion of the persecution of the Pythagorean community by Cylo of Croton in sections 54–57. Porphyry gives more specific dates in his *Vita Plotini* 2: birth came "in the thirteenth year of the reign of Severus"; death in "the end of the second year of the reign of Claudius."

these biographies. Often there is no attempt at all to provide chronological links between events, the authors having been content, apparently, to set down bare lists of the hero's activities, unadorned by contextual setting.[45] The absence of a detailed, progressive chronological framework is, however, a significant feature of these biographies, because it divorces the portrayal of character from dependence on the historical minutiae of the hero's development.

As Leo showed in his *Die Griechisch-Römische Biographie nach ihrer literarischen Form*, ancient biographers generally chose one of two modes for ordering their material: the chronological mode, which involved reporting events in the hero's career in the order of their occurrence, and the topical mode, which ignored the sequence of time and used instead a systematic arrangement of events designed to illustrate various facets of the hero's character. The choice of one of these methods made a significant difference in the way the *akmē*, the productive, creative period in the hero's life, was portrayed.[46] Chronological biographers like Plutarch were dependent upon historical order, and for that reason their judgments about *akmē* had to be tied to specific actions in the hero's career. Further, dependence on history led to a rather straightforward tracing of the life and hence to the convention of placing the *akmē* somewhere in the mature, "career" portion of the hero's life.[47]

Topical biographers were not dependent upon this kind of historical view and so did not portray their heroes' lives as a succession of events that gradually unfolded to bloom in maturity. They tended rather to view the

45. Porphyry's *Vita Pythagorae* provides the best examples of biographical lists:

sections 1–4:	basically a list of patrimony stories;
section 12:	list of sources of Pythagoras' sacred knowledge;
sections 23–26:	list of Pythagoras' communications with animals;
sections 27–30:	list of miracles;
sections 37–45:	list of teachings and maxims.

46. In "Chronological Biography and AKMĒ in Plutarch," *Classical Philology* 69 (July, 1974): 169–177, G. H. Polman reviews the various divisions developed in antiquity to characterize the "stages" of human life. In some, for example, life was divided into seven-year stages (Aristotle *Pol.* 1225b32, *Rhet.* 1390b9; Plato *Laws* 6.722D), while in others the individual was thought to pass through four stages of twenty years each (Diogenes Laertius 8, 10; Plato *Laws* 12.950D). But whatever the schema, the *akmē* was considered to be the individual's mature stage, the time during which his contributions to society were made, and it was often assumed that the period of a person's *akmē* began at age forty. See especially pp. 170–172.

47. See Polman, "Chronological Biography," pp. 172–76.

entire career from the perspective of a single trait or ideal of character in the manner of Aristoxenus and Suetonius respectively, and so developed types rather than historical (and individually developed) personalities. For them the entire career could be treated as the *akmē* of the hero's life.

Biographers of holy men were essentially topical biographers, and their freedom from chronology gave them a broad view of the *akmē*. In fact these biographers portrayed the entire life as an *akmē*. The various aspects of the holy philosopher's perfection did not develop gradually but were persistent features of his personal *topos*. Thus Origen, famous for his allegorical exegesis of Scripture and infamous for his questionable theological positions, was characterized by Eusebius as an orthodox allegorist as a child.[48] And Pythagoras, according to Iamblichus, did not grow into or develop his famed asceticism and "daemonic" bearing; he possessed these qualities "while he was still a youth."[49] The idea of an extended *akmē* helps explain why biographers of holy men resorted so often to lists (of actions, virtues, treatises, disciples, and so on) as devices for characterization. The qualities and talents of ideal figures do not really need an explanatory narrative setting, since there is no causal connection between events in the hero's life and his character. Events are important only in so far as they depict character; they do not shape it.

However, the recitation of events, the *praxeis* of the hero, is crucial to the structure of biographies of holy men. We have just seen that chronology does not provide the structural referent for the narration of the holy man's life. A formal structure is practically nonexistent, apart from concessions to the convention of a birth-to-death envelope.[50] In fact the framework of these biographies is controlled by the ideal of character that the author is using. It is just at this point that form and content are inseparable, for the ideal is, of course, an abstraction, and it is brought to life in the biographies through an assemblage of acts in the hero's life that reveal facets of the ideal. The acts provide the only real structure in the biographies. Each act, whether it is an actual physical deed or a verbal act (a speech, a list of treatises), is a star in the hero's personal constellation; it illumines an aspect of the ideal that his life represents in the biography.

The hero's acts are depicted through the use of a variety of specific literary units (anecdotes, maxims, discourses, and catalogs). Structure has become not a literary pattern or skeleton but a pastiche of literary forms that the

48. Eusebius *HE* 6.2.9–10, 6.2.14–15.

49. Iamblichus *Vita Pythagorica*, 2.10–11.

50. See chap. 3, n. 44 above.

biographer uses to coordinate the elements of his ideal with the activities of his hero.

One of the most important of these forms is the anecdote, a brief biographical narrative that relates a striking or unusual feature of the hero's character. Anecdotes are the major vehicles of biographical characterizations. Not only do they suit the selective nature of storytelling in biographies; they also serve to focus the presentation of the ideal of the holy man by mediating between the stereotype and the historical figure who embodies it. By giving the ideal concrete form in colorful vignettes from the hero's life, anecdotes "demythologize" the ideal. This demythologizing, or personalizing, function of anecdotes is basic to the success of the biographical interplay between the mundane and the ideal. It creates the verisimilitude upon which that interplay depends.

In the early chapters of his "Life of Origen," Eusebius is concerned with developing two themes, themes that in fact relate Origen directly to the godlike model of the holy philosopher discussed earlier. These themes, which express two important aspects of Eusebius' ideal, are Origen's youthful devotion to divine word and deed (the notion of an extended *akmē*), and his special relationship with divinity, which Eusebius defines variously as "divine and heavenly providence," "divine aid," and "divine right hand."[51] Each aspect of the ideal is stated directly, and then is personalized by one or more anecdotes about Origen.

The first theme, the idea of an extended *akmē*, is expressed by Eusebius in the following ways: "In the case of Origen, I think that even the facts from his very cradle, so to speak, are worthy of mention"; and "It will not be out of place to describe briefly how deliberately the boy's mind was set on the divine word from that early age."[52] The young Origen's extreme fidelity is then brought to life in a series of four anecdotes, each of which suggests particular ways in which the ideal showed itself in the real. The first two anecdotes show Origen's eagerness to pursue the divine in deed. The anecdote in *EH* 6.2.3–6 describes Origen's desire to gain the martyr's crown, a desire that is frustrated by divine providence acting through his mother, who hides his clothes and so prevents him from seeking death. The following anecdote (*EH* 6.2.6–7) shows the irrepressible Origen writing to his father on the topic of martyrdom, urging him to seek the glory from which his child has been kept. Both anecdotes are then asserted by Eusebius

51. Eusebius *HE* 6.2.4, 6.2.13, 6.3.4.
52. Ibid., 6.2.2, 6.1.1.

to be "proof of Origen's boyish readiness of mind and geniune love of godliness."[53]

These anecdotes, however, do not simply illustrate Origen's youthful desire to act out the implications of fidelity to religious principle. Rather, they make fidelity real; the character Origen has become a living embodiment of a certain ideal. It is important to note further that the historical veracity of the anecdote is not an essential feature of the dynamic interaction between the character and the model. For example, in the first anecdote we read that Origen lost the chance to become a martyr because his mother hid his clothes "and so laid upon him the necessity of staying at home." The amusing story of the mother's trick and the eager child's modesty has a realistic, believable ring. But Robert M. Grant has pointed out that in an *Apology* for Origen written by Pamphilus and used by Eusebius this vignette is narrated rather differently: Origen was "zealous to strip himself for the stadium of the contests, but his mother, against his will, held him back from his purpose."[54] The stripping motif was originally an athletic metaphor, not a literal use of the word, which Eusebius has either transmitted in a garbled fashion—or reformulated for use in a historical context. In any case, the situation that the anecdote envisages is at least partially legendary. Yet this does not mar the anecdote's success in demythologizing the ideal. Verisimilitude stems not from historical accuracy but from giving the ideal a probable context in which it comes to life. This is not to say, of course, that a biographical hero represented for the biographer simply a personalized or demythologized version of an ideal of the holy man; certainly this is not the case for Eusebius. But with respect to the function that anecdotes serve in biographies, I think that all of our biographers would have agreed with Plutarch's statement: "We must not treat legend as if it were history at all, but we should adopt that which is appropriate in each legend in accordance with its verisimilitude."[55]

Obviously these two anecdotes convey not just the philosopher's active and youthful espousal of religious virtue but also his special connection with a holy force—in this case, providence—that acts as his caretaker (just as the philosopher will himself later be caretaker of his disciples). The two succeeding anecdotes also emphasize this special connection but view it

53. Ibid., 6.2.6.

54. Photius *Bibl.* 118, quoted and discussed by Robert M. Grant, "Eusebius and his Lives of Origen," in *Miscellanea M. Pellegrino* (1975), p. 19.

55. Plutarch *De Isis et Osiris* 374E.

from the perspective of inspiration rather than protection. The anecdote in *EH* 6.2.7–10 recounts the child's introduction to scriptural studies. Here his connection with divinity takes the form of an uncanny wisdom that leads the young scholar to pursue allegorical exegesis, somewhat to the amazement of his father, who thanks God for "such a boy." This anecdote actually finds its climax in the story that immediately follows it (*EH* 6.2.11): "And it is said that many a time he would stand over the sleeping boy and uncover his breast, as if a divine spirit were enshrined therein, and kissing it with reverence count himself happy in his goodly offspring." In the context of a realistic, and rather touching, scene of parental love, a revelation of the theocentric nature of the philosopher is given. The sage is not only inspired and protected by the divine, as in the foregoing anecdotes; he is also intimately connected with it. The kiss of Origen's father represents in fact a revelation, a kind of modified theophany that occurs again and again in different forms as the biography progresses. This story is an excellent example of the way anecdotes function in biographies of holy philosophers. The ideal takes concrete form within an historically framed situation or scene and thus receives credibility.

The biographers' concern for credibility, for the historical credence of their ideal heroes, can be seen not only in their use of anecdotes as literary tools but also in their use of documents. Further, the reference to historical documents helps explain the prominence of two more important literary units in biographies: discourses and maxims.

In the debate between Celsus and Origen over means for legitimating the "son of god" status of particular figures, both men resort to the following dictum: If something in a man's life has had influence on posterity, this lends probability to legends about that man's divinity.[56] This appears to be the kind of thinking that guided the use of sources by biographers who portrayed philosophers as sons of god. Both Porphyry and Iamblichus engage in source-critical discussions of previous historians' and biographers' accounts of the birth and patrimony of Pythagoras.[57] Iamblichus argues against accounts that had suggested Pythagoras' physical descent from Apollo. Porphyry appears concerned to give exhaustive accounts, from both biographies and chronicles, of information on Pythagoras' birthplace, parents, and education. Like Iamblichus, he weaves a reasonably coherent

56. Origen *Contra Celsum* 1.66–67. The point at issue here is divine birth.

57. Porphyry *Vita Pythagorae* 1–6; Iamblichus *Vita Pythagorica* 1.1–2.8.

whole from varied strands of earlier reports. They are, in other words, treating other biographical works as though they were historical documents, and seem to be attempting to distinguish between fact and legend in those documents, at least in so far as birth traditions are concerned.[58]

However, the apparent attack on legendary accretions to the birth story, especially in Iamblichus' biography, breaks down later in the biographies when the revelation of Abaris is recorded uncritically by both authors. That incident, which identified Pythagoras with the Hyperborean Apollo, is at least a partial confirmation of what Iamblichus earlier questions: Pythagoras' Apollonian birthright in a physical sense. What appeared to be, earlier, a critical assessment of legend is later overturned by an uncritical acceptance of the same kind of story. This suggests that both Iamblichus and Porphyry were source critics in a purely formal sense. For Graeco-Roman grammarians and rhetoricians analysed historical narrative on the basis of external or logical principles like "probability," "credibility," and "propriety." History was defined as "an account which sets forth events which took place or as if they took place," whereas myth was an account of something that could not take place.[59] Iamblichus' rejection of Pythagoras' physical Apollonian procreation is not, then, the rejection of a mythical story, since he clearly believes in the historical fact of Pythagoras' Apollonian nature. Rather, it is a technical analysis of an historical narrative, part of which is found to be inappropriate or incredible.[60]

The legacy of the rhetoricians' analysis of myths must have presented quite a problem for authors like Porphyry and Iamblichus because the rhetoricians' rational critiques, which found myths to be unsuitable, impossible, and inconsistent, "left no room," as Grant remarks, "for the operation of nonrational factors in historical events."[61] It is in this context that Por-

58. This obvious sifting and judging of sources also occurs in the reporting of the death stories. In *Vita Pythagorica* 35.248–64, Iamblichus reports the variant accounts of Nicomachus, Aristoxenus, and Apollonius without choosing among them. In *Vita Pythagorae* 54–57, Porphyry chooses the account of Dicaearchus and "the more accurate authorities" (apparently, Nicomachus, since the account Porphyry prefers agrees with Iamblichus' second version, which he attributes to Nicomachus, in *Vita Pythagorica* 35.252–53).

59. Robert M. Grant, *The Earliest Lives of Jesus* (London: SPCK, 1961), pp. 121–22, 39–44.

60. See ibid., p. 41, on the following passage in Theon *Progymnasmata* 76.32: "the incredible is something which can take place or be said, but is not believed to have taken place or to have been said."

61. Ibid., p. 43; see pp. 45–46.

phyry's and Iamblichus' frequent assertions of the credibility and uniformity of their sources are to be understood. The two authors insist upon both the trustworthiness and the accuracy of their sources.[62] That this "probability index" is historical, rather than mythical, is indicated by their use of the verb *historeō*. Significantly, both authors use this verb to justify the historical credibility of Pythagoras' miracles.[63] Here they are clearly revising rationalist rhetorical literary criticism in order to provide a place for the supernatural within history. The "irrational" or supernatural quality of the source material pertaining to Pythagoras is to be accepted as historical because, as Porphyry insists, it is substantiated by uniform stories (*peri t'andros homalōs kai sumphōnōs eirētai*).[64] While he agrees with Porphyry on the issue of uniformity, Iamblichus takes the argument a step further: the supernatural in history is believable because "all things are possible to the gods."[65] The key to his argument is that his historical sources can be regarded as "divine dogma" (*theia dogmata*).[66] For him this is not an issue of interpretation; history has become dogma.

This perspective on sources enables both Porphyry and Iamblichus to call their sources *hūpomnēmata*,[67] memoirs or records, a term related to the use by other authors of *apomnēmoneumata* to denote truthful historical memoranda.[68] True historical criticism is not, therefore, a literary characteristic of these biographies. The success of the biographers' use of sources to validate their biographies in both a literary and a philosophical sense depends on a reinterpretation of the literary-critical view of history. That this reinterpretation is in keeping with traditional biographical techniques is clear in Porphyry's and Iamblichus' use of discourses and maxims. These are major literary components of their biographies that, like the use of documents, give the biographies the appearance of history. Again, the ideal becomes real when the hero's own words are quoted.

Long discourses and lists of Pythagorean maxims make up substantial portions of the Pythagorean biographies; they are important literary build-

62. Iamblichus *Vita Pythagorica* 13.60, 28.134, 29.157; Porphyry *Vita Pythagorae* 10, 28.

63. Iamblichus *Vita Pythagorica* 28.135; Porphyry *Vita Pythagorae* 23, 27.

64. Porphyry *Vita Pythagorae* 28.

65. Iamblichus *Vita Pythagorica* 28.138–39.

66. Ibid., 28.148.

67. Ibid., 19.94, 23.104, 29.157; Porphyry uses variations of the verb *mnēmoneuō* in *Vita Pythagorae* 5 and 29.

68. Grant, *Earliest lives of Jesus*, pp. 119–20 and 15–27 passim.

ing blocks in the construction of character.[69] As Fischel has shown, it is notoriously difficult to locate the origin of maxims historically since the same statement is often attributed to several philosophers from widely divergent cultures and eras.[70] This is also true of discourses. As early as Xenophon (in the *Memorabilia*), biographers attributed to their heroes speeches that they could have made, even if, historically, they did not.[71] That this process has taken place in Iamblichus' reports of discourses is clear from the obvious Neoplatonic cast of certain "Pythagorean" speeches.[72] They are convenient literary vehicles for representing the ideal in the historical figure. The literary-critical notion of historical probability, combined with the view that a man's later stature heightens the "believability" of his deeds, indicates why the conscious reference to sources and use of discourses were important literary tools for biographies of sons of god. They provided means for authenticating legend historically.

These tools were not available to Porphyry for his *Life of Plotinus* nor to Eusebius for his "Life of Origen" since they were writing about more recent figures and could not rely on earlier biographies or well-developed legendary traditions. Their sources were primarily letters and "eyewitness" reports. Porphyry, who in his biography calls himself "one of Plotinus' closest friends," knew many in Plotinus' circle and refers specifically to information that he has obtained from them.[73] Scattered throughout the biography are enigmatic statements of Plotinus', which Porphyry relates in anecdotal

69. Porphyry emphasizes maxims, whereas Iamblichus concentrates on the sage's moral, political, and philosophical exhortations.

70. Henry Fischel, "Story and History: Observations on Greco-Roman Rhetoric and Pharisaism," *American Oriental Society, Middle West Branch, Semi-Centennial Volume*, ed. Denis Sinor, Asian Studies Research Institute, Oriental Series 3 (Bloomington: Indiana University Press, 1969), p. 72. Fischel's focus is on *chriae*, which were borrowed and adapted from Greek literature by Jewish writers and used to characterize such sages as Hillel and Hanina ben Dosa. In *The Sentences of Sextus* (Cambridge: Cambridge University Press, 1959), pp. 143–54, Chadwick has shown that Porphyry's maxims come from Epicurean aphorisms and an alphabetical collection of Pythagorean maxims.

71. See chapter 1, pp. 7–8.

72. See Festugière, "Sur une nouvelle édition du *De Vita Pythagorica* de Jamblique," pp. 470–94; Lévy, *Recherches sur les sources de la légende de Pythagore*, pp. 102–17; Bieler, *ΘΕΙΟΣ ΑΝΗΡ*, 1: 126; and Armand Delatte, *Études sur la littérature Pythagoricienne* (Paris: Librairie Ancienne Honoré Champion, 1915), pp. 12–26. For an alternate view, see C. J. de Vogel, *Pythagoras and Early Pythagoreanism* (Assen, 1966).

73. Porphyry *Vita Plotini* 7; see, for example, 1,2 (Eustochius); 3 (Amelius); 10.

contexts, as well as descriptions of the proceedings of the school, part of which Porphyry has gotten from a collection of notes made by one of Plotinus' earliest and most favored students.[74] He quotes from two letters that he himself received from other philosophers and uses them as a defense of Plotinus' originality and clear thinking; both are part of the polemical accent of his biography, directed against the charge that Plotinus was a confused plagiarizer of Numenius.[75] It is interesting to note that it was after a series of debates with Amelius, Plotinus' apologist, that Porphyry came "to believe" (*episteuthēn*) in Plotinus' writings (*ta biblia*—does he mean "holy documents"?).[76] Porphyry's use of the apologist's letter is clearly related to the usual idealizing tendencies of biographies of holy philosophers.

A final, perhaps most interesting, source, which Porphyry identifies explicitly, is an oracle of Apollo given to Amelius upon Plotinus' death.[77] In it the godlike nature of Plotinus' soul is stated very clearly, and in the following chapter Porphyry indicates the truth of the oracle: "We knew ourselves that he was like this." Poetic truth has become historical fact, authenticated by eyewitnesses. What I find significant about Porphyry's use of documents is that even though his material has a more solid foundation in history (much of it stems from firsthand observation, in good Thucydidean fashion), the same factor of probability evident in his life of Pythagoras is operative here. The letters, anecdotes, Plotinian enigmas, and the oracle are not sources assembled in a haphazard way; they have rather been selected specially, for use in a carefully crafted idealizing portrait.

Like Porphyry, Eusebius also has used letters, though his are by the hero himself,[78] and eyewitness accounts. But the accounts incorporated into the text of his biography were apparently primarily written accounts. At one point he refers to a group of anecdotes as stories that "they tell" (*mnēmoneuousin*) about Origen; the verb here *could* mean either "recall" or "record."[79] This statement concludes the anecdotal series. However, the same section is introduced by Eusebius' admission that some of his material has come from "information" (*historia*) from Origen's pupils. The use of *historia*[80] seems clearly to indicate that his sources are written documents, and that *mnēmoneo* is also used to indicate records, not spoken recollections.

74. *Vita Plotini* 3, collection of notes; 2, 10, 15, enigmatic statements as anecdotal climaxes.

75. Ibid., 17, letter of Amelius. 76. Ibid., 18. 77. Ibid., 22.

78. Eusebius *HE* 6.2.1.

79. Ibid., 6.2.11. See Grant, *Earliest Lives of Jesus*, pp. 119–20 on *apomnēmoneuma*.

80. Grant, *Earliest Lives of Jesus*, pp. 120–21, on *historia*.

Again the notion of probability is relevant. We have already seen that the anecdotal section that is introduced and concluded by these source citations is a product of the biographical idealizing process. Like Porphyry and Iamblichus, Eusebius is certifying the credibility of the divine in the historical by using technical terms that indicate the formal (if not actual) historical provenance of his sources.[81] What the discussion of sources indicates is that, like anecdotes, explicit reference to sources provided biographers with a way to tie together their ideal of the holy man with the historical figure who embodied the ideal.

Thus far, three generic traits of Graeco-Roman biographies of holy philosophers have been discussed: structure, literary units, and source use. Those that remain to be considered—the type of characterization, social setting, and authorial intention—will form the basis for the final three chapters. It should, however, be clear from the foregoing discussion of some of the generic elements of biography that there is a definite continuity in the Greek biographical tradition.

Like earlier biographers of philosophers, those discussed here molded the lives of their heroes to preconceived models. The persistent feature of biography from Hellenistic to Graeco-Roman times was a literary process, the dynamic interaction of fantasy and historical reality whose intent was to capture the ideals suggested by the life of the hero. The specific characteristics of this process also persisted: the dichotomy between *praxeis* and *ēthos*, in which deeds, both physical and verbal, were utilized as a backdrop for the portrayal of character, since character was viewed as the essence of the life; the tendency to extend the *akmē* (developed as early as Xenophon in his *Agesilaus*); and the use of anecdotes and discourses not only as major literary means for depicting character but also as techniques for conveying historical verisimilitude. What was new in Graeco-Roman biographies of the holy man was that the idealizing process assumed a standard face, so that philosophers were depicted not only as superior men but also as figures of holiness. The idea that philosophers were divine represents the reigning mythology of Graeco-Roman biographies devoted to such figures. And, as we shall see, the biographers' adoption of this divine type in their works was directly linked to the social situation in which these biographies were produced, that is, the heated religious conflicts between pagans and Christians in the third and fourth centuries.

81. Eusebius' use of letters will be treated in detail in Chapter 4.

PART II

Myth, History, and the Elusive Holy Man: Two Approaches

CHAPTER FOUR

Eusebius' "Life of Origen": Faces of History

Eusebius of Caesarea devoted most of Book 6 of his *Ecclesiastical History* to a biographical account of his theological hero, Origen of Alexandria. This report contains most of what is known about Origen's life.[1] Though its anecdotal elements do not give us the visual characterization of a Zeno eating green figs and basking in the sun,[2] we might imagine that Origen affected the long hair, beard, and wrinkled forehead of any self-respecting philosopher of his day.[3] This image is evoked by the philosophical pretensions of Eusebius' biography, which casts the Christian theologian Origen in the stereotypical guise of a Hellenistic holy man.

It is ironic that it should have suited Eusebius to depict the life of his mentor within a framework whose literary and ideological conventions served in some respects to mute Origen's identity as a Christian. For it was Origen's fervent desire to be considered a *vir ecclesiasticus*, a man of the Church whose acts as well as his thoughts proclaimed him a Christian in good standing.[4] Eusebius certainly agreed with Origen's portrait of himself

1. Additional facts and fantasies concerning Origen's career are found in the following works: Pamphilus *Apologia pro Origene*; Gregory Thaumaturgus *Panegyric*; Jerome *De viris inlustribus* 54 and 61; *Epistles* 33 and 44; Photius *Bibliotheca* 118; Epiphanius *Panarion* 64; Porphyry *Contra Christianos*.

2. Diogenes Laertius 7.1–160.

3. In *The Cynic* 1, Lucian of Samosata gives a portrait of the typical philosopher: "Why in heaven's name have you the beard and long hair, but no shirt? Why do you expose your body to view, and go barefooted, adopting by choice this nomadic, antisocial and bestial life? Why unlike all others do you abuse your body by ever inflicting on it what it likes least, wandering around and prepared to sleep anywhere at all on the hard ground?" Compare Eusebius *HE* 6.3.9–12.

4. "For my part, my desire is to belong to the church, and not to be called by the name of some heretic, but by the name of Christ, and to carry this name which is blessed on earth; my

as a churchman *par excellence*, and would probably have concurred with those admirers of Origen who thought him not simply a *vir ecclesiasticus* but worthy of comparison with the apostles and prophets.[5] However, Eusebius' biography was not written solely to secure Origen's status within Christian circles. It was also directed at pagan outsiders, with the purpose of establishing Origen's credentials as a thinker worthy of the attention of the philosophical community at large. Hence, while Origen's identity as a Christian is maintained, his eminence derives from those characteristics that define his universal appeal.

Like his contemporary biographers, Eusebius composed his biography with a desire to personify certain revered philosophical and theological precepts. As we have seen, in the Graeco-Roman period the philosophic or religious sage was the enigmatic figure who embodied these precepts, and although his historical accoutrements changed according to the bias and historical circumstances of his various biographers, his idealistic demeanor persisted with few alterations.

In Eusebius' case, the ideal of the sage is imposed on Origen, and to some extent the facts of the churchman's life form a kind of historical clothing for the model Eusebius develops. Thus a stereotype is given the flesh and blood of an historical figure, and as a result the life idealized is infused with a mythic quality that enhances its cross-cultural appeal. Origen, then, appears as a larger-than-life figure able to transcend the confines of his historical Christian identity by taking on the traits of the Hellenistic "divine" philosopher: ascetic, virtuous, and full of wisdom.

This biography is a complex piece of work that cannot be evaluated adequately from a single perspective. It addresses two different communities and attempts to be faithful to two major orientations. The first orientation can be interpreted as a polemical schema directed to Origen's detractors in the Christian community, who were attacking his theological orthodoxy, and to those in the pagan community who were questioning his philosophical integrity. The second appears as a creative apologetic effort to promote unity among the persecuted Christian communities by establishing Origen as a rallying figure, a contemporary "saint," and to present

wish, both in my acts and in my thoughts, is to be a Christian and proclaimed as such by men." (Ego vero, qui opto esse ecclesiasticus et non ab haeresiarchae aliquo, sed a Christi vocabulo nuncupari et habere nomen, quod benedicitur super terram, et cupio tam opere quam sensu et esse et dici christianus.) Origen *Homilies on Luke* 16.1. Origen often referred to himself as a man of the Church. See *Homilies on Joshua* 9.8; *Homilies on Leviticus* 1.1

5. Pamphilus *Apologia pro Origene*, praef.

Origen as an example of a perfect amalgam of pagan and Christian virtues, a kind of proselytizing propaganda to waning paganism. Though the combination of these two schemes in a single literary work might seem paradoxical at first, the tradition of biography writing to which Eusebius was heir provided the thematic conventions that made possible the weaving together of the many faces of Origen that Eusebius presents.

Swaddling Clothes Tales: Legend or History?

Scholarly commentary on Book 6 of Eusebius' *Ecclesiastical History* has not been consistently acute regarding the church historian's ideological stance. Eduard Schwartz, the first scholar to attempt an exposé of the motives behind the entire *History*, found it to be more "ein kirchliches und politisches Pamphlet" than history in the strict sense of the term.[6] In his monumental 1909 critical edition of the *Ecclesiastical History* Schwartz pointed specifically to the biographical character of Book 6, which he thought demonstrated clearly the "apologetic tendencies" of Eusebius' historical efforts.[7] According to Schwartz, Eusebius was the "unqualified partisan" of Origen whose biographical defense of his hero, especially concerning Origen's Alexandrian ecclesiastical situation, resulted in a distorted historical perspective.[8] Although Schwartz's volumes pointed the way to critical examination of Eusebius' portrait of Origen, much of the scholarly work that followed took scant notice of the significance of Schwartz's "Eusebian Origen." In his *Origène, sa vie, son oeuvre, sa pensée* (1923), Eugene de Faye treated Eusebius' biographical evidence erratically, being sometimes sympathetic to his portrait of Origen and sometimes critical. So, for example, when assessing the childhood stories of the biography, de Faye doubted "on the grounds of common sense" that the youth was already allegorizing Scripture and charged Eusebius with a little historical "embroidering"; yet he stated in the same context that "one cannot doubt that he (Origen) was a remarkable child."[9] Obviously de Faye believed that an historical reality underlay Eu-

6. *PW* 6[1], col. 1423, s.v. "Eusebios," by Eduard Schwartz.

7. Eduard Schwartz, *Eusebius: Die Kirchengeschichte*, *GCS* 9, 3 vols. (Berlin: J. C. Hinrichs, 1909), 1:31.

8. Ibid., p. lxvii.

9. Eugene de Faye, *Origène, sa vie, son oeuvre, sa pensée*, 3 vols. (Paris: Éditions Ernest Leroux, 1923), vol. 1: *Sa Biographie et ses Écrits*, p. 6 and n. 1.

sebius' handiwork here, though with regard to the Eusebian Origen as martyr and ardent Christian he was more consistently critical.[10]

The major interpretations of Origen's life that followed did not exercise even a moderate skepticism. Both René Cadiou, *La Jeunesse d'Origène* (1935), and Jean Daniélou, *Origène* (1948), accepted the biography with few, if any, reservations. Daniélou, for example, stated that Eusebius' notion of the worthiness of "even the facts from (Origen's) very cradle" "nous inquiète un peu," yet he accepted the substance of the childhood stories as not simply true but "precious" information.[11] In a similar way he regarded Eusebius' inclusion of the young Origen's encounter with an Antiochene heretic as part of an "apologetic intention," but thought that consistent orthodoxy was characteristic of Origen just the same.[12]

This acceptance of Eusebius' vision of Origen the "Wundermensch" is not to be attributed only to the efforts of French Catholic patrologists to undo Justinian's condemnation of Origen and Origenist theology, for F. J. Foakes-Jackson, a British contemporary of Daniélou and Cadiou, was equally uncritical in his *Eusebius Pamphili, A Study of the Man and His Writings* (1933). In recent years, however, scholars have become increasingly suspicious of the degree of Eusebius' historical detachment, especially where Book 6 is concerned. A remark by Henry Chadwick is indicative of the "Schwartzian" perspective of his approach: "Whenever Eusebius depends on no more than hearsay and oral tradition, his authority is not higher than that of any reasonably conscientious gossip-writer."[13] Foremost among these recent studies on Book 6 are a series of articles by R. M. Grant, which focus primarily on Eusebius' historical subterfuges; a study of Alexandrian and Caesarean legends about Origen by M. Hornschuh; and two works by P. Nautin, an analysis of Origen's letters and a biographical study of Origen. Their insights will be discussed in the course of my own treatment of the "Life of Origen."

Unfortunately it is impossible today to write a true "life" of Origen. We have already seen that the historical facade of biographies of holy men was an intentional artifice; historical data were used to ground an ideal portrait in "real" life, and sources were cited to create the guise of history. Eusebius

10. Ibid., pp. 8–17.

11. Jean Daniélou, *Origène* (Paris: La Table Ronde, 1948), p. 21.

12. Ibid., pp. 23–24.

13. Henry Chadwick, *Early Christian Thought and the Classical Tradition* (Oxford: Clarendon Press, 1966), p. 67.

was no different from his fellow biographers, and what he has given us in his "Life of Origen" is a series of character impressions that follow a vague chronological order and may or may not have some claim to historical veracity. Our problem is whether one can discern a real Origen in all of this. What we know of Origen from his own writings tends to support the conclusion that from time to time the shadow of Origen that haunts the biography may actually be a faithful reflection of the man himself (for example, the materials concerning ascetic practice and martyrdom). At other times, however, the shadow seems to be simply that, a figment of Eusebius' biographical imagination (for example, the childhood stories and materials pertaining to orthodoxy).

The idea that Eusebius' portrait sometimes possesses real substance and sometimes does not is what makes his biography interesting for research into the dynamic of biography writing. Historical information independent of Eusebius' story frequently enables us to see through his idealizing obfuscations and thus to expose in a uniquely detailed manner how biographical portraits were crafted. Two issues will dominate this chapter: one concerns the extent to which we can know the historical Origen; the other concerns the Eusebian Origen and the materials, both historical and imagined, used to create him.

Just as it seemed appropriate to Eusebius to begin his biography of Origen with "swaddling-clothes tales," so it seems fitting to begin this study with the same stories, for they establish the thematic structure of the entire biography. A word of caution is in order, however: though the childhood tales may be examples of Eusebius' lack of historical reserve, they may also be taken as practical applications of statements on literary portraiture that Eusebius makes in his *Against Hierocles*.

In *Against Hierocles*, a critique of Philostratus' biography of Apollonius of Tyana as divine man, Eusebius takes issue not with the idea of biographical eulogy itself but only with what he considers to be the extreme divinization of Apollonius.[14] Eusebius would prefer to see Apollonius portrayed as "a human wise man" (*sophon tina ta anthrōpina ton tuanea gegonenai hēgoumēn*) which Eusebius considers him to have been. Philostratus' interpretative fault is described as "overleaping the bounds of humanity and transcending philosophy."[15] A few chapters later, Eusebius makes two intriguing statements that reveal his own canon concerning the integrity (the believability)

14. Eusebius *Contra Hieroclem* 5.
15. Ibid.

of biographical data. Discussing the juxtaposition of the legend (*mūthos*) of Apollonius' divine nature with the story (*logos*) that certain teachers taught him how to converse with the gods, Eusebius states: "If then he was of a divine nature, it follows that the story of his teachers is spurious. On the other hand if the story was true, then the legend was false, and the account [*graphē*] of his divine nature is not true [*ouk alēthēs . . . gegonenai*]."[16] Here Eusebius appears to be contrasting two kinds of statements, one an historical statement on the part of Apollonius' teachers, the other a transhistorical assertion of Apollonius' divine nature. Yet he actually treats *logos* and *mūthos* as though they were categories of equal value; their transposition must prove one to be false, the other true. The important point is that if *mūthos* can be false, it can also be true. Now *mūthos* as a literary category dealt with likelihood rather than certainty in history. As in the evaluation of historical sources in Book 6,[17] so also here truth is relative, or probable, rather than absolute.

Less than half a chapter later the question of accurate evaluation is still on Eusebius' mind: "I am however quite ready to accept all that is probable and has an air of truth about it [*tois eikosi te kai alētheias echomenois peithomenos*], even though such details may be somewhat exaggerated and highly colored out of compliment to a good man; for it seems to me that they can be admitted and believed [*pista kai paradektea einai moi dōkō*], as long as they are not only full of prodigies and nonsense [*mē mona ta teratōdē kai lērou plea*]."[18] Here Eusebius has linked "the likely" with "the true," "the admissible" with "the believable." The probable in history is worthy of belief; this justifies and makes legitimate the use of hyperbole in panegyric. Since this entire discussion occurs in the context of a critique of a biography, Eusebius' comments are tantamount to a declaration of creative license in biography in which the credibility of historically probable data is affirmed. Based on what he says here, I think Eusebius would equate good biography with panegyric, whose interpretative detail passes beyond the pale of credibility only when incongruous or overly teratological material is related as fact.[19]

Eusebius' theoretical musings on the historical boundaries of biographi-

16. Ibid., 11. 17. See chapter 3, pp. 64–65. 18. Eusebius *Contra Hieroclem* 12.
19. See Eusebius' statement in *Contra Hieroclem* 32: "There are a thousand other examples then which we may select from the same books, where the narrative refutes itself by its very incongruities, so enabling us to detect its mythical and miracle-mongering character."

cal characterization are not intended to rule out the presence of the divine in the human, however. Eusebius finally describes the "bounds of humanity," which he has accused Philostratus of "overleaping" in his divinizing portrait of Apollonius, in chapter 6 of the *Against Hierocles*. Here Eusebius discusses the proper status of nature in cosmic terms: the entire universe is limited and sustained by laws imposed by "the all-wise will of providence," which has decreed for every kind of created being its proper place and order. Ultimately it is the divine providence that prohibits transgressions of natural limits. After giving examples from the animal world (such as the fish which cannot transgress his watery limit and live on land), Eusebius turns to man. Man must respect both physical and spiritual limits: just as he cannot fly, so also he cannot by his own effort ascend to spiritual heights beyond his natural capacity (which is described as fortifying one's soul with philosophy). However, the rule of divine providence (*logos . . . theias pronoias*) allows for man to hope that "some one may come to help him from aloft from the paths of heaven, and reveal himself to him as a teacher of the salvation that is there." In other words, providence allows for a divine nature to associate itself with men because providence, being good, desires to illumine the human soul.

Thus far this is a rather curious discussion, for Eusebius, while trying to indicate the natural limitations of human ability to comprehend the divine, seems to confuse the illumination of the soul by providence with the sending of an illuminator. It is not yet clear whether the "teacher" to whom he refers is an actual figure (Christ) or the gift of spiritual understanding. The concluding portion of the chapter clarifies the ambiguity and is easily one of the most important indications of Eusebius' ideas about the divine-human relationship. I will quote it in full:

> The controller of this universe [one of the names for providence in this discussion] . . . will dispatch the most intimate of his own messengers from time to time, for the salvation and succour of men here below. Of these messengers anyone so favored by fortune, having cleansed his understanding and dissipated the mist of mortality, may well be described as truly divine, and as carrying in his soul the image of some great god. Surely so great a personality will stir up the entire human race, and illuminate the world of mankind more brightly than the sun, and will leave the effects of his eternal divinity for the contemplation of future ages, in no less a degree affording an example of the divine and inspired nature than creations of artists made of lifeless matter. To this extent then human nature can participate

in the super-human; but otherwise it cannot lawfully transcend its bounds, nor with its wingless body emulate the bird, nor being a man must one meddle with what pertains to demons. (*Against Hierocles* 6)

At first this passage appears to be a description of the God-man, Jesus Christ, whom Eusebius has described in an earlier chapter in terms of the lasting effects of his divinity as well of the image of the teacher. In the passage just quoted the teacher that humans can hope for is a messenger whose "eternal divinity" is contemplated by succeeding generations. However, the context of the passage just quoted puts the exclusive identification of this messenger with Christ in doubt.

The entire chapter is intended not to develop a Christian theory of ultimate human divinity but rather to show why Philostratus' portrait of Apollonius is unacceptable. The nature of the holiness attributed to Apollonius is ill-conceived and arrogant because it passes beyond what is possible for the soul to attain, even with the help of providence. Eusebius then sets forth his notion of the "bounds of humanity" (which he also calls in the same chapter the "bounds of divinity"). Jesus may in fact be the ultimate messenger, but Eusebius is here describing a succession of human messengers ("dispatch[ed} . . . from time to time") whose saintly lives ("cleansing understanding and dissipating mortality") show how human nature participates in the superhuman. The intimate messenger is thus a human being whose purified soul bears the image of God, and whose teaching ("the effects of his eternal divinity") survives him. This passage is not about the saving effects of the incarnate redeemer. Its referent is instead a type, the human teacher of salvation, whose greatness of soul demonstrates the outer limits of human ability to relate to the divine as well as to relate the divine to others. What Eusebius has described is a pattern of human divinity; and the man whose life evinces this pattern is the kind of man one memorializes in a biography. At this point Eusebius' literary-critical ideas on probability in history assume their full significance, for the biographer's creative license is legitimate only when he is describing, or "fleshing out," the correct pattern.

That Eusebius has found an exemplar of this pattern becomes clear in the early chapters of his "Life of Origen." In the *Ecclesiastical History* 6.2.4, Eusebius states that the young Origen, a would-be martyr, was preserved from death by "divine and heavenly providence." Four times more in the first four chapters, Eusebius points specifically to a divine power that both saves and protects his hero: in 6.2.13, Origen the impoverished orphan is "found worthy of divine aid"; in 6.3.4, Origen the supporter of martyrs is saved from pagan fury by the "divine right hand"; in 6.3.5, the zealous Origen is saved from heathen plots "again and again" by "this same divine and heavenly grace"; finally, in 6.4.2, Origen is again preserved against a mob attack by "the will of God." In these passages Eusebius has marked out a definite pattern for the relationship between his hero and providence. Providence is the benevolent force that sustains the hero's life, allowing him to teach and to encourage martyrs. Here Origen is shown in an intimate relationship to providence while he at the same time is "teaching salvation" (whose end in this context is martyrdom). Already, then, the life of Origen begins to conform to the pattern that Eusebius has described in *Against Hierocles*: Origen is "a messenger, favored by providence, who stirs up the human race" (both pagan and Christian) by his teaching.

This pattern is not, however, dependent upon providence acting as a *deus ex machina*, simply interceding at critical moments to ensure the hero's continued existence. Origen is not being pictured as a puppet moved by the whims of divine grace. As Glenn Chesnut has shown, Eusebius rejected the pagan notions of fortune and fate as the determining factors in human existence. In his view, they denied the "logos-structure in history."[20] For Eusebius history had both meaning and direction, both of which were supplied by the Logos, "the rational structure of the cosmos."[21] In a general sense, this rational structure is what Eusebius meant by providence, which was responsible for natural laws or limits.

Eusebius recognized, however, that the harmony of history seen in cosmic terms often appeared as a disruptive and random chain of "accidents" when seen in human, historical terms. In order to maintain human history within the benevolent order of the cosmos, Eusebius saw a special providence at work alongside the more general, sustaining providential order. Chesnut argues as follows: Since, according to Eusebius, accidents (the things which happen to us, seemingly as a result of forces beyond our control) "take place in accordance with nature, and the course of natural events is prescribed by the laws of nature contained in the Logos, this means that a sort of general providence specifies the *general* possibilities within which the events of history are allowed to unfold. But there is also a 'special' provi-

20. Glenn F. Chesnut, Jr., "Fate, Fortune, Free Will and Nature in Eusebius of Caesarea," *CH* 42 (June, 1973): 168.
21. Ibid.

dence, because at every historical conjuncture God also chooses exactly which *particular* set of concrete events is going to take place within the manifold set of abstract, purely formal possibilities laid out by the Logos. That is, in every historical conjuncture we see God's providence arranging the *symbebēkota* (accidents) into whatever order (*taxis*) he wishes."[22] In Eusebius' view, providence orders and arranges specific sequences of human events (Chesnut calls it "divine manipulation of the accidents of history")[23] in order to reveal divine purpose and meaning. Providence not only sustains human life according to natural law but actually provides a "life pattern" in a very specific historical sense. Thus in Origen's life the preserving functions of providence that Eusebius delineated were not miraculous interventions in specific historical circumstances but rather evidence of the providential plan for Origen's life. In fact, as Chesnut points out, miracle did not play an important role in Eusebius' historical compositions, and with good reason. Miraculous intervention is erratic intervention, which counters the idea of providence's pervasive cosmic control. "Appeal to the miraculous has never been a good theological device for getting a continuous divine presence in human history."[24]

The idea of a general and a specific providence helps explain how Eusebius conceives of a pattern of human divinity. General providence, responsible for natural law, provided that within the "bounds of humanity" some men may reach the outer limits of those bounds—that is, an intimate association with divinity for the benefit of other men. Providence in the specific sense provided the precise historical conditions within which that specially chosen man operated. Origen, one of those "specially chosen," as Eusebius' frequent mention of providence shows, did not live a life punctuated by miracles that occur just in the nick of time; rather, the very fabric of his life depended upon providential blessing as well as providential control over the historical accidents that affected him.

It must be noted, however, that the sway of providence does not cancel human freedom or free will. Eusebius held to a Platonic psychology of the most extreme kind: the rational soul was completely at variance with the irrational "body."[25] The successful psyche must will the irrational body's

22. Ibid., p. 174. 23. Ibid. 24. Ibid., pp. 173–74, n. 37.

25. Ibid., p. 178. Pertinent in this regard is Eusebius *Contra Hieroclem* 42: "The universe is ordered by the divine laws of the providence of God that controls all things, and the peculiar nature of man's soul renders him master of himself and judge, ruler and lord of himself. . . .

subjection and turn toward the divine (a feat helped greatly by living the ascetic life).[26] In its turning, however, the psyche finds help because by a process called synergism, providence works with and cooperates with the human will.[27] Providence in this sense does not ride roughshod over free will but cooperates with the psyche that has turned in the right way. Eusebius' portrait of Origen provides a good example of this providential dynamic. Origen's breast enshrined a divine spirit (providential blessing); the events of his life showed specific providential ordering; he lived the ascetic life, characterized by an abundance of zeal (proper psychic control over the irrational); and, as Eusebius specifically stated, he enjoyed "the cooperation of the divine power" (synergism: *sunairomenēs autō dunameōs theias*) *as a result of* the manner of his life.[28] The effects of providence on the life of the holy man are thus far reaching. Yet, as Eusebius' biography of Origen shows, the proper human response is a necessary feature of the providential process.[29]

Eusebius' picture of the holy man who works within a providential framework helps explain why the hero of his biography is cast in the godlike, rather than the son-of-god, mold. Providence ensures that the pattern of life, even for a "teacher of salvation," is acted out within fundamentally human, historical limits. Eusebius' divine man is not one who floats freely in some ontological category between God and man; he is, on the contrary,

---

within our control is everything which comes into being in accordance with our will and choice and action, and these are naturally free, unhindered, and unimpeded. But such things as are not in our control are weak and servile, restrained and alien to ourselves; for example, our bodily processes and external objects which are both lifeless and destitute of reason, and in their manner of existence wholly foreign to the proper nature of a reasonable living creature."

26. See *Contra Hieroclem* 42: "As for things which are in our control, each one of us possesses in the will itself alternative impulses of virtue and vice. . . . for the motives on which we act the responsibility lies not with destiny nor fate, nor with necessity. It lies with him who makes the choice."

27. Eusebius *Praeparatio Evangelica* 6.6.45, quoted and discussed by Chesnut, "Fate, Fortune, Free Will and Nature in Eusebius of Caesarea," p. 180.

28. Eusebius *HE* 6.3.7.

29. In his biography, Eusebius insists upon the zeal, boldness, and eagerness of the boy blessed by possession of a divine spirit. See *HE* 6.1, 6.2.3–6, 6.2.9, 6.2.15, 6.3.5–8, 6.3.10–11. Presumably Origen's "excessive zeal" is his response to his gift. He also, of course, turns his psyche properly by following an ascetic lifestyle: *HE* 6.3.6–7 and 6.3.10–12.

located in specific situations that disclose the meaningful direction of history by providence. For Eusebius the life of the holy man reveals a divine *telos*. Thus the kind of divine man portrayed by Philostratus did not, indeed could not, exist for Eusebius. His philosophy of history ruled out fate and necessity as determining factors in human existence. As he clearly stated in one of the concluding chapters of *Against Hierocles*, the doctrine that sees "destiny and the Fates" as the controlling cosmic forces destroys human responsibility for goodness as well as for evil. The divine man who was "a mere toy in the hands of the Fates" was not for Eusebius a very impressive figure.[30] He argued forcefully that Apollonius' wisdom and virtue, as well as his attempts to preach and communicate those qualities, were pointless, for his hearers were fated to be virtuous or wise whether Apollonius spoke or not.[31] But the culmination of his critique was the most damaging, for it destroyed the basis of the Philostratean divine man's uniqueness: none of Apollonius' achievements or characteristics was truly his; destiny alone, who "whirled him idly around," can take credit for this wise man's philosophical and "self"-disciplined life.[32] Eusebius' critique of the son-of-god model adhered to by Philostratus is devastating because it shows that when human responsibility is lacking, there is no pattern of human divinity.

We have seen that, in Eusebius' thinking, there was a specific pattern of human divinity with definite historical boundaries that prevented extreme forms of divinization. Within those boundaries, however, there was great descriptive flexibility, especially for the biographer who attempted to portray a particular man as an exemplar of the pattern. As Eusebius himself stated, the biographer was free to use exaggeration in developing his portrait so long as he maintained at least the semblance of historical truth.

With regard to the stories that Eusebius used to introduce Origen's character in his biography, one might well ask what were the standards governing his own exaggerations. We have already seen how Eusebius used the idea of providential guidance to distinguish Origen's special holiness from that of an Apollonius or a Pythagoras by establishing him within a general type. But the specifics of his characterization (those "compliments" that we would call historical fantasy rather than probable data) were marshaled in favor of two major themes: Origen the ascetic scholar and Origen the orthodox teacher. These themes are introduced in the "swaddling-clothes tales," and they form the ideal standards around which Eusebius' detailed portrait

30. Eusebius *Contra Hieroclem* 41. 31. Ibid. 32. Ibid.

revolves. Both the thematic structure as well as the detailed information supporting it stem from the biographer's creative license, wherein ideal portraits were developed out of "probable" historical data.

The most unusual of the childhood stories does not fit in Eusebius' schema of themes but in fact underpins them all. This is the story in *EH* 6.2.10–11, where Origen's father Leonides kisses his son's breast "as if it was the temple of a divine spirit." Earlier I stated that this story functions as a revelation of the theocentric nature of the philosopher. It is this holy status that justifies Origen's idealistic demeanor throughout the biography and permits the biographer's embellishments and glosses on his personal history. Thus the meaning of this story deserves some further attention.

Recent interpreters of Eusebius' biography have not given much attention to this story of the "divine spirit," perhaps because their objectives have been for the most part historical. In his latest study, Pierre Nautin dismisses the entire section in which the story appears (*EH* 6.2.7–11) as oral tradition: "Cette tradition ne mérite aucune confiance, car personne, à l'époque d'Eusèbe, ne pouvait prétendre avoir connu Origène à cet âge."[33] Because his interest is in historical fact only, Nautin disregards what Eusebius took very seriously, that is, the attempt to frame in historical terms the transcendent quality of his hero's character.[34] Unlike Nautin, Manfred Hornschuh and Robert M. Grant do not dismiss the story but take it to be part of Eusebius' attempt to Hellenize Origen. Both agree that Eusebius' picture of Origen as a temple of a divine spirit comes directly from the *theios anēr* of popular religious expression, a figure whose lofty spiritual capacity was a conventional trait.[35] But neither discusses the story in detail.

Ancient admirers of Origen tended to corroborate Eusebius' impression of the man, though without recounting this story. Jerome, who had certainly read the *Ecclesiastical History* and in fact based much of his biographical notice on Origen in his *On Illustrious Men* on Eusebius' biography,[36] did not mention the story. In that work, however, Jerome made an interesting remark. Speaking of Origen's impressive erudition, he credited him with an

33. Pierre Nautin, *Origène, sa vie et son oeuvre* (Paris: Éditions Beauchesne, 1977), p. 35.

34. See chapter 3, pp. 58–60. This is one of those sections in the biography whose "historicity" Eusebius "proves" by the use of *mnēmoneuousin*.

35. Robert M. Grant, "Early Alexandrian Christianity," *CH* 40 (June, 1971): 134 and "Eusebius and his Lives of Origen," p. 12; Manfred Hornschuh, "Das Leben des Origenes und die Entstehung der alexandrinischen Schule," *ZKG* 71 (1960): 5–6.

36. Jerome *De viris inlustribus* 54. See Nautin, *Origène*, pp. 215–19, for text and commentary.

"eternal genius" (*immortali eius ingenio*). This remark is interesting because it sees Origen as the possessor of a surpassing, divine excellence and because this quality is attributed to him in the context of a discussion of his wisdom, a context like the one Eusebius provided for his own story about Origen's divine spirit. Jerome also complimented the mature Origen by calling him the greatest Biblical commentator[37] as well as the greatest master in the church after the apostles.[38] Further, in one of his letters Jerome stated that Origen was "*from his childhood* a great man."[39] It is intriguing to think that this remark was an allusion to Eusebius' report of Origen the "wunderknaben" and that Jerome thus accepted that report as an historically valid one. But whether this is true or not, certainly Jerome's statements testify to the tenacity of Origen's reputation for greatness.

Another kind of testimony from antiquity, which again corroborates the spirit of Eusebius' story about the divine spirit without mentioning the story itself, is an *hommage* written for Origen by one of his students in the Caesarean catechetical school.[40] This *hommage* was included in the *Apology* that Eusebius and Pamphilus wrote on Origen's behalf, and it expresses clearly Eusebius' own opinion.[41] The student speaks of Origen in superlatives: he possessed a "wise foresight truly divine" concerning the character of his students,[42] and his teaching was so compelling that his students sat transfixed "like men bewitched" by the power of his words, which he spoke with "a kind of divine authority."[43] But Origen was not simply an inspired teacher, for according to this student he was a "*theios anthrōpos*"[44] who, while he seemed to be a man, had actually "gone beyond the human condition to a better state in his ascent to the divine."[45] Obviously this student's testimony corroborates Eusebius' own vision of Origen's divine nature; per-

37. Jerome, "Prologue" to his translation of Origen's *Homilies on the Song of Songs*: "Origenes, cum in ceteris libris omnes vicerit, in Cantico Canticorum ipse se vicit." *Origène: Homélies sur le Cantique des Cantiques*, ed. Dom Olivier Rousseau (Paris: Les Éditions du Cerf, 1966), p. 62.

38. Jerome, "Preface" to his *Onomasticon*: "Origenem quem post apostolos ecclesiarum magistrum nemo nisi imperitus negabit." Jerome, *Works*, ed. D. Vallarsi, 2nd. ed., 3:3.

39. Jerome *Ep*. 84.8 (italics mine).

40. The *hommage* is the *Oration to Origen* whose traditional ascription to Gregory Thaumaturgus has recently been disputed. In *Origène*, pp. 81–86, Nautin suggests that it be attributed to one of Origen's students, Theodore.

41. Socrates Scholasticus *Historia ecclesiastica* 4.27.

42. *Oration* 1064A. 43. Ibid., 1069D. 44. Ibid., 1072B.

45. Ibid., 1053C.

haps it was this kind of witness that provided the impetus for his own anecdote.

One feature of Eusebius' story merits closer scrutiny: it concerns human possession of a *theion pneuma* that is enshrined in the breast. For confirmation of his idea that a holy spirit could dwell in a man, Eusebius could look both to Scripture and to popular religious beliefs. The *Wisdom of Solomon* 7:27–28, for example, states that wisdom "enters into holy souls age after age, and makes them God's friends and prophets, for nothing is acceptable to God but the man who makes his home with wisdom." Paul's first letter to the Corinthians makes this notion of indwelling quite explicit: "Do you not know that you are God's temple, and that God's spirit dwells in you?"[46] In another passage, he identifies the spirit of God with the spirit of Christ, an explicit Christian explanation of indwelling that Eusebius has not followed.[47] Scripture also showed that it was the human heart that provided the holy pneuma's dwelling place. Again Paul's letters provide the clearest testimony: "God has put his seal upon us and given us his spirit in our hearts as a guarantee."[48] The idea that the heart was the seat of a holy spirit was not restricted to the Judaeo-Christian tradition, as a collection of aphorisms called the *Sentences of Sextus* demonstrates.[49] Several of these popular Pythagorean maxims express the conviction that the wise man is holy, and that the mind is a holy temple of God.[50] Philosophers also adhered to this idea: in his biography of Moses, Philo stated that the prophet's mind "was set up in his body like an image in a shrine,"[51] and Porphyry asserted that although "the

46. 1 Cor. 3:16; see also 1 Cor. 6:19: "Do you not know that your body is a shrine of the indwelling holy spirit, and the spirit is God's gift to you?" For a detailed discussion of the idea of spiritual indwelling in antiquity see G. Verbeke, *L'Évolution de la doctrine du pneuma du Stoicisme à S. Augustin* (Paris: Desclée de Brouwer, 1945).

47. See Rom. 8:9: "You are on the spiritual level if only God's spirit dwells within you; and if a man does not possess the spirit of Christ, he is no Christian."

48. 2 Cor. 1:22. See also Gal. 4:6.

49. For a discussion see Chadwick, *Sentences of Sextus*, pp. 4–9.

50. Sextus 450: "The mind of the wise man is a mirror of God"; 394: "Know what God is; perceive the mind [*nous*] in you"; 46a: "The pious mind is a holy temple of God"; 35: "Being select, you have something in your constitution which is like God; therefore treat your body as a temple of God." It is interesting to note that Philo, one of Eusebius' favorite authors, echoes Sextus 35 in his *De opificio mundi* 137, where he says that the human body is a "sacred temple devised for the rational soul," which man must "carry in his mind as the most godly of images [*to theoeidestaton*]."

51. Philo *De vita Moisis* 1.27.

divine is present everywhere and in all men, only the mind of the wise man is sanctified as its temple."[52]

Clearly Eusebius has made use of a rather widespread cultural attitude toward the holy man and his spirit, yet he failed to make explicit the specifically Christian identification of this holy indwelling pneuma with Christ. I think that this part of the story is an instance of the double focus—and perhaps the double appeal—of Eusebius' characterization of Origen as holy man. The child whose breast enshrines a holy spirit could be admired by pagan and Christian alike, since Eusebius' image was supported by popular maxims as well as by Pauline statements about the spirit.

It is interesting to note that the father's act in kissing the child's breast is also dependent upon a cultural convention. In pagan literature, it appears that kisses were bestowed out of familial love, as a mark of honor, and as an act of worship.[53] When the kiss was a mark of honor, it was given on the hands or breast.[54] As an act of worship, the kiss was of course a sign of reverence, though in pagan practice it was statues, temple steps, and cultic objects, not people, that were kissed.[55] In Christianity the holy kiss seems to have played two roles: one was the liturgical or eucharistic kiss attested to in Paul's letters and in later Patristic writings; the other was a means of venerating martyrs.[56] Eusebius' story of the father's kiss is thus not a specifically Christian rendering of the act but is rather an account that draws upon pagan practices of honoring wise or virtuous men and venerating holy objects. His father's holy kiss shows that Origen's divine spirit merited such cultic recognition and veneration.

We have seen that Eusebius' conception of a divine spirit dwelling in a human breast was certainly not a unique conception, since pagans subscribed to this idea as well as Christians. What *is* unique is Eusebius' expression of the idea within a specific historical setting, a scene from Origen's

52. Porphyry *Ad Marcellam* 11.

53. *Theological Wordbook of the New Testament*, s.v. "*Phileō*," by Gustav Stählin, pp. 119–23. See also Karl-Martin Hofmann, *Philema Hagion* (Gütersloh: Verlag C. Bertelsmann, 1938), pp. 74–76.

54. Stählin, "*Phileō*," p. 121; Petronius *Satyrion* 91.9: "I kissed his breast full of wisdom."

55. Stählin, "*Phileō*," p. 123, and Hofmann, *Philema Hagion*, pp. 74–83.

56. Stählin, "*Phileō*," pp. 139, 142, gives quotations citing the eucharistic kiss in Justin *Apology* 65.2 and in Tertullian *De oratione* 18. Hofmann, *Philema Hagion*, p. 139, cites passages indicating the kissing of martyrs: Tertullian *Ad uxorem* 2.4; Eusebius *Martyrs of Palestine* 11.20 and *HE* 6.3.4, where Origen himself gives martyrs the holy kiss.

childhood. Though it is not possible to find the origin of the story itself, it is significant that Eusebius has made the anecdote central to his exposition of Origen as divine man. Its function in the biography is not only to clothe Origen's holy spirit with historical dress but also to justify the divinizing view of Origen's entire career. To that career we now turn, beginning with the theme of Origen as ascetic scholar.

The Faces of Origen

As one might expect, Eusebius' vision of Origen's childhood did not produce anecdotes relating the normal, playful activities of a young boy. In this respect Eusebius was no different from other biographers who, while they showed a concern to depict the holy man's passage through life's stages like other men, seem to have avoided the creation of scenes that could not be used to reveal the hero's numinous qualities in a serious way. In fact, out of all the biographies discussed in earlier chapters, there is only one childhood story that does not have a revelatory function. This is Porphyry's anecdote about Plotinus' refusal to be weaned until his eighth year, a curious story that reflects Porphyry's almost desperate search for information about Plotinus' past in the face of his mentor's adamant refusal to supply it.[57] The only biographical works that do contain pictures of the hero as a child at play are New Testament apocryphal books like *The Infancy Story of Thomas*, and even here Jesus' childish pranks are simply vehicles for miraculous displays. The accomplishments of the mature holy man have been read back into his childhood.

The technique of reading back, or extending the *akmē*, has also been used by Eusebius, but unlike the apocryphal writers he has produced a somber rather than a playful child in keeping with his theme of asceticism. The childhood story introducing the biographical theme of Origen the ascetic scholar pictures the young boy laboring ceaselessly at studies both secular

57. Porphyry *Vita Plotini* 3. E. R. Dodds uses this story to make a connection between Plotinus' mysticism and Freudian theory: "so prolonged a refusal to grow up would seem to be significant. It would fit Freud's suggestion that mystical experience, with its sense of infinite extension and oneness with the Real, may represent a persistence of infantile feeling in which no distinction is yet drawn between 'self' and 'other.'" *Pagan and Christian in an Age of Anxiety* (New York: W. W. Norton, 1970), p. 91, n. 2.

and divine, attending the latter with his usual "excessive zeal" and plumbing the scriptural depths for allegorical meaning.[58] The story provides an obvious entrée to the mature scholar's literary achievement, but it is also an indication of the man's ascetic bearing, for in this story Eusebius describes Origen's education twice as "training," an *askēsis* that dominates the hero's entire life.[59] In no other book of the *Ecclesiastical History* does Eusebius use the word *askēsis* and its cognates so frequently; in fact, almost every occurrence of the term is located in the "Life of Origen." In this story, the training is linked with the study of Scripture; Eusebius is giving *askēsis* a Christian context and a Christian interpretation. As the biography progresses, however, Eusebius does not maintain the specifically Christian context of Origen's *askēsis*. The Christian ascetic Origen whom we meet as a child appears later in a more ambiguous ascetic guise.

Earlier I pointed out that imitation was an important feature of the holy philosopher's asceticism; his ascetic lifestyle not only attracted students but also provided those followers with a pattern or model for their own lives.[60] But the holy men themselves were imitators. They too looked back to exemplars of the ascetic-philosophical life. Apollonius, for example, took Pythagoras as his model, and Plotinus looked back with veneration to both Socrates and Plato.[61] Origen, however, was unabashedly Christian in his choice of model. Although in *Against Celsus* he noted the virtue evident in the lives of Socrates and Pythagoras, he emphasized the fact that they were simply men, and that the models they established were inadequate for centuries-long influence.[62] Origen's own model was Jesus, whose "message of salvation and moral purity was sufficient to prove his superiority among men."[63] The following passage from his *On First Principles* shows clearly Origen's acceptance of Jesus as ascetic model: "so, too, should each one of

58. Eusebius *HE* 6.2.7–10.

59. The two passages in this story are as follows: "*tais theiais graphais ex eti paidos enēskēmenos*"; "*tois hierois enaskeisthai paideumasin.*"

60. Chapter 2, pp. 25–28. On Origen as a model-provider, see Eusebius *HE* 6.3.13: "And by displaying proofs such as these of a philosophic life to those who saw him, he naturally stimulated a large number of his pupils to a like zeal, so that, even among the unbelieving Gentiles and those from the ranks of learning and philosophy, some persons of no small account were won by his instruction."

61. Philostratus *Vita Apollonii* 1.7; Porphyry *Vita Plotini* 1.2.

62. *Contra Celsum* 1.3, 1.29, 3.66, 4.97, 6.8 (virtues of Socrates and Pythagoras); 1.64, 3.68 (Socrates and Pythagoras only men).

63. Origen *Contra Celsum* 2.40.

us, after a fall or a transgression, cleanse himself from stains by the example set before him [Christ's example], and taking a leader for the journey proceed along the steep path of virtue, that so perchance by this means we may as far as is possible become, *through our imitation of him*, partakers of the divine nature."[64] Origen also speaks of faith in Christ, his model, as a spiritual circumcision of the heart and body and often refers in a mystical way not simply to imitation but to a kind of union with "Dominus meus Iesus Christus."[65]

In his own writings, then, Origen declared Christ to be the model for his own ascetic life. Eusebius, however, did not present a consistent picture of Origen's *imitatio Christi*. In fact in the chapter following the childhood *askēsis* story, Eusebius presents Origen as an imitator of Socrates, albeit in an oblique way. In *EH* 6.3.7, Eusebius states that Origen's conduct revealed "the right actions of a most genuine philosophy" and that the maxim "as was his speech, so was the manner of his life" could be fittingly applied to him. This maxim is an allusion to (and an interpretation of) a statement made by Socrates in the *Republic*, a statement that became a proverb among the Greeks, as Seneca noted. Cicero, who also attributed the statement to Socrates, showed by his discussion that the proverb took its meaning from an ascetic context: the man whom this maxim characterized was a model of Stoic (or later Pythagorean) asceticism, the dispassionate sage with a balanced disposition of soul.[66] By applying this popular Socratic maxim to

64. Origen *De principiis* 4.4.4 (italics mine). The following passage from *De principiis* 4.4.10 is also pertinent in this regard: "The marks of the divine image in man may be clearly discerned, not in the form of his body, which goes to corruption, but in the prudence of his mind, in his righteousness, his self-control, his courage, his wisdom, his discipline, in fact, in the whole company of virtues; which exist in God essentially, and may exist in man as a result of his own efforts and his imitation of God."

65. Origen *Homilies on Genesis* 3.6 and especially 3.7, where Origen quotes with approval Paul's statement in Gal. 6:17, "I bear on my body the marks of Jesus." See Louis Doutreleau, trans. and ed., *Origène: Homélies sur la Genèse*, Sources chrétiennes, no. 7 (Paris: Les Éditions du Cerf, 1976), pp. 142–43, n. 1, for several examples of Origen's use of the phrases "*my* Lord" and "*my* Christ." Origen's mystical Christocentrism and his theology of the image of Christ have been the subject of several studies. See, among others, Henri Crouzel, *Origène et la 'connaissance mystique'* (Paris: Desclée de Brouwer, 1961) and *Théologie de l'image de Dieu chez Origène* (Paris: Aubier, 1956) and F. Bertrand, *Mystique de Jésus chez Origène* (Paris: Aubier, 1954).

66. Plato *Republic* 400D. See Seneca *Ep.* 114.2: "here is a phrase which you are wont to notice in the popular speech—one which the Greeks have made into a proverb: 'Man's speech is just like his life.'" Cicero's comments are in his *Tusculanae Disputationes* 5.47.

Origen, Eusebius has created for his readers an Hellenic Origen, a man whose daily conduct was characterized by harmony of soul. As we have seen, this was exactly the picture that Porphyry and Iamblichus presented in their biographical descriptions of Pythagoras' ascetic bearing.[67] Again, one can discern in Eusebius' biography a double focus—a combining of traits that results in a Janus-faced Origen, at once Christian and Hellenic, at least in the revered Socratic sense.

It must be noted, however, that the Christian "face" tends to dominate the portrait of Origen as an ascetic, for soon after alluding to the Socratic image, Eusebius describes exactly what Origen's philosophical life was like. It was a literal *imitatio Christi* in terms of specific gospel passages. "And above all he considered that those sayings of the Savior in the Gospel ought to be kept which exhort us not to provide two coats nor to use shoes, nor, indeed, to be worn out with thoughts about the future."[68] The extremes of Origen's asceticism are attributed to his literal rendering of scripture; it is an image that does not accord either with Socratic balance or with Origen's own vision of his *imitatio*, which emphasized not a physical but a spiritual pattern of activity.

The issue of Origen's literal-minded asceticism also appears in Eusebius' story of his hero's self-castration. In the *Ecclesiastical History* 6.8.1–3, Eusebius states: "At that time, while Origen was performing the work of instruction at Alexandria, he did a thing which gave abundant proof of an immature and youthful mind, yet withal of faith and self-control. For he took the saying, 'There are eunuchs which made themselves eunuchs for the kingdom of heaven's sake,' in too literal and extreme a sense, and thinking both to fulfil the Savior's saying, and also that he might prevent all suspicion of shameful slander on the part of unbelievers (for, young as he was, he used to discourse on divine things with women as well as men), he hastened

67. See chapter 2, p. 29.

68. Eusebius *HE* 6.3.10. In this respect it is interesting to consider one of Origen's remarks in his *Homilies on Luke* 25.3, where he wistfully compares the rough clothing of John the Baptist with "we who live in the city among crowds and pursue elegance in clothing, food and housing." Eusebius' vision of Origen the barefooted, ill-clothed ascetic philosopher was simply a vision, a part of his biographical image-making. A further indication that Origen himself was rather divorced from real ascetic or monkish desert life of the kind Eusebius had in mind is his allegorization of "life in the desert." For him the desert life signified the adoption of a spiritual attitude. See *Homilies on Luke* 11.4 and the comments by Henri Crouzel *et al.*, trans. and eds., *Origène: Homélies sur S. Luc*, Sources chrétiennes, no. 87 (Paris: Les Éditions du Cerf, 1962), p. 192, n. 1.

to put into effect the Savior's saying, taking care to escape the notice of the greater number of his pupils." Here Eusebius has given two explanations for what he calls Origen's "rash act": one involves a literal reading of Matthew 19:12; the other pertains to the sage's self-control in sexual matters.

The second explanation seems unconvincing in light of a section in *Against Celsus*, in which Origen implies that sexual continence is not meritorious if sexual activity or desire have been rendered physical impossibilities.[69] When Origen writes about chastity and speaks disparagingly about our "sensible nature" and the "futility" of our bodies, he does so in the Pauline sense of bodily life as a sinful affliction that we must endure.[70] However, the early history of modes of celibacy in the church shows that self-castration was an ascetic option, though the practice was officially condemned at Nicaea and by the fourth-century Apostolic Canons.[71] Like Origen, the church decided that forced chastity was without moral value.

Eusebius' other explanation, that of Origen's scriptural literalism, is equally suspect. One of Origen's predecessors in Alexandria, the Gnostic teacher Basilides, interpreted Matthew 19:12 as a classification of male celibates into three groups: those who have a natural revulsion from women; those who practised the ascetic life to provoke the admiration of others; and those who remained celibate in order to pursue the work of the church without domestic distractions.[72] Basilides did not, apparently, take the word "eunuch" in a literal sense. Origen also refused to accept the literal meaning of the passage. In his *Commentary on Matthew*, Origen quotes with disapproval the maxims in Sextus that state that castration is preferable to impurity[73] and states firmly that "one must not believe in them [that is,

69. Origen *Contra Celsum* 7.48.

70. Ibid., 7.49–50. See also Origen *Selections on Genesis* 8.58 and *Contra Celsum* 4.40 for the theory that the "coats of skins" with which Adam and Eve were clothed after their fall were in fact bodies.

71. See Chadwick, *Sentences of Sextus*, p. 111. The first canon of Nicaea prohibited those who had been mutilated from being ordained; the twenty-third Apostolic canon condemned castration as a rebellion against providential order, since the body is a God-given gift. For early Christian references concerning castration see R. P. C. Hanson, "A Note on Origen's Self-Mutilation," *Vigiliae Christianae* 20 (June, 1966):81–82.

72. Basilides quoted by Clement of Alexandria *Stromateis* 3.1.

73. Origen was referring to the following maxims in *Sextus*: No. 13: "Every member of the body that would persuade you to be unchaste cast away; for it is better to live chastely without the limb than to live for destruction with it"; No. 273: "You see men cutting off and casting away parts of their bodies in order that the rest may be strong; how much better to do this for the sake of chastity."

other exegeses] since they have not understood the meaning of the Holy Scriptures concerning these matters. For if self-control was listed among the fruits of the spirit with love, grace, patience and the rest, one must rather bear the fruit of self-control and one must preserve the male body given from God."[74] In opposition to his biographer, then, Origen rejected the literal exegesis of the passage.

Scholarly opinion on the historical nature of this story has been divided. Hanson, for example, saw no reason to doubt the story and felt that Origen's later exegesis in his *Commentary on Matthew* represented a change of opinion.[75] Chadwick, on the other hand, thought that the story was "malicious gossip" passed on thoughtlessly by Eusebius.[76] However, what is interesting about this story is not its historicity,[77] which Origen's own testimony makes dubious, but rather that Eusebius used it as a vehicle to characterize Origen. The story seems to establish two major aspects of Eusebius' image of Origen's asceticism: the first is that his ascetic practice was Christian, based this time not on *imitatio Christi* but on a fervent acceptance of the Savior's words; the second is that his ascetic practice emphasized the self-control characteristic of all good Greek philosophers. Again the two-dimensional focus of the biography is clear.

Eusebius makes a direct link between Origen's asceticism and his life as a scholar in the following way. He describes as part of Origen's *askēsis* a day-and-night routine of teaching and studying.[78] This passage seems to fit admirably Eusebius' idealization of Origen as a zealous devotee and propagator of Christian truth, giving his entire life to his pursuit. However, this aspect of Origen's *askēsis* may be due not simply to Eusebius' image-making

74. Origen *Commentary on Matthew* 15.3.

75. Hanson, "A Note on Origen's Self-Mutilation," p. 82.

76. Chadwick, *Sentences of Sextus*, p. 68. See also Grant, "Eusebius and his Lives of Origen," pp. 15–16.

77. This legend was repeated by Jerome *Ep.* 84.8 and by Epiphanius *Panarion* 64.3.9–13, where one can see an amplification of the story: "They say that this Origen had something in mind against his own body. For they say that he cut off his penis in order not to be troubled by sensual pleasure nor to burn with passion in bodily movements. But others tell another story, that he contrived to apply a drug to his genitals to dry them up, on the ground that he discovered an herb which was efficacious as far as regards the memory." Interestingly, in Epiphanius' version the notion of a literal reading of Scripture has disappeared, but the connection between asceticism and the philosophic life (self-control; memory) has been not only retained but reinforced. For a discussion of this passage in Epiphanius see Nautin, *Origène*, pp. 210–11.

78. Eusebius *HE* 6.3.9, 6.8.6, 6.15.

but possibly to Origen's own view of himself. For there is extant a letter fragment in which Origen, describing his relationship with his patron Ambrose, paints a scholarly ascetic picture of his own daily routine:

> The holy Ambrose . . . supposing that I am a zealous worker and utterly athirst for the word of God, convicted me by his own zeal for work and passion for sacred studies . . . for neither when we are engaged in collating can we take our meals, nor, when we have taken them walk and rest our bodies. Nay, even at the times set apart for those things we are constrained to discourse learnedly and to correct our manuscripts. Neither can we sleep at night for the good of our bodies, since our learned discourse extends far into the evening. I need not mention that our morning studies also are prolonged to the ninth, at times to the tenth, hour.[79]

Even though this text stems from an apologetic interest of Origen's, it provides an interesting perspective on Eusebius' image of Origen, if indeed, as Nautin has proposed, Eusebius did use this text (or a fragment of it from the *Apology*) as a source for his biography. For Eusebius sees Origen's ascetic zeal as an essential feature of his character, welling up out of his scriptural and scholarly devotion. Yet Origen's view of his own strict routine shows another's zeal, that of his patron Ambrose, as the motivating force behind his ascetic regimen. In this context, Origen's own words at least show him as a more human figure, needing encouragement to sustain rigor. Yet, if Nautin is correct in assuming that Origen himself was pleading a specific case, and defending his innocence concerning documents published (and ideas thought?) at the instance of an overzealous Ambrose, we still have not touched the real Origen but are left simply with two idealized versions of an ascetic life whose historical provenance remains a mystery.

Even though Origen's early scholarly training was connected to asceticism in Eusebius' introductory childhood story, Origen's actual activities as teacher and scholar form a separate theme, that of Origen the schoolman. The first issue of interest here is Origen's philosophical-religious training.

79. English translation quoted in H. J. Lawlor and J. E. L. Oulton, trans., *Eusebius: The Ecclesiastical History and the Martyrs of Palestine*, 2 vols. (London: SPCK, 1927–28), 1:213f; Greek text quoted in Pierre Nautin, *Lettres et écrivains chrétiens des IIe et IIIe siècles* (Paris: Les Éditions du Cerf, 1961), p. 251. In the discussion in this work as well as in *Origène*, pp. 39–41, Nautin has proposed that this letter fragment, preserved in part in Pamphilus' *Apology for Origen*, was originally part of an apologetic letter to Pope Fabian in which Origen defended his orthodoxy in part by blaming Ambrose's zeal in publishing texts without Origen's approval or knowledge.

Apart from the pious legend of the father's formative influence on the child's Christian training, what can we glean from Eusebius' biography? The only point of historical importance is his note on Origen's period of study with "the teacher of philosophy," Ammonius Saccas.[80] A figure almost completely shrouded with mystery, Ammonius seems to have been as much a "great shadow"[81] for Eusebius as he is for modern historians.[82] Eusebius introduces Ammonius by quoting a passage from Porphyry's *Against the Christians* in which the great pagan commends Origen's Greek training only to deplore his fall into "barbarian recklessness."[83] According to Porphyry, Ammonius was originally a Christian, having been "nurtured" (*anatropheis*) in Christian doctrine by his parents, whereas Origen was a Greek, "educated" (*paideutheis*) in Greek philosophy, whose embrace of Christianity was a dire apostasy. As one commentator has shown, the contrasting parallel that Porphyry drew between *anatropheis* and *paideutheis* is important: "the *paideia* stands higher than the *anatrophē*; because of that, the growth of Ammonius, who attained *paideia* in spite of his Christian *anatrophē*, is the more admirable, and the falling away of Origen, who was already acquainted with Greek *paideia*, the more to be disapproved."[84] To combat this picture of an apostate Origen, Eusebius takes a position opposing Por-

80. Eusebius *HE* 6.19.6–10.

81. E. R. Dodds, "Numenius and Ammonius," *Entretiens sur l'antiquité classique* 5: *Les sources de Plotin* (Geneva: Fondation Hardt, 1960), p. 32.

82. The most judicious detailed treatment of Ammonius is that of Dodds, "Numenius and Ammonius." In a section dealing with "Ammonius the Protean," Dodds discusses, and largely dismisses, scholarly reconstructions that have viewed Ammonius as an Indian missionary, a Pythagorean ecstatic, and an heretical Christian theologian. Dodds himself feels that Ammonius belonged to the Platonic camp and bases his supposition on Ammonius' student Longinus' statement to that effect in a passage quoted by Porphyry in his *Vita Plotini* 20 and on a passage in Nemesius *Of the Nature of Man* 2.12 which contrasts Numenius, a Pythagorean, with Ammonius "the master of Plotinus" (the latter being an undoubted Platonist). Unfortunately, Ammonius wrote nothing, nor were his lectures recorded. Even Dodds' assiduous handling of the material does not move beyond Ammonius' shadow, and the attempt of Henri Crouzel (in "Origène et Plotin élèves d'Ammonius Saccas," *Bulletin de littérature ecclésiastique* 57 [1956]: 193–214) to reconstruct Ammonius' philosophy from points of agreement in the thought of his two most famous students is highly questionable, since it ignores the students' individual creativity and in any case produces only philosophical generalities to which any Platonically oriented thinker would have subscribed.

83. Eusebius *HE* 6.19.5–8.

84. W. C. Van Unnik, *Tarsus or Jerusalem?* trans. George Ogg (London: Epworth Press, 1962), pp. 32–33.

phyry's. He affirms Origen's training under Ammonius but counters Porphyry by asserting both Origen's and Ammonius' Christian upbringing and lifelong faithfulness to that tradition.[85] Whether in the heat of controversy, out of ignorance, or with an apologetic desire to defend Origen's Christian integrity, Eusebius has painted a picture of Ammonius which is certainly erroneous. Whatever his *anatrophē* may have been, Ammonius was not a Christian teacher but a Platonizing or Neopythagorean master.[86]

What is intriguing about the Ammonius issue is not so much Eusebius' historical mistake, though it is suggestive of an apologetic motive, but rather his failure to pursue the issue of Origen's Greek erudition, which was the context for the Ammonius discussion. Eusebius seems to be treading a fine line concerning this issue, for on the one hand Origen's identity as a *Christian* scholar is emphasized,[87] while on the other hand his understanding of, in fact his devotion to, Greek learning is also clearly affirmed.[88] In Eusebius' opinion, Origen managed to combine the best of both worlds, yet there is reason to doubt whether Origen really achieved or even aspired to the "happy medium" suggested by Eusebius' biography.

As the height of his praise, Eusebius makes the following statement about Origen's philosophical acumen:

And numbers of the heretics, and not a few of the most distinguished philosophers, gave earnest heed to him, and, one might almost say, were instructed by him in secular philosophy as well as in divine things. For he used to introduce also to the study of philosophy as many as he saw were naturally gifted, imparting geometry and arithmetic and other preliminary subjects, and then leading them on to the

85. Eusebius *HE* 6.19.10.
86. See Grant, "Early Alexandrian Christianity," p. 139. Note that Porphyry, too, was mistaken in part of his account. Though we know from Eusebius (*HE* 6.2.7 and 6.2.15) that Origen studied the usual Greek scholastic curriculum, we also know that his *anatrophē* was Christian, not pagan. The idea that Origen was born and raised a Christian is based on the fact that his father, Leonides, was martyred during the Severan persecution in 203, a persecution apparently aimed primarily at Christian converts. See W. H. C. Frend, "Open Questions Concerning the Christians and the Roman Empire in the Age of the Severi," *JTS*, N.S., 25 (October, 1974): 333–51. Origen himself stated in his *Homilies on Ezekiel* 4.8 that his father, to whom he did not refer by name, had been a martyr for the faith. (In *Origène*, pp. 31–32, 208, and 414–15, Nautin states that the identification of Origen's father with the Alexandrian martyr Leonides is legendary.)
87. See especially Eusebius' attempt at an exhaustive list of the master's scriptural works in *HE* 6.15–17, 23–25, 31–32, 36.
88. *HE* 6.19.1–2, 11–15.

systems which are found among the philosophers, giving a detailed account of their treatises, commenting upon and examining into each, so that the man was proclaimed as a great philosopher even among the Greeks themselves.[89]

Although Eusebius has not supplied the details of Origen's philosophical learning (for example, *which* systems did he expound, and why?), certainly the general impression of this passage is unmistakeable: Origen was an immensely erudite scholar in the Greek philosophical tradition. Origen himself, however, gave a more somber reason for his philosophical teaching. In his *Homilies on Jeremiah*, Origen said that in fact he often had to cloak his Christian identity with Greek erudition because some of his pagan acquaintances were so hostile to Christianity that an explanation of its principles had first to be undertaken in the guise of traditional philosophy.[90] While this confirms Eusebius' idea that Origen was learned in things Greek, it also suggests that Origen viewed his own exposition of philosophy as an apologetic and proselytizing tool, not as proof of his standing as an intellectual virtuoso. Further, as Nautin has shown by an artful reading of Origen's comments on preaching, Origen did not distinguish between the roles of preacher and teacher.[91] The role of the master was to convert, that is, to move the student's soul.[92] And true conversion was effected, not by studying philosophy, but by reading the Scriptures both old and new, inscribing their words on one's heart, and modeling one's life on their examples.[93]

The vision of education as conversion, expressed by the mature Origen,[94] is confirmed at least in part by the eulogy written by one of his students.[95] Noting that in his relations with students Origen showed not only "grace and gentleness" but "persuasion and force" as well,[96] the student praises

89. Eusebius *HE* 6.18.2–3.

90. Origen *Homilies on Jeremiah* 20.5.

91. Pierre Nautin, "Origène Prédicateur," in *Origène: Homélies sur Jérémie 1–11*, ed. Pierre Nautin, Sources chrétiennes 232 (Paris: Les Éditions du Cerf, 1976), p. 152.

92. Origen *Homilies on Jeremiah* 20.6.21 and especially 19.14.108, where Origen states that one who explains the words of a prophet prophesies himself. The task of the modern teacher/prophet is "to teach, to denounce, to convert" (ibid., 15.2.8).

93. Ibid., 4.6.18.

94. Nautin, "La Date des Homélies," in *Origène: Homélies sur Jérémie*, pp. 15–21, dates the Jeremiah homilies between 241 and 244.

95. See chap. 4, n. 4 above.

96. *Oration* 1069C.

Origen for attending to his students' souls.[97] Inspired by the Holy Spirit and by "the saving Logos," Origen led his students to contemplate true divinity.[98] In a statement that closely parallels Origen's own idea of the prophet-teacher, the student reported about his teacher that "everything he said had its source, in my opinion, in a communication with the divine spirit: the same power is in fact necessary to those who prophesy and to those who hear the prophets; and no one can hear a prophet unless the same spirit which prophesied in him gives him the meaning of his words."[99] These comments, reflecting so well what Origen himself wrote in his *Homilies on Jeremiah*, give us what appears to be a genuine reflection of the man himself.

However, Origen the prophesying magister, who once lamented that "very few people are enthusiastic about rational thought,"[100] was not in the habit of plunging his students directly into divine studies. As his student describes it, Origen's school in Caesarea had a "ladder" arrangement, whose first rungs were occupied by an elementary scholastic curriculum ("all the sciences," e.g., geometry and astronomy).[101] Next came every conceivable kind of philosophy (except that which was atheistic), followed finally by study of the Scriptures themselves.[102] The student describes this curriculum as a kind of dialectic, whose aim was first to pattern and train the intellect, but ultimately to lead to an understanding of "God and his prophets."[103]

In his Caesarean school, then, Origen did not emphasize the study of philosophy but regarded it as a propaedeutic tool. This is not the picture suggested by the sections in Eusebius' biography dealing with Ammonius and with Porphyry's comments on Origen's philosophical being. For in order to refute what he conceived to be Porphyry's calumnies, Eusebius showed Origen teaching Greek philosophy for its own sake, a practice not characteristic of the mature magister. However, if the mature Origen was decidedly Christian in his teaching and preaching, there is evidence that

97. Ibid., 1061C. 98. Ibid., 1093D, 1072A, 1080A. 99. Ibid., 1093D.
100. Origen *Contra Celsum* 1.9. 101. *Oration* 1077C. 102. Ibid., 1077B–C.
103. Ibid., 1077B, 1088A–C, 1093B. See Origen *Contra Celsum* 6.10: "There are some people to whom we preach only an exhortation to believe, since they are incapable of anything more; but with others we do all we can to approach them with rational arguments by questions and answers." For a discussion of the school in Caesarea see Henri Crouzel, "L'École d'Origène à Césarée," *Bulletin de littérature ecclésiastique* 71 (January–March, 1970): 15–27. Eusebius' only comment on the organization of Origen's Caesarean school occurs in *HE* 6.30: "Origen instilled into them a passion for philosophy and urged them to exchange their former love for the study of divine truth."

suggests that as a young man he was in fact intoxicated by pagan learning, though this issue too is treated ambiguously by Eusebius.

The nature of Origen's Alexandrian teaching activities is unfortunately clouded in Eusebius' biography by two kinds of apology. The first stems from an apologetic motivation of Eusebius' that results in arguments very different from, in fact diametrically opposed to, the arguments raised in conversation with Porphyry's charges. Again Ammonius is relevant, for in crafting his portrait of Origen the Alexandrian teacher, Eusebius is extremely reticent about the precise character of Origen's introduction to a teaching career and about the content of that teaching. Because Eusebius' overriding concern in this section is to show Origen as the most prominent successor in the Alexandrian catechetical school, he emphasizes the Christian aspects of Origen's scholastic activity. The second kind of evidence comes from portions of one of Origen's letters that Eusebius has preserved, a letter in which Origen felt compelled to defend his Greek erudition by showing its role as a complement to his Christianity.

Eusebius approached the issue of Origen's entry into a teaching career with a story about the youth's fate after his father's martyrdom. *EH* 6.2.12–15 is one of the narratives in which Eusebius demonstrated the guidance of providence over Origen's life. Whereas earlier, providence acted through his mother to save him from early martyrdom, here providence acts through a wealthy Alexandrian patroness, who provides the youth with "welcome and refreshment." Eusebius does not explain in historical terms the reason for this offer of shelter. Yet he notes that the patroness also had living with her "as her adopted son" a noted heretic whose skillful speech attracted "very great numbers, not only of heretics but also of our own people" to hear his teachings. Eusebius uses the story to make a point about Origen's youthful orthodoxy: in spite of his house-mate's fame, Origen would not even pray with him, so great was his loathing of heresy. But this story can bear more than one interpretation, for Eusebius appends to this story a rather curious passage: "His father had brought him forward in secular studies, and after his death he applied himself wholly with renewed zeal to a literary training, so that he had a tolerable amount of proficiency in letters; and, not long after his father's perfecting, by dint of application to these studies, he was abundantly supplied, for a person of his years, with the necessaries of life."[104] This is certainly a roundabout, if not evasive, way of stating that Origen's early career as a teacher was not in fact

104. *HE* 6.2.15.

Christian but secular. But it is also a way of diverting attention from the young Origen's early association with heterodox Christianity, especially if, as Nautin has surmised, Eusebius is depending here on Origen's apologetic letter, part of which was a defense of his youthful, somewhat suspect attachment to a wealthy patroness who apparently surrounded herself with the "bright young men" of Alexandria regardless of their "orthodoxy."[105]

Eusebius' desire to emphasize the Christian aspects of Origen's teaching profession is also clear in his account of Origen's school in Alexandria. Unfortunately for modern historians, he gives two conflicting explanations to account for Origen's position as a Christian instructor. The first, in *EH* 6.3.1–2, implies that Origen assumed the task of catechesis as a result of the approach of "some of the heathen to hear the word of God." This occurred during the Severan persecution, when the catechetical post was vacant. In this version of the story, Origen's first teaching experience was that of proselytizing, and Eusebius has depended on erroneous (or foreshortened) dating to show Origen's secular career as simply a brief prelude to his "real" teaching activity,[106] which is depicted as being crowned by the number of Origen's students who achieved martyrdom.[107]

The second explanation for Origen's Christian teaching role, in *EH* 6.3.8–9 and 6.6.1, is dependent upon Eusebius' vision of a continuing Alexandrian catechetical school with an unbroken succession of teachers, a real *diadochē* beginning with Pantaenus and followed by Clement and Origen. In this view, the school was part of the ecclesiastical establishment, and its head held his position by appointment of the bishop. Thus the second explanation is that Origen was actually appointed by the bishop Demetrius to head the school and that only when he received this appoint-

105. This is Origen's letter to Pope Fabian. See chap. 4, n. 79 above. In "Das Leben des Origenes und die Entstehung der alexandrinischen Schule," p. 7, Hornschuh does not doubt that the young Origen associated with a famous heretic. He regards Eusebius' inclusion of this story as an occasion to mount an apologetic defense—in other words to revise history in the light of his own convictions concerning his hero: "This story serves Eusebius as the occasion to submit to proof Origen's irreproachable ecclesiastical views, and to give proof of Origen's firmness against all temptations. The motif of dangers and temptations, which the hero endures and in which his virtue and superiority are proven, is typically legendary."

106. See the article by T. D. Barnes, "Origen, Aquila, and Eusebius," *Harvard Studies in Classical Philology* 74 (1968): 313–16, which proves that if Origen was sixteen years old when his father died in 201/202 (*HE* 6.2.12), then he was older than seventeen (*HE* 6.3.3) when he started his proselytizing-teaching activity during the reign of the prefect Aquila, whose office did not begin until 205/206.

107. *HE* 6.4–5.

ment did Origen cease to "teach letters"—only then did he give up his secular teaching. This abandonment of secular studies is related by Eusebius in rather drastic terms: Origen "disposed of all the volumes of ancient literature which formerly he so fondly cherished."[108] Even if this last statement stems ultimately from Origen's apology,[109] its dramatic effect was certainly not lost on Eusebius, who followed it with an account of the stringent "philosopher's life" Origen began to lead, a link between his teaching and his asceticism. What seems odd is that the abrupt abandonment of the philosopher's course of study, if not its attendant lifestyle, fits better with Eusebius' first explanation of Origen's turn to Christian teaching, which deemphasized the scholastic nature of Origen's "conversion" in favor of a proselytizing-teaching venture.

In any case, what we know of Origen's Alexandrian period does not support the notion of an abrupt turn away from philosophy. It is possible that Eusebius' reliance on Origen's own apology was a means of avoiding the issues that prompted his hero's self-defense in the first place. For in fact parts of Porphyry's comments on Origen, which Eusebius so vigorously refuted, were true: Origen *did* "play the Greek"; he *was* conversant with the Platonic and Pythagorean philosophers; and he *did* use "the figurative interpretation, as employed in the Greek mysteries, and applied it to the Jewish writings."[110] Two of Origen's Alexandrian works attest to the truth of those statements: *On First Principles*, whose fourth book is an elaborate defense of the use of allegory to interpret Scripture; and *Miscellanies*, which also promoted allegory and used Platonic language to interpret scriptural ideas.[111]

108. *HE* 6.3.9.

109. Nautin, *Origène*, pp. 39–40.

110. Porphyry *Contra Christianos*, quoted in Eusebius *HE* 6.19.8.

111. On Origen's *Stromateis*, see Robert M. Grant, "The *Stromateis* of Origen," in *Epektasis: Mélanges patristiques offerts au Cardinal Jean Daniélou*, ed. Jacques Fontaine and Charles Kannengiesser (Paris: Éditions Beauchesne, 1972), 285–92; Chadwick, *Early Christian Thought and the Classical Tradition*, pp. 71–72; and Nautin, *Origène*, pp. 293–302. Jerome's comment on Origen's *Stromateis* is instructive: "Origen wrote ten *Stromateis*, comparing the views of Christians and philosophers with one another and confirming all the doctrines of our religion out of Plato and Aristotle, Numenius and Cornutus" (*Ep*. 70.4). As Chadwick pointed out in *Early Christianity and Classical Culture*, p. 97, Origen was aware of his innovative stance. In *Homilies on Leviticus* 1.1, 7.4–5, and 13.3, he refers to critics who characterized his allegories as subjective, fanciful interpretation. In his *Homilies on Jeremiah* 20.8, Origen, sympathizing with the prophet, asked, "If it gets me into trouble when I teach and preach, why do I not rather retire to the desert and to quiet?"

Further, as Robert M. Grant has shown, Alexandrian Christianity was not the monolithic entity described in Eusebius' *Ecclesiastical History*. In fact what Alexandria nourished during most of the second century was a luxuriant variety of Gnostic sects, and even those teachers who did not associate themselves directly with Gnosticism, that is, Pantaenus, Clement, and Origen, were like their Gnostic brethren strongly influenced by Neopythagorean and Middle Platonic ideas. Origen's own school in Alexandria was organized along Pythagorean lines, with an emphasis on philosophical studies that were not simply "preliminary" (as Eusebius says) but rather part of the core curriculum.[112]

So Origen was a Christian teacher with a truly philosophical approach; this seems to have been the reality behind Eusebius' confusing explanations. Most modern scholars have accepted this general picture, but in trying to unwind the tangled skeins of Eusebius' accounts, they have emphasized different aspects of the Eusebian portrayal. Grant's approach, as we have just seen, attempts to fill in presumed lacunae in Eusebius' report, pointing out his deliberate omission of information that might damage Origen's credibility as a Christian teacher. Like Grant, M. Hornschuh finds apologetic motives lurking behind Eusebius' school account, but he criticizes especially the first explanation, finding that Eusebius has crafted the accounts of Origen's proselytizing and his martyr-students in favor of his Christian vision of the *theios anēr*, in which the hero triumphs over political adversity.[113] Hornschuh has also doubted both that the school was a formal institution and that its leadership constituted a *diadochē*. For these arguments he is dependent upon a seminal essay by Gustave Bardy,[114] which showed that the Alexandrian teachers were freewheeling theological masters whose followers constituted more a society than a school. Bardy showed further that there was no Alexandrian *diadochē*, since it is highly doubtful that Origen studied with Clement, and in any case, as Hornschuh demon-

112. Grant, "Early Alexandrian Christianity," pp. 135–40.

113. See Hornschuh, "Das Leben des Origenes und die Entstehung der alexandrinischen Schule," pp. 9–15, for the detailed argument. On p. 13, Hornschuh states a telling argument: "If one considers, in conclusion, that around 202 Septimius Severus forbade the conversion to Christianity altogether by an edict, it is highly unlikely that during the persecution in Alexandria a Christian institute was flourishing, which had no other duty than to train pagans for admission to the Christian church."

114. Gustave Bardy, "Aux origines de l'école d'Alexandrie," *Recherches des sciences religieuses* 27 (1937): 69–90.

strated, until the rise of Demetrius as bishop, the spiritual leaders of the Alexandrian Christian community had been a group of presbyter-teachers who maintained their positions by force of intellect and personality,[115] not by official ecclesiastical sanction.[116]

Eusebius' portrait of Origen as Christian teacher fails for two reasons: his own explanations are conflicting, and, as scholars have shown, they are not true to the historical situation. Further, his desire to emphasize Origen's Christianity in a scholastic context conflicts with his pride in Origen's Greek and ascetic accomplishments. What Eusebius' biography lacks is a sustained account of Origen the churchman, which would certainly have been an easier way to suggest his orthodoxy. For at least in his Caesarean period, Origen's homiletic output was prodigious, and there were times when he preached every day.[117] Origen himself once stated that "throughout the period of this mortal life we are dependent on the sacramental, external forms of Bible and Church; secondary as they may be, they are an indispensable vehicle."[118] This clear affirmation of churchmanship was bolstered by moving treatises such as *On Prayer* and *On Martyrdom*, which firmly attest to his piety and zeal.

Perhaps part of the problem was that the context of Eusebius' ideal Origen, in fact the ideal of the holy man itself, was not ecclesiastical but philosophical. Eusebius seems to have placed himself in the uncomfortable position of explaining how a *theios anēr* could be orthodox. Ironically, what we can surmise about the historical Origen in his Alexandrian phase seems to fit the picture of the holy man rather well. That is, at least in his early career, Origen really did wear the Janus mask, combining two worlds, the Greek and the Christian, with flair. He was a philosophical maverick, operating in a heterodox, creative theological climate. But in his Caesarean period, he was more Christian in the ecclesiastical sense, combining scho-

115. Hornschuh, "Das Leben des Origenes und die Entstehung der alexandrinischen Schule," pp. 198–205. See also E. W. Kemp, "Bishops and Presbyters at Alexandria," *JEH* 6 (1955): 125–42.

116. Note that Demetrius' displeasure with Origen, which resulted in his official condemnation by the Alexandrian church establishment, had nothing to do with Demetrius' jealousy over Origen's scholastic fame, as Eusebius states in *HE* 6.8.4–5. In fact his excommunication was due to his ordination to the presbyterate in Palestine, an act that disregarded episcopal authority and jurisdiction. See Eusebius *HE* 6.8.5 and 23.4; W. Telfer, "Episcopal Succession in Egypt," *JEH* 3 (1952): 1–13; and Nautin, *Origène*, pp. 103–105.

117. Crouzel, ed., *Origène: Homélies sur S. Luc*, p. 79.

118. Origen *On Prayer* 5.

lastic activity with church duties. Perhaps Eusebius' biographical difficulties grew out of his attempt to impress his ideal on the whole of Origen's life. Had he been more sensitive to the nuances in Origen's life history, he might have been able, for example, to counterbalance the radical youth with the more conservative older man. Yet biography was from its inception characterized by its single-minded vision of its subjects, and in this respect Eusebius' biography does not differ from other biographies of holy men. Historical distortion, whether intentional or not, was seemingly an inevitable by-product of the biographical dynamic. Further, Eusebius' own addition to the vision of the holy man, namely providential guidance, served mainly to enhance biography's rather free treatment of history. For Eusebius was clearly aware of criticisms of his hero, especially concerning the issue of orthodoxy, yet how could divine providence nourish a Greek-minded heretic? Thus was Eusebius moved to separate the faces of the Janus mask, highlighting and then obscuring *both* the "pagan" *and* the "orthodox" Origens when it suited his own apologetic purposes.

It is with these points in mind that one can begin to understand the conflicting features of the biography discussed in this chapter. For Eusebius, Origen was truly a cultural hero, a "man for all seasons." Depicting his hero as a Christian holy man involved two main procedures. One was to show Origen's command of virtues admired by his (and Eusebius') contemporaries regardless of religious antagonisms or commitments. This was the philosophical Origen, a figure developed in the biography by emphasizing ascetic and spiritual character traits. The other procedure was to show Origen's command of virtues respected in his own tradition. This was the Christian Origen, who appears primarily in scholastic and martyr-related situations. As we have seen, Eusebius did not succeed in showing how these two figures were one; the Origen of the biography, like the Origen of history, is Janus-faced, yet he does not integrate the two worlds in which he is shown to participate. The Origen whom Eusebius has created is at times almost unrecognizable in instances when historical evidence throws light on Origen's sometimes shadowy career and personality. But Eusebius' task was not a quest for the historical Origen. Like that of other biographers, his goal was to create a convincing portrait of a magnificent man by capturing in prose the ideals which that man represented.

CHAPTER FIVE

Porphyry's *Life of Plotinus*: Interior Familiars of Myth

The question as to what is meaningful, or the question as to how (and in what way) things mean, or the question as to what the question is that we are asking when we ask what is meaningful—all this is just the question.[1]

These questions about the quest for meaning, posed here by a modern philosopher–scholar, reflect what was for Porphyry and other thinkers of his time a central concern: the riddling nature of reality and the difficulty of giving it verbal expression. So Plotinus had said, speaking about the recognition of God in the self, that "the vision baffles telling," since it is our inclination to make this supreme mystery into a "common story."[2] Porphyry's story about the meaning of Plotinus' life expresses the same sentiment in a poignant way. After recording one of Plotinus' oracular statements about his relation to the gods, Porphyry says, "What he meant by this exalted utterance we could not understand and did not dare to ask."[3] Such meaning resists direct questioning.

The idea that the oracular quality of life cannot be told as a common story, that true understanding is an initiation into a mystery,[4] had been offered long before by one of the Neoplatonists' presiding spirits, Socrates. In the *Euthydemus* 291b, Socrates makes a speech on the capturing of knowledge:

Find it, good heavens! No, you would have laughed at us—we were like children after larks, always thought we were going to catch each knowledge by the tail, and

1. Stanley Romaine Hopper, "'Le Cri de Merlin!' Or Interpretation and the Metalogical," in *Yearbook of Comparative Criticism*, vol. IV: *Anagogic Qualities of Literature*, ed. by Joseph P. Strelka (University Park: Pennsylvania State University Press, 1971), p. 14.
2. Plotinus *Enn*. 6.9.10–11.
3. Porphyry *Vita Plotini* 10.
4. Plotinus *Enn*. 6.9.11.

the knowledge always got away. . . . Then it seemed like falling into a labyrinth; we thought we were at the finish, but our way bent round and we found ourselves as it were back at the beginning, and just as far from that which we were seeking at first.

The issue here involves a contrast between practical knowledge and the art of knowing. Against what might be called the "scientific" method of generals and hunters, whose skill lies in the hunt that has capture as its goal, Socrates suggests that when knowing is an art, knowledge is like an animal—it can be tracked, but not captured. Further, the tracking involves one in a labyrinth that has no end. When the winding path of the art of knowing is followed, meaning cannot be stated propositionally or in direct statements that "catch" it.

Plotinus repeated this Socratic wisdom again and again in his warnings against equating language with the realities it attempts to evoke. "Everywhere we must read 'so to speak'," he once said.[5] And, in his own way, Porphyry echoed his teacher's conviction that the revelation of meaning is allusive rather than declarative, for in *On the Cave of the Nymphs* he remarked that what is "dark and obscure," or resistant to shaping, comes to expression as a "shadowing forth in form."[6]

For Porphyry as for so many others of his era, the art of knowing had as its climax knowledge of God, an evocation of divine fullness in the soul.[7] However, even though the presence of divinity could be described as a "shine" so radiant that adepts at the art of knowing were thought to be "like God" and "divine,"[8] the lives of such sages still remained enigmatic, neither transparent nor open to rational scrutiny. We have already seen Eusebius weaving Origen's lifelines—and tangling the skeins! Eusebius' play with patterns of images, which from an historical perspective obscures as much about character as it reveals, suggests that the repose in the soul might really be a "divine desolation,"[9] both for the sage and for his interpreter. As Porphyry suggested, the forms of things are shadows, shades of the mystery of divine presence whose meanings ghost our perception and mock straight-minded attempts to tell the story plainly.

5. Ibid., 6.8.13. 6. Porphyry *De antro nympharum* 5.

7. See chapter 2, pp. 17–19.

8. On the shining of soul in bodies, see Plotinus *Enn.* 1.1.8, 1.6.9. Porphyry remarks that Plotinus' intellect "visibly lit up his face" and that his gentleness "shone out from him." See *Vita Plotini* 13.

9. Numenius as quoted by Eusebius *Praeparatio evangelica* 11.22.

Porphyry's own odyssey with regard to the art of knowing speaks eloquently to this point. In one of his frequent reflections on his own life in the *Life of Plotinus*, Porphyry remembers his early days in Plotinus' circle. Accustomed as he had been to the compelling logic of rhetorical discourse, he objected to the meandering course of Plotinus' lectures, which were "like conversations." His response to these conversation-like lectures was a treatise directed against his teacher, in which he attempted to show "that the object of thought lies outside the mind."[10]

This is a curious passage, for it is not immediately obvious why an objection to style should call forth a treatise devoted to a philosophical issue. What does Porphyry mean by this connection? I suspect that Porphyry's memory of his early objection to Plotinus' style, and his consequent response, contains an implicit assumption about an intimate relation between one's style of presentation and the content of that presentation. That is, one's vision of reality, of *what* one knows, is inseparable from one's way of expressing that vision. Style and substance, method and content, thinker and thought, are one. If this is the awareness that had dawned on Porphyry, we can see his objection more clearly. For, as Armstrong has shown, he had learned from Longinus, his first teacher, that what we know is somehow distinct from the mind—a separation of thinker and thought. For the logician, the art of knowing is like the hunter's "science" described by Socrates; it "captures" thoughts and catalogs, classifies, orders them into a clear-cut system. What, then, had Porphyry seen in Plotinus that irritated (and finally unsettled) his logical convictions?

First, Plotinus was not systematic: "He treats the same subjects in different ways in different places," as his student Amelius said.[11] Plotinus himself recommended not logic but dialectic as the way to the "winged" contemplation of the philosopher. This method, which works by "weaving together" all that issues from "the plain of truth," "leaves what is called logical activity, about propositions and syllogisms, to another art."[12] Further, the art of dialectic, unlike logic, is not a mere tool: "It is not just bare theories and rules; it deals with things and has real beings as a kind of material for its activity. . . . It does not know about propositions—they are

10. Porphyry *Vita Plotini* 18. On the whole issue raised by the title of Porphyry's treatise, see A. H. Armstrong, "The Background of the Doctrine 'That the Intelligibles are not outside the Intellect'," in *Entretiens sur l'antiquité classique* 5: *Les Sources de Plotin* (Geneva: Fondation Hardt, 1960), pp. 391–425.

11. Porphyry *Vita Plotini* 17.

12. Plotinus *Enn.* 1.3.4.

just letters. . . ."[13] Finally, Plotinus suggests that the dialectic method, which is the interweaving activity of perfect mind, "knows the movements of soul."[14] It is just at this point that Plotinus' style, his way of knowing, becomes one with the matrix of thought itself—soul—whose movement is a labyrinthine dance of "real beings" within.[15] For Plotinus "every soul that knows its history" is aware that its true motion is a circling around its source; real knowing is a divine wandering within, not a straightforward march toward some external object. It is we who are contained within reality, we who think only insofar as we are in soul; and when we break away from that containing presence—for example, by supposing that our dualistic language, by separating thinker and thought, has captured reality—we break away not only from the source but from ourselves.[16]

This, then, was the new thinking with which Porphyry had to contend. And his contending was, as he says, an agony. For he had been trained to catch larks, but now found that that way of knowing leaves the hunter far away from that which he seeks, like "a distraught child who does not recognize his father."[17] Following his conversion to the Plotinian way,[18] Porphyry seems to have given up the effort "to tell the story plainly" to such an extent that he was once accused of madness after reading to his colleagues his own poem, a "mysterious and veiled" interpretation of sacred marriage. Plotinus, however, remarked that he had become "at once poet, philosopher, and hierophant."[19] Seized by the madness that is heaven-sent,[20] Porphyry now saw thinking as a *poiesis*, a poetic working that is an imaginative act, not a logical exercise. Perhaps he had come to see what Plotinus knew, that the "divine desolation," the dark mystery of being, manifests itself enigmatically, "like a face seen in many mirrors."[21] The faces are images, phantoms of the soul's interior, the "real beings" through which God is seen,[22]

13. Ibid., 1.3.5.
14. Ibid.
15. On the circling motion of soul, see *Enn.* 2.2. On dancing, see *Enn.* 1.8.2; 2.9.7.
16. On the soul and its history, see Plotinus *Enn.* 6.9.8; on being in soul, see *Enn.* 1.1.13; 1.1.9; on knowing and seeing within, see, for example, *Enn.* 5.8.2 and 10; 5.9.13; on breaking away from ourselves, see *Enn.* 6.9.7; on duality, *Enn.* 6.9.10; 2.9.1.
17. Plotinus *Enn.* 6.9.7. On Porphyry's agony see *Vita Plotini* 18.
18. On Porphyry's conversion, see chapter 3, p. 64.
19. Porphyry *Vita Plotini* 15.
20. Plato *Phaedrus* 244a–b.
21. Plotinus *Enn.* 1.1.8.
22. In *Enn.* 2.9.2, Plotinus suggests that soul is "one nature in many powers." Elsewhere he says that the soul is filled with images that, if considered properly, are likenesses of archetypal realities in the divine realm. See *Enn.* 2.9.6 and 3.5.1. Finally, one must see not only

and our thinking—indeed, our very being—is likewise veiled with images, for "living things are all conformed to the complete pattern of the All."[23]

Porphyry's new vision of the "pattern of the All" may account for the change in his allegorical method that one scholar has detected. In his *On Images*, written before the sojourn with Plotinus, the figures in the text being interpreted do not bear multiple significations; whereas in *On the Cave of the Nymphs*, written after the encounter with Plotinus, the terms in the source text give rise to pleromatic meanings in the interpretation.[24] The change, it seems to me, is significant. Allegory, formerly a tool for the one-to-one correspondences of "plain telling," became for Porphyry part of the dialectic of the vision that baffles direct telling. Interpretation had itself become a winding path, a "pattern of the All," a labyrinthine tracing of the faces of a text's "dark and obscure" presence.

The idea of interpretation as the key to life's "Garden of Plenty"[25] might be seen as a response to one of our opening questions: "the question as to how (and in what way) things mean." What I am suggesting is that for Plotinus and for Porphyry, there is meaning in life when one is possessed by its metaphoric power, by the nuances and shadows of its riddling nature, by the plenty of its garden. It is a question of possession and identity. As Plotinus said, "Did 'we' investigate by having soul? No, but in so far as we *are* soul."[26] That "primal nature"—what we have been calling the mystery at the heart of life—is always present, and "we are always before it," and within it.[27]

Unfortunately, there is a tragic flaw in our investigations: "We do not always attend"; "we do not always look."[28] We forget "the question as to what the question is that we are asking when we ask what is meaningful." Our modern questioner, following C. G. Jung, has taken the mysterious cry of Merlin in the forest of Broceliande as a figure for this painful failure to attend: "Men still hear his cries, so the legend runs, but they cannot understand or interpret them. . . . This cry that no one could understand im-

---

the images, but the correspondences among them as well: "All things are full of signs, and it is a wise man who knows one thing out of (by way of) another" (*Enn.* 2.3.7).

23. Plotinus *Enn.* 2.3.13.

24. See Jean Pépin, "Porphyre, exégète d'Homère," in *Entretiens sur l'antiquité classique* 12: *Porphyre* (Geneva: Fondation Hardt, 1966), p. 247 and passim.

25. See Plotinus, *Enn.* 3.5.8–9.

26. Ibid., 1.1.13.

27. Ibid., 6.9.8.

28. Ibid.

plies that he lives on in unredeemed form. His story is not yet finished, and he still walks abroad."[29] Only by placing ourselves within the "magnetic field" of that cry, within the echoes that the cry evokes, can we hope to redeem our interpretative looking.[30] Like Plotinus' primal nature, which is always present, Merlin's cry sounds; if only the hearer will attend, its echoes will compose "a choral song full of God."[31]

In the following pages, biography will be considered as a quest for meaning, an interpretative effort that resists making a "common story" out of the "vision which baffles telling." The text, in this case, is a life, the life of Plotinus, and the vision is the dark and obscure cry of the man's being that sounded through Porphyry and made of his interpretation a song full of echoes. The biographical telling is indeed baffling, for the echoes come forth as "real beings" like Odysseus and Socrates, who give shadowed form to the mystery we call Plotinus. Nature, we have said, is riddling; so too is the meaning of a man's life. In Porphyry's biography, the soulfulness of Plotinus shines like a face reflected in many mirrors. What we can know about a life is its veil of images; biographical interpretation is a labyrinthine tracing and a weaving together of the tracks of soul in life.[32]

Shadows of Life: Interior Familiars

"All things," said Plotinus, "are full of signs."[33] Visible things are linked by a "chain" of sympathy to the invisible, such that visible nature is the mask of God. In fact, the earth is itself a god, and the primal nature is expressed

29. Hopper, "'Le cri de Merlin!'," p. 10; the quotations are from C. G. Jung, *Memories, Dreams, Reflections*, p. 228, and *Psychology and Alchemy*, p. 228.
30. See Hopper, "'Le cri de Merlin!'," p. 26: "In the case of the poem, [I must] stand within the magnetic field of the elements in tension, and see as the poem sees. . . . What is miraculous here in the moment of recognition is the sudden sense of identification with that which is beyond conceptualization."
31. Plotinus *Enn.* 6.9.8.
32. A note on our way of proceeding: in Chapter 4, Eusebius' "Life of Origen" was read in context with other writings of Eusebius (especially his *Contra Hieroclem*) as well as works of Origen. So here, other writings of Porphyry, especially his *De antro nympharum*, as well as the *Enneads* of Plotinus, will be used to throw light (or cast shadows) on his *Vita Plotini*. I assume that biographies were not isolated phenomena but rather one face of the whole world of an author's thought.
33. Plotinus *Enn.* 2.3.7.

through it in signs. What is fundamentally whole shows itself here, to us, as a fullness of lucid images.[34] Even the human body, part, after all, of the earth, can function as such a soul sign: "We can come to conclusions about someone's character, and also about the dangers that beset him, and the precautions to be taken, by looking at his eyes or some other part of his body. Yes, they are parts, and so are we; so we can learn about one from the other."[35]

The idea that the whole might unfold and blossom in the part seems to have had a powerful effect on Porphyry. We can see it at work in a humorous way in the anecdote with which he opens his biography of Plotinus:

> Plotinus, the philosopher of our times, seemed ashamed of being in the body. As a result of this state of mind he could never bear to talk about his race or his parents or his native country. And he objected so strongly to sitting to a painter or sculptor that he said to Amelius, who was urging him to allow a portrait of himself to be made, "Why really, is it not enough to have to carry the image in which nature has encased us, without your requesting me to agree to leave behind me a longer-lasting image of the image, as if it was something genuinely worth looking at?" In view of his denial and refusal for this reason to sit, Amelius, who had a friend, Carterius, the best painter of the time, brought him in to attend the meetings of the school—they were open to anyone who wished to come, and accustomed him by progressive study to derive increasingly striking mental pictures from what he saw. Then Carterius drew a likeness of the impression which remained in his memory. Amelius helped him to improve his sketch to a closer resemblance, and so the talent of Carterius gave us an excellent portrait of Plotinus without his knowledge.[36]

Porphyry seems to relish the trick played on the master as much as the portrait itself! But what of this portrait, and Porphyry's obvious delight in its existence? Was he guilty of a literal appreciation of "an image of an image," thus depriving of its soul signs that part of earth fashioned as "Plotinus"? The words he uses to describe the portrait suggest otherwise. The artist Carterius is described as working with "striking fantasies" (*phantasias plēktikōteras*); what he drew is characterized as a "likeness of his mental impression" (*indalmatos to eikasma*; *indalma* can also mean "hallucination"!); what Amelius helps him improve "to a greater likeness" (*eis homoiotēta*) is his "sketch" (*to ichnos*: literally, "footprint," "track").

34. Ibid., 4.4.26. 35. Ibid., 2.3.7. 36. Porphyry *Vita Plotini* 1.

All of these terms suggest that for Porphyry the portrait was not an opaque image of the man, nor was it merely an imitation of his physical features. It might better be described as a creative mirroring, an act of the imagination more true to reality than direct perception. This kind of portrait could be described as a visual text full of signs, footprints of the man's deep self.

A passage from another of Porphyry's works provides a more discursive sense of the portrait art: "If a man makes an image of a friend, of course he does not suppose that the friend is in it or that the parts of his body are included in the various parts of the representation. Honor is shown toward the friend by means of the image."[37] Although it reads, curiously, like an apology for the biography's opening anecdote, this statement from *Against the Christians* comes in the context of a defense of images—statues—of the gods. As with the image of a friend, so with representations of the gods; one would not suppose "that the god is in the wood or stone or bronze from which the statue is manufactured."[38] Further, "even supposing that any one of the Greeks were so light-minded as to think that the gods dwell within the statues, his idea would be much purer than that of the man who believes that the divine entered into the womb of the virgin Mary and became an embryo before being born and swaddled in due course; for this is a place full of menstrual blood and gall and things even more unseemly."[39]

What Porphyry seems particularly adamant about here is the nature of the space framed by the image. We may not imagine that the statue becomes the place for the physical dwelling of the god, nor may we think that the portrait of the friend captures him in a tangible way. Rather, just as the image of the friend shows honor, so statues of the gods are for the sake of remembrance and knowledge; thus to honor the statue with sacrifices is actually to evoke one's own divine inclination.[40] In this regard, Porphyry's remarks about the birth of the Christian god demonstrate graphically what was, for him, the sacrilege of supposing that the presence or indwelling of the gods is in any way physical.

37. Porphyry *Contra Christianos* fr. 76 (Harnack).
38. Ibid.
39. Ibid., fr. 77. This was, of course, an old argument between pagans and Christians. Porphyry is here following in the footsteps of Celsus: see, for example, Origen *Contra Celsum* 7.62 (Chadwick, pp. 446–47) and 8.17–24 (Chadwick, pp. 464–70). On the whole issue, see E. Bevan, *Holy Images* (London, 1940).
40. Porphyry *Contra Christianos* fr. 76 (Harnack).

Images, then, do not place gods or men in frames that define them in temporal or spatial dimension. The province of these visual images is not actual place, but a placing that leads inward, through the representation, to a "realm of inner space," an "interior geography" where meaning is gathered and from which it can flow.[41] There is a paradox here, perhaps even an absurdity. For it is the face, the image, that gives face to what is fundamentally faceless. Further, it is not meaning that is placed in the object, but rather we who are placed within the realm for which the image provides a frame. The portrait of Plotinus, for example, was an object, an image that gave face to the inward mystery of the man. Yet it was not Plotinus who delighted in this image, but Porphyry; through the image of his friend he was placed within a geography that expressed his own interior inclination. In honoring Plotinus in this way, he was at the same time honoring the memory, and evoking the knowledge, of a face of his own soul.

We might think of the portrait of Plotinus as a "shadowing forth in form," a visual image that, paradoxically, both masks the man's "inner realm" *and* takes us into it. But we no longer have this visual portrait; it has been transformed by Porphyry into a literary image so powerful for him that he chose it to begin the winding path of his biography. Not only the biography as a whole, but each anecdote, each image, serves as a face whereby Porphyry faced the "dark and obscure" meaning of Plotinus that lived on as part of his own "interior geography." By giving face to Plotinus in the biography, Porphyry has, like the artist Carterius, placed himself within the "striking fantasies" that impressed him as appropriate framings, or footprints, of his master's nature.

The biography, then, is the baffled telling of a vision, a "placing" of soul through image and type. As one of Porphyry's Gnostic contemporaries said, "Truth did not come into the world naked, but it came in types and images. One will not receive truth in any other way."[42] And Plutarch, a less rash voice and one more squarely in Porphyry's own tradition, said the same: naked truth wounds, and is too harsh; thus the Delphic oracle spoke in the "equivocations and circumlocutions" of metaphor.[43] Oddly enough, this

41. For these phrases I am indebted to David L. Miller, "Utopia, Trinity, and Tropical Topography," a lecture at the colloquium on "Utopia" sponsored by the Protestant Theological Faculty of the University of Human Sciences of Strasbourg and the Department of Religion, Syracuse University, 13–15 March 1980, Strasbourg, France, Manuscript, p. 6.

42. *Gospel of Philip*, in Robinson, *Nag Hammadi Library*, p. 140.

43. Plutarch *De pyth. orac.* 26, 407e (and see the discussion of Plutarch's position on these issues by Jean Pépin, *Mythe et allégorie*, 2nd ed. (Paris: Études Agustiniennes, 1976), p. 180.

"placing of truth under poetic form"[44] places the hearer within the very meaning that would evade him otherwise. We suggested above that a paradox surrounds "imaging truth" and the "placing which places." It is a paradox that characterizes the biographer's mythic art of weaving fact with fiction; as Plutarch said, it is the gesture that speaks worlds, not the obvious act, and it is precisely the gesture that the biographer must capture, for then, dissimulating, he tells the truth.

The paradox of poetic placing was not a stranger to Porphyry's thought, nor to that of his master. Plotinus once called *topos* ("place") "the source and spring of true soul and knowing."[45] Yet he also said that "the world of sense moves in soul—there is no other place for it than soul."[46] Taken together, these sentences read like a play on the word "place," for how can soul be both what places and what springs from place?

What sustains this paradox, and carries its meaning, is Plotinus' idea of double *energeia*. The idea of *energeia* is of course connected to Plotinus' famous theory of emanation, the procession of a chain of beings from a single, ultimate principle, the One. This chain, however, is not a series of flat links but rather appears as groups of trinities, with *energeia* as the focal point, the "third" between any two related links.[47] One feature of this procession that seems to have interested Plotinus in particular is the *double* nature of *energeia*: that what does the forming is itself informed by its activity—visions envisioning themselves! In *Ennead* 6.2.22, Plotinus turns to the double *energeia* of the embodied soul: soul fashions body, or "places" it within its containing embrace, and at the same time soul is given "place," or expression, by the body into which it shines. The body is placed by the energy of soul, and is a living expression, and expressing, of its activity.[48]

In his *Sentences*, Porphyry picked up and expanded upon these Plotinian thoughts. What is present in us, he says, are the *energeiai* of soul; body is in soul, and soul is "in" body not as *ousia*, as a substantive thing, but as activity.[49] Further, the relating of body and soul cannot be described in terms of actual place—only bodies can be "in a place"—but rather in terms of the energy of placing. The emphasis is on the *relation* between soul and body, a relation which is a dance of "living energies" like Plotinus' "real

44. Ibid. 45. Plotinus *Enn.* 2.5.3. 46. Ibid. 3.7.11.

47. See the discussion in Andrew Smith, *Porphyry's Place in the Neoplatonic Tradition* (The Hague: Martinus Nijhoff, 1974), pp. 9–16.

48. On the outer and inner man, see *Enn.* 1.1.3, 3.6.5, 4.3.10, 6.4.14–15; on archetypes, see *Enn.* 6.7.4–5; see also Smith, *Porphyry's Place*, pp. 11, 23.

49. Smith, *Porphyry's Place*, p. 2.

beings" within.[50] The paradox of placing, then, is kept in tension by a relating, an energy of mutual illumination.

The matter goes farther, and deeper, than an ontology which is only cosmic, however. For the metaphor of "placing," which envisions a simultaneous juxtaposition of soul and body, idea and object, intellect and sense, such that each is seen through the other, also has psychological and literary implications. It is Plotinus who makes psychological sense of this metaphor, and because his ideas give sharper focus to Porphyry's more explicitly literary enterprise, it will be useful to consider them first.

In his reflections on the human psyche, Plotinus makes it clear that true knowing is a poetic knowing with "the inner sight."[51] It is a seeing that makes one "at home" (*endon*), like dwelling within the familial hearth. And when one looks deeply within the self, what is seen is *theoeidēs aglaia*,[52] literally the splendor or shining of divine form. The seeing is not single, however, but multiple, for in its weavings through body, soul leaves tracks, footprints of a shimmering presence. We are each a whole universe (for "soul is many things, and all things"[53]), and our task is to polish our way of looking, until the hearth shines with likenesses of the relating activity of soul in body.[54]

Plotinus had a striking metaphor for the way of looking that lets the hearth, the dark mystery of our being, shine with familial images: it is the "mirror of Dionysus."[55] Plotinus shared Porphyry's view of the evocative power of visual images, and it was a discussion of statues as receptacles for the presencing of soul that seems to have called forth this metaphor. After remarking that statues "serve like a mirror to catch an image of [the pres-

50. See the following fragment preserved in *Stobaeus* 1.354.4f. (text and translation in Smith, *Porphyry's Place*, p. 3 and n. 7): "The life-giving activities [*hai zōtikai energeiai*], by accepting the arrangement of the different activities into parts which is imposed upon them by their acceptance of the enharmonising power of soul, have added the 'possession of parts' even to the soul. And perhaps soul is to be thought of and to have life in two ways, its own life and life in relation; the 'parts' exist in the related life. . . . Thus in the sowing (embodiment) the parts exist, alongside soul which remains indivisible."

51. *Enn.* 1.6.9.

52. Ibid.

53. Ibid., 3.4.3; see also 2.2.2: each man is a "private universe" (*oikeion holon*: a "domestic whole"!).

54. On polishing, see *Enn.* 1.6.9; on likeness, *Enn.* 3.3.6: "Correspondence holds all things together" (especially when the things are "opposites" like form and matter, heaven and earth, body and soul); see further 2.9.6 and 2.3.13: "living things are all conformed to the complete pattern of the All."

55. *Enn.* 4.3.12.

ence of] soul,"[56] Plotinus turns to another kind of statue, the human being. "Nothing, in fact, is far away from anything," and although our bodies, like statues, are in place and have a tangible reality, true self-hood, like the reflecting, receptive statue, "has nothing to do with spatial position."[57] Selfhood, rather, is a placing, a unity "in which there is distinction."[58] It is the metaphor of the "mirror of Dionysus" that itself mirrors the inner realm of self along with its variegated "distinctions."

Why this particular mirror? In the early Dionysus stories, the mirror was the favorite toy of the young god, and when he was ripped apart by the Titans, his mirror reflected his altered image. It was a trick or magic or even lying mirror that, showing an altered image, yet showed the real one—perhaps like Plutarch's "gesture," which tells the truth while lying.[59] In late Orphic-Neoplatonic interpretations, the mirror was symbolic of a way of looking in which heavenly truth was revealed: the mirror's images "caught in figures the transparence of heaven."[60] In a similar vein, Proclus says that the mirror symbolizes "the characteristic way in which the universe abounds with intelligence," for out of the image in the mirror flowed the particulars of creation.[61]

These reflections on the mirror are at work in Plotinus' use of the metaphor, too: "the souls of men, seeing their images in the mirror of Dionysus as it were, have entered into that realm in a leap from above; yet they are not cut off from their origin. . . ."[62] Mirrored images are creative, and it is through them that contact with the origin is maintained. Thus the mirror of Dionysus suggests that our truest way of looking at life is to look poetically, in figure and image, for it is through these "particulars" that the single hearth of self manifests its presence and becomes a home. Plotinus might well have agreed with one of his modern heirs, who has suggested that "the imaginal sense turns the world to trope, not so much in seeing images as in sensing all things imaginally. The place of image and its sense is a center in which everything is contained, as if center were circumference, the horizon a point pointing. If God [the hearth] is *topos*, the *topos* is trope."[63] Images are the tracings that give shape and contour to the relation, the "placing," between what is hidden within and plain without.

56. *Enn.* 4.3.11. 57. Ibid. 58. Ibid.

59. Nonnus *Dionysiana* 6, quoted in Pépin, *Mythe et allégorie*, p. 202, n. 111.

60. John Lydus *Mens*. 4.51, quoted in Pépin, *Mythe et allégorie*, p. 202. n. 111.

61. Proclus *In Tim.* 33b, 163, quoted in Pépin, *Mythe et allégorie*, p. 202. n. 111.

62. *Enn.* 4.3.12.

63. David L. Miller, "'I know a place . . .'," a lecture at the Symposium, "Religion after

This imaginal sensing that reveals the true self through its tracings can be found in Porphyry's literary way of knowing, where text is hearth and interpretation its imaginal reflections. In the opening sections of his *On the Cave of the Nymphs*, Porphyry argues against two ways of interpreting Homer's description of the Cave of the Naiads in *Odyssey* 13. On the one hand, he says, it is not a mere fiction (*plasma*: "delusion"); nor is it geography, a literal history of a place (*historia topikē*). Both of these interpretative approaches are absurd, since the one accuses the poet of a poetic license run wild, while the other accuses the gods of an arbitrary act, "opening by a new art a path to gods and men in the region of Ithaca."[64] What Porphyry recommends is a third way, the way of unfolding the concealed meaning of the text by exploring its symbols and the meaning that shines through them. Porphyry sets out to seek the "wisdom" of the cave through its images.[65]

This interpretative perspective is reminiscent of a statement that Porphyry makes in his *Life of Plotinus*. Immediately after he quotes and explicates the Delphic oracle about Plotinus, he says, "This, then, is my account (*historētai*) of the life of Plotinus."[66] Here is a very different use of the word "history" from the one we saw above. For what kind of history speaks in the poetry of Pythian frenzy? Although the oracle is an obvious example, I would suggest that the entire biography is characterized by the kind of poetic thinking that allows for history a soulful depth, a hearth that shimmers forth in images. Porphyry's biography is a mirror of Dionysus!

Looking in the mirror of Dionysus is the making of a world in images. When the world is a human life, the images body forth the relation between the man's hidden soulfulness, the dark presence within, and the facts of his life, his "statue." The biographical mirror, then, reflects images of the activities of soul in life, creating what a modern literary thinker has called "the phantasmal real."[67]

What are the phantasms that, ghosting Porphyry's biography, make Plotinus real? One of them is Socrates. He is mentioned twice by name, at

---

Freud and Jung," sponsored by the Center for Twentieth-Century Studies, University of Wisconsin-Milwaukee, 15–16 April 1980, Manuscript, pp. 9–10.

64. Porphyry *De antro nympharum* 2–4.

65. Ibid., 4.

66. *Vita Plotini* 24; see above, chapter 3, pp. 63–64.

67. J. Hillis Miller, "Ariadne's Thread: Repetition and the Narrative Line," *Critical Inquiry* 3 (1976): 76.

the beginning and at the end of the biography, giving it a kind of Socratic "envelope." His first explicit appearance comes in the context of Plotinus' refusal (as in the case of the portrait) to celebrate himself: instead of honoring the date of his own birth, he celebrated Socrates' birthday, "receiving his friends at his hearth" (*hestiōn tous hetairous*).[68] His second appearance comes as the prologue to Apollo's oracle about Plotinus: "When Amelius asked where the soul of Plotinus had gone, Apollo, who said of Socrates, 'Socrates is the wisest of men,'—hear what a great and noble oracle he uttered about Plotinus."[69]

In both of these instances, the appearance of Socrates gives a sense of Plotinus' soulful identity. They are evocations of a daemonic "other" that most truly reveals the heart of the man himself. The first appearance of Socrates is an example of Porphyry's Plutarchian way of depicting character. It involves a gesture that speaks more faithfully than grand actions on the world stage. Here it is the context that is especially revealing, for instead of recording the celebration of Socrates' birthday as part of the normal Platonic academic practice,[70] Porphyry has made this gesture serve as a face of Plotinus' interior inclination. Thus it is not academic practice that we hear about, but a gathering of friends at Plotinus' own hearth, where Plotinus is host, not to himself, but to Socrates. The second appearance is a similar evocation of Plotinus' Socratic self; here the soul of Plotinus is directly linked with "Socrates the wisest of men," a placing that gives authority to "the immortal song" Apollo sings in honor of Plotinus.

These two explicit appearances of Socrates are not, however, the only shapes of the biography's Socratic ghost. If, as we have suggested, images are phantoms, reflections in the mirror of Dionysus, their epiphanies are likely to be varied, being sometimes obvious, as we have just seen, and sometimes more subtle. The changeable nature of these daemonic "others" seems to have been well known to Porphyry. His thinking on this matter has been summarized as follows: "*daimones* have misty (*aerōdes*) *pneuma*, which alters its form in response to their momentary imaginings, and thus causes them to appear to us in ever changing shapes, sometimes acting the parts of gods or higher spirits or the souls of the dead."[71] Taking Porphyry at

68. Porphyry *Vita Plotini* 2.
69. *Vita Plotini* 22.
70. See John Dillon, "The Academy in the Middle Platonic Period," *Dionysius* 3 (December 1979), p. 76.
71. Dodds., *Proclus*, App. II, p. 319.

his word, we can say that the appearance of Socrates by name is but one form of "momentary imagining"; other shapes of Plotinus' Socratic phantom will follow.

The opening chapters of the biography, with their suggestion that Plotinus disdained the frivolous pleasures of the world, announce another way in which Socrates gives figure to Plotinus. Behind what Porphyry reports about Plotinus' contempt for bodily things lies Socratic advice on freeing the soul from the shackles of body.[72] This is the way, for Socrates, to the contemplative life of the true philosopher, who "everywhere seeks the true nature of everything as a whole, never sinking to what lies close to hand."[73] That Plotinus lived the contemplative life where everything is seen as a whole is most strikingly suggested by Porphyry's account of Plotinus' four unions with "the God who is over all things."[74] But there are other indications as well.

Porphyry reports that when Plotinus was speaking, his intellect "visibly lit up his face." Further, he was so full of thought (abounding in ideas such that he did not even notice his own grammatical mistakes) that Porphyry was led to describe his presentations in terms of "rapt inspiration."[75] Like Alcibiades with Socrates, Porphyry had been "bitten in the heart" by Plotinus' philosophy *and* by his presence, and Socrates' "sacred rage" and "philosophic frenzy" ghost his account of his own teacher.[76]

The clearest picture of Plotinus' contemplative Socratic face comes in chapter eight of the biography. Here Porphyry says that his mentor "was wholly concerned with thought. . . . Even if he was talking to someone, engaged in continuous conversation, he kept to his train of thought. He could take his necessary part in the conversation to the full, and at the same time keep his mind fixed without a break on what he was considering." "Present at once to himself and to others," Plotinus "kept the connection." "Never, while awake," did Plotinus relax his "intent concentration upon the intellect." Again the Socrates of the *Symposium* comes to mind. Not only is there the picture of Socrates still "keeping the connection" at the end of

72. Plato *Phaedo* 67c; 83a.

73. Plato *Theaetetus* 173e; see also *Republic* VI.486a.

74. *Vita Plotini* 23.

75. Ibid., 13–14. Note that the rapture that failed to attend to grammar also had its humorous side. Porphyry reports, in *Vita Plotini* 7, Plotinus' play with the name of one of his students, reminiscent of Socrates' playfulness with words (especially names) in the *Cratylus*.

76. Plato *Symposium* 218a–b.

the banquet when everyone else has succumbed to wine and sleep; there is also Alcibiades' story of Socrates during the campaign at Potidaea.[77] There Socrates took care of what "lay close to hand," enduring hardships and fighting bravely, yet he did not lose his philosophical concern with contemplation of the whole, standing for a whole day "lost in thought, wrestling with some problem or other." This "absolutely unique"[78] Socrates, who kept the connection so faithfully, echoes poignantly as the contemplative melody in Porphyry's Plotinian song.

Yet another Socratic echo sounds in Porphyry's story about the visible manifestation of Plotinus' companion spirit (*oikeios daimōn*: his "familiar daemon").[79] The scene was a temple of Isis, and the ceremony of evocation was presided over by an Egyptian priest giving a "display of his occult wisdom." In Porphyry's words, "when the spirit was summoned to appear a god came" and not a "mere daemon." Thus the "companion [*ton sunonta*: 'the one with him'] was a daemon of the more godlike kind [*theioterōn daimonōn*], and he continually kept the divine eye of his soul fixed on this companion."

The idea of the personal daemon, occupying the peak of a hierarchy of invisible "real beings" within the self, was, of course, a popular one. One scholar has remarked that "the invisible world was as real as the visible," and the daemonic companion "lodged contact with the divine in the structure of the personality itself."[80] As Porphyry notes in this section of the biography, Plotinus wrote a whole treatise on the companions after his experience, remarking about these daemons that "what works in a man leads him."[81]

The specifically Socratic character of Plotinus' invisible familiar is suggested by its divinity, its godlikeness. Socrates' famous voice, his "constant companion,"[82] is described as a "divine or supernatural experience," a "prophetic voice," "my familiar divine sign."[83] Further, as Socrates notes often,

77. Plato *Symposium* 220a–221b. 78. Ibid., 221c. 79. *Vita Plotini* 10.

80. Peter Brown, *The Making of Late Antiquity* (Cambridge, Massachusetts: Harvard University Press, 1978), pp. 10, 69; cf. pp. 63–75. On p. 121, n. 64, Brown remarks that in Christian thinking on this topic, the guardian angel came to be seen as "the principle of a person's identity," such that *angelus* came to be used as a "courtesy phrase" for a person instead of his name!

81. *Enn.* 3.4.3.

82. Plato *Apology* 40a.

83. *Apology* 31c; 40a; *Phaedrus* 242c. See also *Republic* VI.496c.

his companion was truly a guardian: it warned him of danger, thus protecting him from it. This is exactly the kind of role that Porphyry ascribes to Plotinus' daemon, for he introduces the story of the summons in the temple with an anecdote about the great power of Plotinus' soul in repulsing a magical attack, remarking wryly that "Plotinus certainly possessed by birth something more than other men." Plotinus' familiar daemon, then, lived on in Porphyry in such a way that in the ceremony of his biography, he summoned it through an image of Socrates.

Like Porphyry, Alcibiades said about *his* mentor, Socrates, that he was "godlike,"[84] and in Alcibiades' touching words about his love for Socrates, a final face of the Socratic ghost who embodies Plotinus in the biography comes forth. In chapter 15, Porphyry is relating the events of one year's feast of Plato in the school. After telling about the reading of his own poem, "The Sacred Marriage," and Plotinus' approval of it ("You have shown yourself at once poet, philosopher, and hierophant"), he reports what followed:

> The rhetorician Diophanes read a defence of Alcibiades in Plato's *Symposium* in which he asserted that a pupil for the sake of advancing in the study of virtue should submit himself to carnal intercourse with his master if the master desired it. Plotinus repeatedly started up to leave the meeting, but restrained himself, and after the end of the lecture gave me, Porphyry, the task of writing a refutation. Diophanes refused to lend me his manuscript, and I depended in writing my refutation on my memory of his arguments. When I read it before the same assembled hearers I pleased Plotinus so much that he kept on quoting during the meeting, "So strike and be a light to men."

What Diophanes read to the school was a defense of sexual love between teacher and student, based on a misreading of Alcibiades' speech in the *Symposium*.[85] Alcibiades had not actually suggested that Socrates had desired to be his lover and that he as the student had submitted willingly, but rather that he had been so deeply moved by Socrates' philosophy, "which clings like an adder to any young and gifted mind it can get hold of," that he desired his body as well, confusing inner beauty with its exterior appearance. As Socrates himself says to Alcibiades, "You're trying to exchange the semblance of beauty for the thing itself."

Presumably Plotinus shared this Socratic sentiment, and it was his dis-

84. *Symposium* 219c; *Vita Plotini* 23 and 10.
85. *Symposium* 222a.

may at hearing Diophanes' gross misreading, which must, after all, have been aimed directly at him, that prompted his repeated inclination to leave the meeting. Porphyry, who had just finished reading an inspired poem on sacred marriage, also disagreed, and wrote such a dazzling refutation that Plotinus called him "a light to men."

What was Porphyry's refutation like? It is tempting to imagine that he extended his thoughts on sacred (as opposed to profane) marriage to Alcibiades' speech. For, in his conclusion, Alcibiades says about Socrates that "if you open up his arguments, and really get into the skin of them, you'll find that they're the only arguments in the world that have any sense at all, and that nobody else's are so godlike, so rich in images of virtue. . . ."[86] Here "getting into the skin" involves a soulful connection, an interior seeing in images that is most truly expressive of the relationship's beauty. It is a marriage of teacher and student that is figured by the "bite in the heart" of "sacred rage,"[87] not by physical frenzy.

Alcibiades' reference here to godlike images within is a play on the image with which he opens his eulogy. There he had compared Socrates to a statue of Silenus: "they're modeled with pipes or flutes in their hands, and when you open them down the middle there are little figures of the gods inside." It is, says Alcibiades, an apt comparison: "I don't know whether anybody else has ever opened him up when he's been being serious, and seen the little images inside, but I saw them once, and they looked so godlike, so golden, so beautiful, and so utterly amazing that there was nothing for it but to do exactly what he told me."[88]

Because Porphyry's refutation is lost to us, we will never know whether he countered Diophanes' view of the profane marriage between teacher and student with Alcibiades' Silenic perspective. We do know, however, that in the biography Porphyry calls himself "one of Plotinus' closest friends," and that, while he calls attention again and again to Plotinus' care for him, he makes it clear that what Plotinus really "loved with all his soul" was the God "who has neither shape nor any intelligible form, but is throned above intellect and all the intelligible."[89] What the Diophanes anecdote suggests in the context of such statements is that the relation between Porphyry and Plotinus was like that between Alcibiades and Socrates. Again the Socratic phantom has given shadowed form to the mystery of Plotinus, this time as a

86. *Symposium* 222a. 87. Ibid., 218a–b. 88. Ibid., 215b and 217a.

89. *Vita Plotini* 7 and 23. For instances of Plotinus' care for Porphyry, see 7: editing of treatises; 13 and 18: solving intellectual difficulties; 11: preventing suicide.

figure for Plotinus the teacher. And the Silenic figure within which golden images shimmer lives on also, for Porphyry had "seen the little images" inside Plotinus, and has in his biography let one of those images come forth as the Socratic face of Plotinus.

As we saw earlier, Porphyry believed that each daemon can appear in "ever changing shapes in response to their momentary imaginings." Thus the various Socratic shadings of Plotinus that we have just seen might suggest that what one scholar has called "the sense of the multiplicity of the self"[90] can be evoked by a single image, an interior familiar with several faces. In Porphyry's biography, however, there is another important familiar, who figures the hearth of Plotinus in equally powerful fashion. It is Odysseus, whose wanderings through the biography we will follow shortly, tracing first his appearance in Plotinus' own thinking.

Reflecting on his conviction that the primal nature, when it shines into beings, does not get "stuck" in their matter, Plotinus says that the true nature of Being is "to work [*poiein*] on beings."[91] The primal nature is the "poetry" of our being, and it is our task to discern the working of that nature in us. The path to this discerning is described by Plotinus often as a turning (*epistrophē*),[92] a looking within that is a return to our true selves: "To real Being we go back, all that we have and are; to that we return as from that we came."[93] The turning is a journey within, a homecoming that, recognizing as it does the *poiesis* of Being, Plotinus can only describe poetically.[94]

90. Brown, *The Making of Late Antiquity*, p. 68.

91. *Enn.* 3.6.14.

92. See, for example, *Enn.* 3.7.12; 4.7.10; 4.8.4; 5.1.1.; 5.5.11.

93. *Enn.* 6.5.7. On the return to the true self, see 1.6.9: when you see ultimate beauty, then you are "wholly yourself, nothing but true light," which in 5.8.11 Plotinus calls "perfect self-identity." See also *Enn.* 5.8.10: "All that one sees as a spectacle is still external; one must bring the vision within and see no longer in that mode of separation but as we know ourselves; thus a man filled with a god . . . need no longer look outside for his vision of the divine being; it is but finding the strength to see divinity within."

94. Consider the poetic ecstasy of the following passage, which describes the vision of those who have "turned." *Enn.* 5.8.10: "This vision Zeus takes, and it is for such of us also, as share his love and appropriate our part in the Beauty there, the final object of all seeing, the entire beauty upon all things; for all there sheds radiance, and floods those that have found their way thither so that they too become beautiful; thus it will often happen that men climbing heights where the soil has taken a yellow glow will themselves appear so, borrowing color from the place on which they were. The color flowering on that other height we speak of is Beauty; or rather all there is light and beauty, through and through, for the beauty is no mere

One of the most striking of Plotinus' figures for this journey home is Odysseus at sea. In the work of the Neoplatonists, as well as that of many other thinkers in Late Antiquity,[95] Odysseus had been subjected to another odyssey, envisioned as the journey of the soul to its inner home. Odysseus lived on as an image of the soul longing for divine vision. The context of Plotinus' use of this image is particularly engaging, not only because it shows clearly Odysseus' transformation into a figure for soulful wandering, but also because it lays the ground for Porphyry's use of the image. The text is as follows:

> When [a man] sees the beauty in bodies he must not run after them; we must know that they are images, traces, shadows, and hurry away to that which they image. For if a man runs to the image and wants to seize it as if it was the reality . . . then this man who clings to beautiful bodies and will not let them go, will . . . sink down into the dark depths where intellect has no delight, and stay blind in Hades, consorting with shadows there and here. This would be truer advice: 'Let us fly to our dear country.' What then is our way of escape, and how are we to find it? We shall put out to sea, as Odysseus did, from the witch Circe or Calypso—as the poet says (I think with a hidden meaning)—and was not content to stay though he had delights of the eyes and lived among much beauty of sense. Our country from which we came is there, our Father is there. How shall we travel to it, where is our way of escape? We cannot get there on foot . . . You must not get ready a carriage, either, or a boat. Let all these things go, and do not look. Shut your eyes, and change to and wake another way of seeing, which everyone has but few use.[96]

Plotinus has called forth Odysseus the wanderer, the one who "turned in many ways" (*polūtropos*),[97] as an image for *epistrophē*, the turn within which is the turn toward home, here described as the "country" that is our "Father."[98] There is a very close connection between the "way of escape" (the "putting out to sea") and the "dear country," a connection that can be

bloom upon the surface. . . ." Those who truly see are here described as "drunken with this wine, filled with the nectar."

95. For references to the appearance of Odysseus in many other writers of the period, see Hugo Rahner, *Greek Myths and Christian Mystery*, trans. Brian Battershaw (New York: Harper and Row, 1963), Chapter VII: "Odysseus at the Mast." See also F. Buffière, *Les mythes d'Homère et la pensée grecque* (Paris, 1956).

96. *Enn*. 1.6.8.

97. So Odysseus is described in the first line of his epic.

98. Note that this passage in Plotinus is a play on Book Five of the *Odyssey*, where Odysseus, tossed by the sea, thinks of land as life and as father.

explained by the "much-turned" character of Odysseus. As Plotinus points out in this passage, the error of the man who sees the beauty in an image is not that he sees the image, but that he clings to it, deluding himself with the thought that the image has captured beauty itself. What must be done, rather, is to "let all these things go," *as things*, or, as he says elsewhere, to cease being "intent upon the fragment."[99] Then we wake another way of seeing, a return through a multiplicity of "images, traces, shadows" to that which they reflect. And all of this happens within. We cannot get there on foot or in an actual boat, Plotinus says. As one scholar has remarked, the Neoplatonic "turn" is an "introversion" and "the 'self' which is thus known is not an isolated individual, but contains *in potentia* the whole range of reality."[100]

Now transformed into one who was not captured by images of the primal nature, but rather put out in its sea on an imaginal journey, Odysseus serves as an image of the soul's wakeful wandering within, a wandering through which the return home is accomplished. In his *On the Cave of the Nymphs*, Porphyry turns to the same image.[101] Porphyry's rendition of it, however, is less eirenic than Plotinus', since he sees the sea as the rough water of life within which the soul's *pathos*, its passionate attractions, can become "treacheries" (*epiboula*). Where Plotinus saw a kind of blind sinking into Hades, Porphyry sees an active plotting on the part of the soul, a willing embrace of sensuous form.

However, though he seems to have a more pessimistic sense of the difficulty of the sea journey, Porphyry uses the Odysseus image to the same end as Plotinus had: the journey is an exploration of the true self; the entire sea of images must be traversed; and one must learn to see through life's images to what they image so thoroughly that, as Porphyry remarks, one "puts together an oar with a fan" (that is, mistakes one for the other), so deep is the concentration on what is imaged rather than on the image itself—truly a Plotinian "letting go"! Finally, again as with Plotinus, the journey takes one home. What Plotinus called "Father" and "dear country," Porphyry calls "the domestic seat" (*kathedra oikeia*). Odysseus comes home to his familial "sitting," the "posture" of his hearth.[102]

In the biography, the Odysseus who found his hearth comes forth as one of the familiars of Plotinus' hearth. Again it is Odysseus as sea-wanderer

99. *Enn.* 4.8.6. 100. Dodds, *Proclus*, p. 203. 101. *De antro nympharum* 34–35.
102. Liddell, Scott, and Jones, *A Greek-English Lexicon*, give the following possible meanings for "*kathedra*": seat, chair, sitting part, posterior, base, sitting, posture, session, throne.

who appears. Odysseus, originally summoned by Apollo's oracle on Plotinus' behalf, is summoned again by Porphyry's inclusion of the oracle in his biography. The pertinent passages of the oracle are as follows:

> 'Spirit, man once, but now nearing the diviner lot of a spirit, as the bond of human necessity has been loosed for you, and strong in heart, you swam swiftly from the crowd of the wicked, there to set your steps firm in the easy path of the pure soul, where the splendor of God shines round you and the divine law abides in purity far from lawless wickedness.
>
> 'Then too, when you were struggling to escape from the bitter wave of this blood-drinking life, from its sickening whirlpools, in the midst of its billows and sudden surges, often the Blessed Ones showed you the goal ever near. Often when your mind was thrusting out by its own impulse along crooked paths the Immortals raised you by a straight path to the heavenly circuits, the divine way, sending down a solid shaft of light so that your eyes could see out of the mournful darkness. Sweet sleep never held your eyes, but scattering the heavy cloud that would have kept them closed, borne in the whirl you saw many fair sights which are hard for human seekers after wisdom to see.'[103]

This oracular evocation of Plotinus' soulful nature is an allegorical play on the *Odyssey* 5.307–493.[104] Odysseus has just left Calypso, and Poseidon has sent great waves to crush his ship. Left with only a "poor planking" to hold to, Odysseus is heaved to and fro in the tempestuous sea, finally loses even the raft, and is forced to swim and drift "in the solid deep-sea swell" for three days. Four times during this ocean odyssey he is aided and instructed by divine figures, with whose help, along with his own "self-possession," he at last reaches "the soil of earth," and kisses it.

The oracle's description of the odyssey of Plotinus' soul is much the same. Like Odysseus, Plotinus is pictured "in the midst of billows and sudden surges"; his Odyssean life was a journey through "sickening whirlpools" and "bitter waves." Also, the gods often intervened, making his "crooked paths" into "heavenly circuits," the tumultuous sea into a divine "whirl," reminiscent of Plotinus' own thoughts about the circling whirl of the wise soul around its source. Finally, both swim free—Odysseus to land, Plotinus to wisdom, the "fair sights" that are truly home.

While this is the most ecstatic appearance of Plotinus' Odyssean wan-

103. *Vita Plotini* 22.

104. For the *Odyssey* passage, I have used *The Odyssey*, trans. by Robert Fitzgerald (Garden City, New York: Doubleday and Co., Inc., 1963).

derer, there are yet other ways in which the "turning" of Odysseus moves Porphyry's account of Plotinus. One is Plotinus' death scene, which comes at the beginning of the biography.[105] It seems odd that Porphyry has chosen to begin the story of his teacher's life with the story of his death, until one notices that here it is not Porphyry the historian, but Porphyry the hierophant who is speaking. For the death-bed scene has become, in Porphyry's telling, the setting for a remarkable statement by Plotinus on how to live: "Try to bring back the god in you to the divine in the All!" In his death, Plotinus was truly alive, still engaged in the inward turning toward the sacred home. There is a similar shock to our normal expectations in the oracle with which Porphyry has chosen to close the biography: in the context of a story about Plotinus' birth into the "company of heaven," what is emphasized is a certain kind of death, the death of Plotinus to a false way of looking that drowns the spectator in life's crooked paths. Just as Plotinus' death at the beginning of the biography shows how to live, so his birth at the biography's end shows how to die. The life-in-death, death-in-life paradox serves as an Odyssean frame for the biography's own journey through Plotinus' story. Porphyry the narrative poet has "turned" his history to suit the Odyssean character of his hero.

At another point in the biography, Porphyry notes as an example of Plotinus' philosophical asceticism, standard fare for any holy man,[106] that "even sleep he reduced by taking very little food, often not even a piece of bread, and by his continuous turning [*diarkēs epistrophē*] in contemplation to his intellect."[107] The locus of Plotinus' discipline, his *askēsis*, is placed by Porphyry in his turning, his contemplative wandering within. Interestingly, it is not only Plotinus who is ghosted by this Odyssean metaphor of turning, but Porphyry and his biography as well.

In chapter twenty of the biography, Porphyry includes a long quotation from a book by his old teacher Longinus, which evaluates Plotinus and other philosophers of his era. In the course of his critical assessment, Longinus makes an implicit comparison between the two outstanding students of Plotinus', Amelius and Porphyry himself, and it is this comparison which Porphyry picks up and explains in his comments on Longinus' remarks. That passage reads as follows:

He (Longinus) said of Amelius that 'he walked in Plotinus' footsteps [*kat' ichnē*], but was diffuse in exposition and in his roundabout method of interpretation [*tē tēs*

105. *Vita Plotini* 2. 106. See above, chapter 2, pp. 25–30. 107. *Vita Plotini* 8.

hermēneias peribolē] was led by an inclination opposed to that of Plotinus'; and at the same time, in referring to me, Porphyry . . . he says, 'my friend and theirs, Basileus of Tyre, who has himself written a good deal in the manner of Plotinus.' He put it in this way because he really recognized that I altogether avoided the unphilosophical circuitousness [*tēs peribolēs to aphilosophon*] of Amelius and looked to the style [*pros zēlon*] of Plotinus as my standard in writing.[108]

What is intriguing here is the connection between Plotinus' footsteps, his "tracks," and the roundabout method of interpretation. Porphyry does *not* seem to be implying that Plotinus' method of interpreting was not roundabout; he has already quoted sympathetically from a letter in which Amelius says that Plotinus "treats the same subjects in different ways in different places."[109] He wants, rather, to distinguish his own roundabout Plotinian style from the *unphilosophical* (hence un-Plotinian) wandering of Amelius' style.

This distinction between two different kinds of *peribolē*—a word that refers to various kinds of "turning"[110]—does not appear in Longinus' remarks. It is Porphyry's own construction on the reality of the comparison between Amelius and himself. What is he saying? I would suggest that in this passage Porphyry has become part of the Odysseus complex himself. The footprints of Plotinus show themselves in the roundabout nature of his own literary style. Consider, for example, the journeys through Plotinus' works that open and close the biography. In chapters 4 through 6, we are given a chronological listing of Plotinus' treatises, while in chapters 24 through 26 a systematic grouping of the treatises is given. First there is the procession of the works through time, then there is their constellation by likeness. This is another Odyssean frame: two journeys, and two ways of wandering, through contemplative images that express Plotinus' literary voyage in the sea. So the biography is itself a literary voyage, and its anecdotal footprints trace a turning path through the life whose soulfulness it attempts to express.

Thus, as with Plotinus himself, so with Porphyry's biography. In its turning is its home. As the discussion in an earlier chapter on the "extended

108. *Vita Plotini* 21. Note that in literary criticism, *zēlos* is used to mean "style," especially in the sense of the spirit, taste, or interest of a thing. See Liddell, Scott, Jones, *A Greek-English Lexicon*, s.v. *zēlos*.

109. *Vita Plotini* 17.

110. Liddell, Scott, and Jones, *A Greek-English Lexicon*, s.v. *peribolē*.

akmē" of holy man biographies showed,[111] there is in these works no true beginning or end but only the "latent mysteries and intermittent radiances"[112] of their extended middle. Every turn in the biography's journey—another anecdote, another letter, another speech, and so on—discloses what Plotinus called "real beings," real presences that make familiar the mysterious hearth of the biography's own hearth, the holy man to whom its journey is devoted.

There is a final Odyssean footprint in Porphyry's *Life of Plotinus* that has directly to do with the hearth. We have already seen that the main vehicle for Plotinus' Odyssean self, the Pythian oracle, is an allegory on the final scene in the *Odyssey*, Book Five. There, reaching land is understood in terms of Odysseus' struggles in the sea, just as, in the oracle, the "dance of immortal love," "kinship with most blessed daemons," "being crowned with mighty life"—all homecoming metaphors—are seen in context with Plotinus' "many contests."[113] It is as though the struggling journey of life is inextricably linked with the hearth, and it is only the man who truly wanders whose home can be described as a hearth.

The identity between the wandering man and the hearth is given striking expression at the close of the Odyssey passage upon which the oracle plays. The Homeric poet shows Odysseus, now out of the angry waters, groping his way up a slope to a grove. Here Odysseus rakes together a bed of leaves, and, with laughing heart, buries himself completely in this leaf-bed. The text continues:

> A man in a distant field, no hearth fires near, will hide a fresh brand in his bed of embers to keep a spark alive for the next day; so in the leaves Odysseus hid himself while over him Athena showered sleep that his distress should end, and soon, soon. In quiet sleep she sealed his cherished eyes.[114]

Odysseus is his own hearth! He has within himself the spark alive for the next day's wandering, the brand which gives life to the bed of embers.

Like Odysseus, Plotinus is also figured by the hearth image. The context in Porphyry's biography is a letter from Amelius, which sets forth one

111. See chapter 3, pp. 56–57.

112. I owe this phrase to Kermode, *The Genesis of Secrecy* (Cambridge: Harvard University Press, 1979), p. 122.

113. *Vita Plotini* 22.

114. Fitzgerald, trans., *The Odyssey*, p. 95.

aspect of both Amelius' and Porphyry's work on Plotinus' behalf: to explain how the journey through Plotinus' thought must be undertaken, especially to those who misconceive its character. In the course of his letter, Amelius says that finding the right path through Plotinus' thought is not always easy, because "he treats the same subjects in different ways in different places." Plotinus, as we have seen, followed the winding way. Yet, in practically the same breath, Amelius characterizes this wanderer, his teacher, with a phrase which, from an Odyssean perspective, we might have expected: he calls Plotinus *tēs oikeias hestias*, "our familiar hearth," "our domestic Hestia."[115]

Porphyry has used the word *hestia* twice to characterize Plotinus: once when Plotinus is host to his friends on Socrates' birthday, and now again when he speaks through his quotation of Amelius' direct naming of Plotinus by this term. In the midst of his biographical calling forth of "daemonic others" who figure the essential mystery of the man, Porphyry has also given the mystery a divine name. Appropriately, this mystery, the hearth, is presided over by a goddess, not by daemonic images (for it is their function to show the traces of the mysterious hearth in an individual life). It is Hestia who figures the matrix of Plotinus' being and provides the foundation for the biography's wandering daemonic evocations of the man's soulfulness.

When a Greek thinker said *hestia*, "hearth," he petitioned at the same time Hestia, the goddess.[116] Who was she? One of Socrates' playful etymologies in the *Cratylus* gives serious voice to the significance of this goddess:

> That which we term *ousia* is by some called *essia*, and by others again *ōsia*. Now that the essence of things should be called *hestia*, which is akin to the first of these (*essia* = *hestia*), is rational enough. And there is reason in the Athenians' calling that *hestia* which participates in *ousia*. For in ancient times we too seem to have said *essia* for *ousia*, and this you may note to have been the idea of those who appointed that sacrifices should be first offered to *hestia*, which was natural enough if they meant that *hestia* was the essence of things.[117]

In this passage, it is clear that for Plato, Hestia names the essence of things, and that which we consecrate first with our sacrifices is life's *ousia*, the

115. *Vita Plotini* 17.

116. Liddell, Scott, and Jones, *A Greek-English Lexicon*, s.v. *hestia*.

117. Plato *Cratylus* 401c–d.

"primary real" that underlies that which is our own.[118] Further, not only is Hestia our underlying reality, she is a dwelling place. Plato remarks elsewhere that "Hestia abides alone in the gods' dwelling place," while the rest, the "host of gods and daemons," proceed outward, "ordering all things and caring therefore."[119] As one interpreter has said, Hestia is "the center that sustains the place of return."[120] She is the archetypal home of the gods themselves. Thus when a human being is called by her name, she figures a realm of inner space, the divine hearth within, that both embraces and unleashes a procession of divinities, the "daemonic others" that give familial expression to the deep self.

The Platonic Hestia lived on in Plotinus' thoughts about the heart of our reality. In *Ennead* 5.5, Plotinus is trying to explain what "the One" is, and how we (and everything else that exists) are related to it. It is, he suggests, a difficult task, and he finds himself "in agony for a true expression," since he is "talking of the untellable."[121] Yet, in spite of the agony, we must make the attempt to name ultimate realities anyway, "for our own use." It is in this context that he discusses *hestia*. He begins by saying that "the trace [*ichnos*] of the One gives birth to reality [*ousia*]: existence [*einai*] is a trace of the One." He then goes on to point out, as Socrates had, that there are relationships among such words that are not merely etymological. Rather, the etymologies suggest the power of language to take us into the reality it attempts to express:

> What we call primary being advanced a little outward from the One, so to speak, then chose to go no further, turned inward again and comes to rest and is now the reality and hearth [*ousia* and *hestia*] of all things. Pressing (with the rough breathing) on the word for being [*on*] we have the word "one" [*hen*], an indication that in our very form of speech we tell, as far as may be, that being is that which proceeds from the One. Thus both the thing that comes to be and being itself are images, since they flowed out from the power of the One; and language, under the influence of this sight, tries to represent what it sees and breaks into sound: existence [*on*, *einai*], essence [*ousia*], hearth [*hestia*]. These words try to express the

118. Liddell, Scott, and Jones, *A Greek-English Lexicon*, s.v. *ousia*.

119. Plato *Phaedrus* 247a.

120. Stephanie Demetrakopoulos, "Hestia, Goddess of the Hearth," *Spring 1979*, p. 61. Demetrakopoulos remarks on p. 74, n. 37, that "Hestia becomes the 'spatial archetype' of home for the Gods themselves."

121. *Enn.* 5.5.6.

essential nature of what the One produces, and they try to represent, as far as they can, the origin of reality.[122]

What our agonized telling tells us, according to Plotinus' meditation, is that our hearth, the inner reality of ourselves (and our language), images in us the primal nature that underlies everything. Further, the reality that comes to life within that hearth traces the flow of Being in living things. Our Hestia-nature might be described as both hidden (resting in its inwardness) and revealed (the outflowing of traces that "break into sound"). Like the paradox of poetic placing by soul in soul, Hestia at rest is moved by what breaks forth from her silence.

In his paradoxical statement about the hearth, Plotinus has given deeper resonance to Socrates' musings about Hestia and the essence of things. The philosophical depths of this paradox can also be found in images from Hestia's mythology. As we have seen, for Plato, Hestia is the dwelling from which the divine host proceeds and to which it returns, and for Plotinus too the hearth is established as a presence in connection with outward and inward turning. So also in the mythic accounts: Hestia is Rhea's firstborn, and the first to be swallowed by Cronos; she is the one to whom "Cronos in his craftiness first gave birth (and also last—thanks to Zeus)."[123] Yet in the face of, or because of, these comings and goings, her place is described as "in the center," and the symbol most frequently associated with her is the circle, a roundness in which beginning and end are common, as Heraclitus said.[124] Further, the round hearth is in the center of a house, and its presence confers Hestia's blessing on that dwelling. It is as though a building is "only a building until it receives its Hestian soul,"[125] and as though the comings and goings in that dwelling have no inward reality without her divine presence.

Hestia is not, however, merely a symbolic presence, although part of her mystery, and her meaning, lies in her hiddenness and in her virginal secrecy.[126] She is a circle, but there is a fire in that center. Her virginal emptiness is full of the warmth that turns raw nature into a human feast.[127] Again

122. *Enn.* 5.5.5.
123. *Homeric Hymns*, "Hymn to Aphrodite (I)," discussed by Demetrakopoulos, "Hestia," p. 56.
124. Ibid., pp. 56, 71. 125. Ibid., p. 58. 126. Ibid., pp. 60–68.
127. Ibid., p. 58.

Heraclitus comes to mind: when visitors found him warming himself by the hearth fire, he is reported to have said, "Here too are gods."[128] In this respect Hestia is a figure for "the silent pondering of the soul, that sits and prods the fire." She gives expression to the "central and ever-abiding origins of the self" out of which we proceed, and to which we return.[129] It is her fire that gives our comings and goings their divine shadows.

In Porphyry's biography, Plotinus is called *hestia*. We have taken time to "prod the fire" of philosophical and mythological thinking about Hestia and the hearth in order to suggest the significance of that designation. For what might be taken as a "mere" image or metaphor in fact carries within itself a whole world of associations whose wandering path leads to deeper insight about what is so imaged. By naming Plotinus *hestia*, Porphyry has named the underlying reality, the divine fire, of the man. As we remarked at the beginning of this chapter, that underlying reality is an obscure cry that resists direct telling, and its evocation involves one in enigma and mystery. We could say, paraphrasing Heraclitus, that the sacred hearth, like the Lord at Delphi, neither speaks nor conceals, but gives signs.[130] Thus when Porphyry calls Plotinus *hestia*, what we sense is the mystery of his inwardness, the silent soul prodding its fire, forever turning toward the "divine in the All." For Hestia's only frame of reference is herself; she is the dwelling that turns on its own center. Yet she is also the home of "interior familiars," that daemonic host through whom the hearth comes to expression in life.

The daemonic figures that come forth as Plotinus' interior familiars, Socrates and Odysseus, are thus ways of looking, faces that give face to a vision that is, finally, baffling. It is these shadowy phantoms, whose comings and goings trace the round path of the hearth, that turn the "raw nature" of Plotinus' mystery into a "human feast." But it is not a mundane feast. The Hestian perspective is a release from that false way of looking that drowns the one looking in a sea of opaque images. For the biographer, it is a release from the history that chronicles into the history that "sounds soul to the depths."[131] Hence the particularities of a life become images, thresholds upon which meaning turns, human gestures that bear the imprint of a life's

128. Philip Wheelwright, ed., *The Presocratics* (Indianapolis: Bobbs-Merrill, 1960), p. 75, fr. 74 (from Aristotle *De part. animalium* I.5 : 645a, 17).

129. Demetrakopoulos, "Hestia," pp. 59–60.

130. Heraclitus fr. 14, Marcovich (93 Diels-Kranz): "The Lord at Delphi neither conceals nor reveals, but gives signs."

131. Plotinus *Enn.* 6.9.5.

soulfulness. Odysseus and Socrates, then, give shadowed form to those gestures in Plotinus' life that most truly reflected the glow of his hearth. In the poetic working of the biography, these "daemonic others" are the signs that carry the concealed hearth in the life's speaking.

Myth and History

The discovery of "Hestia" in Porphyry's text became the occasion for considering not only the depth of Plotinus' character but also the biographical enterprise itself. The word became a figure for, and took us into, the depths of the text within which it appears. This dynamic has been described by one interpreter in the following way: "The metaphors we believe we choose for describing archetypal processes and ideas . . . are inherently part of those very processes and ideas themselves. It is as if the archetypal material chooses its own descriptive terms as one aspect of its self-expression. This would mean that 'naming' is not a nominalistic activity, but realistic indeed, because the name takes us into its reality."[132] This perspective suggests that the metaphoric power of Hestia, which we thought we chose, has in some sense chosen us and has taken us into the very reality of which it is a part.

What is that reality? That is, how are we to understand the procession and return of the biography's Plotinian phantoms if the reality of the biography is Hestia's silent hearth? Plotinus' name for this kind of understanding is myth. In his treatise "On Love," he asserts that "myths, if they are really going to be myths, must separate in time the things of which they tell, and set apart from each other many realities which are together. . . . The myths, when they have taught us as well as they can, allow the man who has understood them to put together again that which they have separated."[133] Thus myth works initially by focusing on—even isolating—particular images, distinct faces of the reality it wishes to express. Yet finally what it wants to show is the oneness—"the One"—of that reality.

For Plotinus, myth seems to work by a simultaneous placing together of fullness and unity. As Pépin remarks, myth respects the mystery by evoking

132. James Hillman, *The Dream and the Underworld* (New York: Harper and Row, 1979), p. 25.
133. *Enn.* 3.5.9.

its riches.[134] Myth flowers in the heart of obscurity and, as Plutarch said, protects those who would know that heart from the heart's fatal darkness, its "naked truth," by speaking with an equivocal voice. The mythic vision, then, is tropical; it gives rise to constellations of tropes, the imaginal ways of seeing whose turnings upon the hearth of meaning constitute the embrace of the hearth itself.

In earlier chapters, we have spoken about the "creative license" of the biographer, and the "air of truth" that such an imaginative approach presents.[135] Biography has been viewed throughout as a mythologizing of a man's life that works by drawing poetic truth out of historical fact. Presiding over this perspective was Aelius Theon's definition of myth: "*logos pseudēs eikonizōn alētheian.*"[136] Myth is the false word, the dissimulating gesture, that images the truth. In the preceding chapters, moreover, we have imagined the false words of the biographer's mythic voice speaking mainly through the holy man model, and this model named our understanding of the expression of the real through the ideal, which gives the biography's sense of a life's meaning. Now, however, with the tropical phantoms of Hestia ghosting our perspective, we can offer another name for understanding the reality of biography: "daemonic history."

I have suggested in this chapter that Porphyry's biographical method can be understood as an evocation of Plotinus' interior familiars; it is a poetic placing that calls forth the daemonic faces of the man's soulful presence. From this perspective, method is really a style. It is what one author has called "a metaphorical style where consciousness is one of innuendo, reflection, echo, tone, and elusive movements."[137] Porphyry's method—indeed, the method of any ancient biographer—does not, after all, entail telling a story with a plot; there is no narrative movement from beginning to middle to end. Instead, events are recorded to lay bare a structure, and what sounds within the elements of this structure are echoes of the hero's divine nature. When method does not tell a story but exposes a structure of images that underlie a life, it "slows the parade of history."[138] Daemonic history is monumental history, which enhances by its selectivity, by its very refusal to attempt "the whole story."

134. *Mythe et allégorie*, p. 482.

135. See above, pp. 61–62 and 74.

136. See chapter 1, n. 15.

137. James Hillman, "The Fiction of Case History," in James B. Wiggins, ed., *Religion as Story* (New York: Harper and Row, 1975), p. 145.

138. Hillman, "The Fiction of Case History," p. 150.

Recently myth has been defined as the "boundary line where fantasy and reality meet," a "mixture of the magical and the banal." Further, "the actual starting point" of this mixing is "arbitrary," for "the point of enlightenment is the transition, the motion across the threshold in either direction."[139] These remarks capture succinctly the biographical dynamic sketched in this chapter. Porphyry's daemonic history is poised on a boundary, the boundary between the facts of Plotinus' life, his history, and the model of holiness which Porphyry used, his fantasy. Across that boundary, back and forth, Porphyry traced Plotinus' footprints, the tracks of his sacred inner mystery in life. The boundary is the biography's hearth, and seeing the daemonic others that dwell there plunged us into a turning path, a tracing of the movements of Plotinus' interior familiars in the biography. As in Socrates' labyrinth, we ended up where we began (where we already were). Traveling the full circle of the biography, we can find no "actual starting point," either for Porphyry's writing or our own, but the turning has given deeper perspective, more nuanced vision. Hestia now presides, along with Merlin, over the "question as to what the question is that we are asking when we ask what is meaningful," and daemonic history as a style of consciousness suggests an answer to "the question as to how (and in what way) things mean."

139. Wendy Doniger O'Flaherty, "Inside and Outside the Mouth of God: The Boundary between Myth and Reality," *Daedalus* 109 (Spring, 1980), pp. 95, 99, 96.

CHAPTER SIX

Conclusion: The Creative Use of History

The biographies of holy men of Late Antiquity were literary celebrations of the virtues of certain eminent individuals, and they accomplished their goals by seeing their heroes through ideal traits, images that tended to cluster around two basic models of holiness. Biographers saw their heroes, not "through a glass *darkly*," but through prisms of divine sonship or godlikeness. In Chapter 4, a detailed study of one of these biographies showed that the prism of the character model worked to distort the historical situation of the hero so that the ideal facets of his life might be emphasized. In Chapter 5, we took the refracted historical situation for granted, and looked instead at how the riddle of a man's life comes to expression in a biography's images. Both of the biographers considered in these two chapters looked *through* a glass *into* darkness. For both authors, it was an imaginative looking whose light figured the darkness.

We have described what they saw through this glassy divine-man prism as "faces" (Eusebius' Janus-faced Origen) and as "phantoms" (Porphyry's daemonic Plotinus), which are literary elements in a biographical structure presented as a faithful journey through a life's meaning. Biographers present their works as true stories, and Plotinus' dictum about the metaphoric reality of language—"everywhere we must read 'so to speak'"—does not break into either Porphyry's or Eusebius' biographical speech. Their biographies presume to be faithful tellings. Yet, as we have tried to show in a variety of ways, these "faithful" tellings are reflected, refracted, shadowed, and ghosted, and we must now ask, in a pointed way, what the impulses for this prismatic biographical looking might be.

Underlying the present study is the conviction that these biographies were not exercises in literary dexterity; the biographers were not manipulating their prisms—the cluster of ideals that defined their models—simply to rewrite history. For if the prisms worked to distort the actual lives of the biographers' subjects, they also worked to reflect the motivations and historical concerns of the biographers themselves. Biographies were personal statements, statements which, though couched in religious and philosophical terms, addressed sociopolitical and cultural concerns as well.

The view that biographies reflected the personal convictions of the biographers brings up the issue of intent. If these works functioned not only to recall the significance of the life of a hero of the past but also to make sense of contemporary life, we must attempt to describe the historical context of the authors in order to discover situations that may have prompted their literary activity. This will be, of course, a speculative journey, yet as the history of biography writing in Chapter 1 showed, biography was from its inception a genre that found its home in controversy. Biographers like Aristoxenus were self-conscious mediators of specific traditions, and their works had both apologetic and polemical aims, apologetic in defending, affirming, and sometimes correcting opinion about a hero; polemical in suggesting by the strength of the defense, and sometimes by outright attack, the unworthiness of other traditions by comparison. The social sphere of early biographies was one in which the biographers sought to promote specific philosophical traditions by elaborate confirmations of past representatives of those traditions. It was a battle of school against school. The writers of biographies of holy men were also engaged in a battle, yet theirs involved not only philosophical conviction but religious belief as well. We could say that their heroes had become emblems in a holy war.

But it is not only the cultural, cultic context of these biographies that will interest us in this chapter. Earlier we remarked that the divine man who was "a mere toy in the hands of the Fates" was not for Eusebius a very impressive figure.[1] What, then, of the divine man who is a toy in the hands of his biographer? By discussing biographies as vehicles for the social and political concerns of the biographers, we might ourselves be guilty of suggesting that Plotinus and Origen were mere toys in the hands of their biographers. In order to avoid the idea that an author's impulse to write is a conscious manipulation of his material merely for objective, sociopolitical ends, we will look at an author's intent not only as a way of imagining his

1. See chapter 4, p. 80.

work's context, but also as a reflection of the author's deep sense of himself. With this perspective, we need not think of biographers as manipulative puppeteers. For puppets are lifeless and opaque things, whereas Plotinus and Origen were translucent presences who lived, not in the misty past, but in the creative moment of their biographers' imaginations. In that creative moment, it is not only the depths of cultural situations that are sounded, but also the soulful depths of the author.

In what follows, we will consider first how the biographers' idea of the holy man can be seen as ways of understanding and organizing the cultural situations in which they were embroiled. Our particular interest will be to show how Eusebius and Porphyry have used images of other lives to express their own immediate concerns. Further, we suggest that not only does the biographer look *through* a prism, but in a way he might himself *be* the prism through which he is looking. Prisms do not create light, they reflect it; and by their reflecting, images are produced. And if the reflected images sometimes look like shadowed distortions, we have learned from the mirror of Dionysus that the altered image is often the true one. In other words, as he creates, the author is himself created; his reflections are shadings of his own soul.

The Holy War

In an article devoted to exposing the "strictly apologetic historiography" practiced by Eusebius in his *Ecclesiastical History*, Robert Grant remarked that Eusebius was "far too ready to find the judgments of God clearly imposed within the historical process to vindicate saints and crush sinners." [2] This observation has particular significance for Book 6, the "Life of Origen," since there the battle lines between saints and sinners are clearly drawn, and two apologetic concerns, both with polemical overtones, can be identified. One of the apologetic themes is directed inward to the Christian community; the other is addressed to the pagan community.

The "Life of Origen," as Eusebius himself intimated,[3] was based on an *Apology for Origen* that he wrote in conjunction with his friend, the Caesa-

2. Robert Grant, "The Case against Eusebius, or, Did the Father of Church History write History?," *Studia patristica* 12 (1975): 418, 413.
3. See *HE* 6.23.4, 6.33.4, 6.36.4.

rean presbyter Pamphilus, sometime between 308 and 310, the period of the latter's confinement in prison during the Great Persecution.[4] The *Apology* was dedicated to Christian confessors who as a result of the persecution had been condemned to the copper mines in Phaeno in southern Palestine.[5] This dedication, plus the *Apology*'s setting during the persecution, provide clues to the meaning of the biography's apology directed to Christian insiders. For in the *Ecclesiastical History* Eusebius remarked at one point that he and Pamphilus had composed their *Apology* "because of the fault-finders."[6] That the "fault-finders" were Christians is clear both from the context of Eusebius' remark in the biography, where he is emphasizing Origen's position as a standard-bearer of orthodoxy, and from the dedication of the *Apology* to the Christians in Phaeno, a group of rigorist confessors from Egypt who had been relegated to the mines for their refusal to sacrifice. These martyrs had organized themselves into a "Church of the Martyrs"[7] and were critical of philosophical theologians and of people who were not martyrs.[8] The memory of Origen was subjected to bitter attacks, perhaps because of the tradition, reported by Epiphanius, that Origen had sacrificed during one of the persecutions of his own day,[9] but certainly because of his infamous excommunication and the speculative nature of his theology.

The *Apology*, which consisted of a life of Origen followed by a detailed defense of his theology,[10] was, as an answer to the rigorists' attacks on Origen, motivated by self-preservation, since Pamphilus and Eusebius were both adherents of an Origenist theology and had attended the school that Origen founded in Caesarea. In an interesting and, I think, quite plausible reconstruction of the situation that prompted the writing of the *Apology*, Nautin has suggested that the opposition of the martyrs in Phaeno was in fact inspired by one or more of Pamphilus' episcopal enemies in Caesarea, who detested his theological stance and feared the veneration that might develop for him as a result of his martyr's life in prison. By exposing his unorthodox theological views, especially since they stemmed from a man who had incurred the wrath of the ecclesiastical establishment, Pamphilus'

4. Photius *Bibl.* 118: the *Apologia* written while Pamphilus was in prison; Eusebius *Martyrs of Palestine* 7.4–6, 11: on Pamphilus' imprisonment.

5. See Nautin, *Origène*, p. 135.

6. Eusebius *HE* 6.33.4.

7. Epiphanius *Panarion* 68.3.6.

8. See Grant, "Early Alexandrian Christianity," pp. 133–34.

9. Epiphanius *Panarion* 64.2.1–6.

10. Nautin, *Origène*, p. 107.

enemies could thereby separate him from authentic confessors and thus stem the tide of admiration.[11] A look at the charges against Origen in the *Apology*,[12] which were presumably directed against his intellectual heir Pamphilus as well, shows that the instigators of the opposition at Phaeno knew well what kind of theological opinion was likely to arouse furor in a situation in which a high premium was being placed on the various forms of Christian martyrdom. The force of the attack fell in large part on the supposed subordinationist tendency in Origen's Christology; the rigorists objected strongly to the idea that the Son was not complete in his Godhood. Coming from a group of martyrs, this objection seems especially revealing, since to diminish the divinity of Christ would be to diminish the quality of the martyr's own *imitatio Christi*.[13] Two other telling features of the attack dealt with Origen's repudiation of the resurrection of the flesh and of eternal punishment, which in the context of the martyr's fervor to witness for the faith could be interpreted as denying the martyr his "crown" and whitewashing the persecutor's evil. In the situation in which the Christians in Phaeno found themselves, the serene world of allegory simply had no place.

Eusebius and Pamphilus' *Apology*, then, consisted mostly of defenses of Origen's orthodoxy and was addressed to a group of Christian dissidents, a powerful group of martyrs which, because of its esteemed status, threatened to create a serious rift within the Church. Based on the *Apology* and also published during the Persecution,[14] the "Life of Origen" takes its place within this context. It can be read not only as a defense of the Origenist tradition but also as an attempt to close the rift, to heal internal wounds in order to present a united front to the pagan enemy. In the biography, the defense does not argue specific theological points, but presents the Origenist tradition as the only tradition representative of, and present in, the Alexandrian-Caesarean area. As we discussed in chapter 4, Eusebius' picture of Origen's school activities used the biographical "pars pro toto" technique to create the guise of unity and continuity; the bishop Demetrius—the voice of opposition with which he was forced to deal—he simply con-

11. Ibid., pp. 133–34.

12. See the Greek texts and translation in Nautin, *Origène*, pp. 108–33.

13. In *HE* 8.10.3, Eusebius quotes a letter of one of the martyrs of the Great Persecution which refers to martyrs as *Christophoroi*. Ironically, Origen himself saw martyrs as imitators of Christ. See his *Exhortation to Martyrdom* 14, 35, and especially 42.

14. For a discussion of the date of the first edition of the *Historia ecclesiastica*, see Jean Sirinelli, *Les vues historiques d'Eusèbe de Césarée durant la période prénicéene* (Dakar: Université de Dakar, 1961), p. 23.

demned as a sinner, a Satanic aberration whose opposition stemmed only from personal spite. Origen and his latter-day supporters then appear as the true saints within the Christian community; and Eusebius' emphasis on Origen's orthodoxy, his lifelong desire for martyrdom, and his proselytizing teaching activities begins to make good apologetic sense. This mode of apology represents the most basic orientation of the biography's appeal to Christian insiders. However, the biography can also be read as an attempt, once the defense was achieved, to create a hero figure around whom all Christians could unite. Here the persecution context is especially important, for as one scholar has remarked, the *Ecclesiastical History* as a whole views the history of Christianity as the history of a spiritual nation engaged in battling demonic forces;[15] it was a history marked by a continual overcoming of odds, as Eusebius' careful recounting of the history of persecution in the *History* makes clear. If the history of the Church in this sense can be viewed as an historical paradigm, then Origen's own life, as Eusebius tells it, represents a personal imitation of the ecclesiastical model. For as we have seen, Origen was constantly overcoming obstacles, or being saved from disaster by providence. In the biography he is a kind of symbol of courageous survival and so could serve Christians in a time of trouble as a sign of hope, a reminder that providence would not abandon the saints.[16]

This context suggests further a second kind of apologetic intent, one aimed at the pagan opposition. In Eusebius' eyes, the pagan opponents of Christianity found their chief philosophical spokesman in Porphyry, the "false one" whose attack on Origen was refuted as "calumny" in the biography.[17] That in a later work Eusebius could refer to Porphyry not by name but simply as "our enemy" suggests the infamy, as well as the danger, of this person's writings.[18] Porphyry's *Against the Christians* was a monumental exposé of the alien nature of the Christian religion. Not only was Christianity neither Greek nor Barbarian, it relied on faith rather than rational demonstration and even managed to pervert its one claim to antiquity, the

15. Arnaldo Momigliano, "Pagan and Christian Historiography in the 4th c. A.D.," in Momigliano, ed., *The Conflict between Paganism and Christianity in the Fourth Century* (Oxford: Clarendon Press, 1963), p. 90.

16. See *Martyrs of Palestine* 13.13–14 for Eusebius' remarks on providential guidance of Christians through the persecution.

17. *HE* 6.19.11.

18. Eusebius *Demonstratio evangelica* 3.6. Eusebius in fact devoted a treatise of twenty-five books to a refutation of Porphyry's *Contra Christianos*, but it is no longer extant. See Sirinelli, *Les vues historiques d'Eusèbe de Césarée durant la période prénicéene*, pp. 27–28.

Jewish Scriptures, by false and inharmonious interpretation. The picture of Jesus presented by the gospels is constantly ridiculed not only because of its inconsistencies but also for absurd statements like Jesus' Eucharistic command, which Porphyry says could never be accepted by anyone with a liberal education.[19] It was to this attitude that Eusebius responded in his "Life of Origen." By defending Origen's Greek philosophical erudition, by showing the value of his allegorical interpretation of Scripture, and by developing an image of Origen the rational schoolman, Eusebius was in fact answering Porphyry's charges against the Church. Although it is not known whether Porphyry himself participated in the "war council" that immediately preceded the outbreak of the Great Persecution,[20] one of those who did participate, Sossianus Hierocles, carried on the Porphyrian assault with a treatise "The Lover of Truth." Eusebius answered this with his *Against Hierocles*, an attack on the heroic picture of the pagan hero Apollonius, favored by Hierocles, which is certainly indicative of Eusebius' recognition of the persuasive power and danger of pagan propaganda.

Finally, Eusebius' biography should also be seen in the light of Porphyry's own biographical activity. The *Life of Plotinus* and the *Life of Pythagoras* were written before Eusebius' work, and Eusebius had definitely read

19. For representative texts from the *Contra Christianos* see Adolph Harnack, *Porphyrius 'Gegen die Christen'* (Abhandlungen der preussischen Akademie der Wissenschaften zu Berlin, Philosophisch-historisches Klasse, 1916), no. 1, fragments 1, 73, 43, and 69. See also Robert L. Wilken, "Pagan Criticism of Christianity: Greek Religion and Christian Faith," in *Early Christian Literature and the Classical Intellectual Tradition*, ed. by William R. Schoedel and Robert L. Wilken (Paris: Éditions Beauchesne, 1979), pp. 117–34, for a suggestive discussion of Porphyry's *Philosophy from Oracles* as an attack on the foolishness of Christian interpreters who elevate Jesus (truly a Hero) above the rank possible for a human being to attain.

20. This council was a meeting of Diocletian's *consilium principis* during the winter of 302/3 in Nicomedia, the result of which was the first edict of persecution against the Christians. See Lactantius *De mortibus persecutorum* 11–12. Porphyry's participation is based on an ambiguous phrase in his *Ad Marcellam* 4, which mentions a journey undertaken at this time on behalf of "the affairs of the Greeks." See Chadwick, *Sentences of Sextus*, pp. 142–43, and Walter Pötscher, "Porphyrios *Pros Markellan*," *Philosophia antiqua* 15 (1969): 66. It has been argued recently that Porphyry's *Against the Christians* was published just before the beginning of the persecution and so might have been an influence on it. See T. D. Barnes, "Porphyry *Against the Christians*: Date and Attribution of the Fragments," *JTS*, N.S., 24 (October, 1973): 424–42. See also Joseph Bidez, *Vie de Porphyre* (Ghent: n.p., 1913; reprint ed. Hildesheim: Georg Olms Verlagsbuchhandlung, 1964), p. 105, n. 5, who felt that Hierocles, then *praeses* of Bithynia, might actually have been one of Porphyry's students.

the latter.[21] Both of those biographies claimed for their heroes the usual qualities one would expect in a Graeco-Roman holy man. In this context it is intriguing that Eusebius' biography presents the Christian theologian Origen in Graeco-Roman dress as a typical ascetic philosopher full of wisdom and virtue, and I would suggest that Origen's Greek dress represents one of Eusebius' apologetic attempts to counteract the propaganda of the pagan intelligentsia.

Eusebius' biography is best understood in its social sense as a response to the time of persecution in which he lived, a persecution that had aroused antagonisms both within and without the Christian circle. Ironically, the prophet of the persecution was himself enmeshed in a threatening situation, for if, in a benevolent mood, Porphyry could simply "pity the folly" of those who had fallen into the error of the Christians,[22] he could also bemoan their loss to his own tradition. What we call the Great Persecution of Christians actually took place within a series of three pagan religious revivals spearheaded by the emperors Diocletian, Galerius, and Maximin Daia, whose reigns spanned the years from 284–313.[23] The need for revival, especially when it went to the extreme of outlawing and then killing those in other religious traditions, points to the fact that the pagan camp was in disarray.[24] The Christian movement had made serious inroads, the old allegiances were failing, and, as much of Diocletian's legislation shows, thoughtful pagans feared the loss of the favor of the immortal ancient gods.[25] It is within Neoplatonism, and especially in the work of two of its chief exponents, Porphyry and Iamblichus, that one can best see how paganism responded to its own plight.

Olympiodorus summed up the movement within Neoplatonism in this

21. See Grant, "Eusebius and his Lives of Origen," p. 8, and Barnes, "Porphyry *Against the Christians*," p. 431.

22. Porphyry *On the Philosophy of Oracles*, quoted by Eusebius *Demonstratio evangelica* 3.7.

23. Robert M. Grant, "The Religion of Maximin Daia," in *Christianity, Judaism, and Other Greco-Roman Cults, Studies for Morton Smith at Sixty*, ed. Jacob Neusner, 4 vols. (Leiden: E. J. Brill, 1975), 4:143.

24. The best treatment of this topic is W. H. C. Frend, *Martyrdom and Persecution in the Early Church* (London: Basil Blackwell, 1965), especially ch. 4: "The Triumph of Christianity 260–303."

25. See Diocletian's "Edicts" on marriage, maximum prices, and Manichaeism, all of which attack dissension from the traditional Roman ethos. For texts of the "Edicts" see Naphtali Lewis and Meyer Reinhold, eds., *Roman Civilization*, 2 vols. (New York: Harper and Row, 1966), vol. 2: *The Empire*, pp. 455–74.

period when he stated that "some put philosophy first, as Porphyry and Plotinus; others the priestly art, as Iamblichus, Syrianus, Proclus, and all the priestly school."[26] The revival within Neoplatonism took the form of a new religious orientation that found redemption less and less in Plotinian *theōria* and more and more in cultic *theourgia*.[27] However strongly Porphyry might protest the Christian emphasis on belief, the fact is that in his own tradition authority had begun to replace reason. Plato the hierophant replaced Plato the rationalist, and his authority was augmented by revelatory knowledge from Pythagorean, Hermetic, and Chaldean materials.[28] Like the very group they opposed, the pagan intelligentsia began to expound upon and collate sacred texts, and "to neutralize Christian miracles" with miracles of their own.[29] As Dodds has remarked, Neoplatonism was transformed from its abstract philosophical character in Plotinus' day into "a religion with its own saints and miracle-workers,"[30] a movement that resulted from "the desire to create a single Hellenic philosophy which should supersede the jarring warfare of the sects" and "to construct within the framework of traditional Greek rationalism a scheme of salvation capable of comparison and rivalry with those offered by the mystery religions."[31]

Porphyry's writings provide a revealing example of this shift within Neoplatonism, for the same man who wrote a scathing critique of theurgy in the *Letter to Anebo* also wrote a commentary on the Chaldean Oracles and in *On the Return of the Soul* even recommended the purificatory, though not the salvific, powers of theurgical practices.[32] His biographies especially illustrate Porphyry's midway position between Neoplatonism as a philosophical

26. Olympidorus *In Phaed.* 123.3, quoted by E. R. Dodds, *Proclus: The Elements of Theology*, 2nd ed. (Oxford: Clarendon Press, 1963), p. xxiii.

27. Dodds, *Proclus: The Elements of Theology*, p. xx.

28. Dodds, *Pagan and Christian in an Age of Anxiety*, p. 122; R. E. Witt, *Albinus and the History of Middle Platonism* (Cambridge: Cambridge University Press, 1937), p. 123.

29. Arnaldo Momigliano, "Popular Religious Beliefs and the Late Roman Historians," *Studies in Church History* 8 (1972): 11.

30. Dodds, *Pagan and Christian in an Age of Anxiety*, p. 109.

31. Dodds, *Proclus: The Elements of Theology*, p. xviii. See also Joseph Bidez, "La liturgie des mystères chez les Néoplatoniciens," *Academie Royale de Belgique, Bulletins de la classe des lettres* (June 1919): 417–18.

32. Dodds, *The Greeks and the Irrational*, p. 287. What Dodds called Porphyry's "incurable weakness for Oracles" seems to have been held in abeyance during his years of tutelage in Plotinus' school. See Robert M. Grant, "Porphyry among the Early Christians," in *Romanitas et Christianitas*, ed. W. Den Boer *et al.* (Amsterdam: Northern Holland Publishing Company, 1973), pp. 181–83.

school and as a religion; for the *Life of Plotinus* is concerned above all to emphasize the rational, philosophical calm of Plotinus' school, whereas the *Life of Pythagoras* is a good example of the turn toward saints and miracles. The *Life of Plotinus* was, of course, written as the preface to Porphyry's edition of the master's works and can thus be seen as an attempt to show the harmony between the hero's life and his thought. But I would suggest, further, that Porphyry's emphasis in this biography on school and disciples shows that he, like Eusebius, was concerned to create a scholastic tradition that might serve as a solid foundation for uniting his peers. For we know that in Porphyry's day the idea of a single school was an illusion; there were factions within Neoplatonism just as there were within Christianity.[33] The creation of a school tradition also entailed, of course, the creation of a revered founder. Plotinus' godlike image in the *Life* might be interpreted as Porphyry's apologetic statement to fellow pagans whose commitment was flagging; it reminded them that disciples are measured by the greatness of their founder.

Porphyry's *Life of Pythagoras* tells quite a different story, for here, as we have seen, Porphyry has created a son of god for the Neoplatonic tradition.[34] This biography is a kind of sacred text that relates uncritically the god's miracles, healing powers, philosophical tenets, and ascetic program for daily living and ends with an account of the strength and friendliness of the Pythagorean community through several generations. If Plotinus was the historical founder, Pythagoras has become for Neoplatonists the spiritual revealer. Porphyry's biographies appear to answer conflicting needs within the paganism of his day. One addressed its philosophical heritage; the other is a witness to Neoplatonism's attempt to respond to Christianity's encroachment by showing that it did not lack what the other tradition claimed.

Porphyry's biographies show him as a middle man, caught between two tendencies within the Neoplatonic community. Such was not the case for his onetime pupil Iamblichus, an exact contemporary of Eusebius who studied first with the Aristotelian philosopher Anatolius, then with Porphyry, and later set up his own school in Apamea.[35] Iamblichus' works show him to have been a decided partisan of *theourgia*, not *theōria*; he took the step that

33. See John Dillon, ed. and trans., *Iamblichi Chalcidensis: In Platonis dialogos commentariorum fragmenta* (Leiden: E. J. Brill, 1973), p. 8–14.
34. See chapter 2, pp. 34–36, 40.
35. Dillon, *Iamblichi Chalcidensis*, pp. 5–12.

Porphyry did not take and combined the scholastic with the cultic, revelatory tendency within Neoplatonism. Even though his philosophical system was "essentially an elaboration of Plotinus' Platonism,"[36] he thought that Plato was a Pythagorean; he composed at least two treatises on the Chaldean Oracles and wrote a four-volume commentary on Pythagorean materials, one volume of which consisted of his *Pythagorean Life*.[37] One of his most important works, *On the Mysteries*, was a detailed refutation of Porphyry's critique of theurgy. Called by one scholar a "manifesto of irrationalism" because it finds the key to salvation "in ritual rather than in reason,"[38] *On the Mysteries* envisions a priestly order of theurgists whose communication with the gods comes not through philosophical contemplation but through ritual acts. The philosophical master has here been transformed into the priest who is the sole interpreter of divine knowledge.[39]

Iamblichus' *Pythagorean Life* was, like Porphyry's *Life of Plotinus*, an introduction to the philosopher's thought. But we know that in his school Iamblichus interpreted Neoplatonic philosophy through Pythagorean eyes.[40] Hence the biography itself is an exposition of Iamblichus' own thought and goes far beyond Porphyry's *Life of Pythagoras* in its detailed and sympathetic portrait of the Pythagorean community and its successors and in its magnification of Pythagoras' status as a son of god. It is interesting that, unlike Porphyry, Iamblichus was not much of a polemicist, though in *On the Mysteries* he does refer to the *atheoi* who revile worship of the gods, probably a reference to Christians.[41] His efforts were devoted to building the cult, and his biography, over half of which discusses the range of virtues promoted by Pythagoras and continued, in his eyes, by Neoplatonists, can best be read as a clarion call to waning paganism that its tradition was worthy of adherence.

As Herbert Musurillo once remarked, "It is frequently difficult to deter-

36. Ibid., p. 28.

37. Ibid., pp. 18–25, for a list of Iamblichus' writings. See also Eduard Des Places, "La Religion de Jamblique," in *Entretiens sur l'antiquité classique* 21: *De Jamblique à Proclus* (Geneva: Fondation Hardt, 1975), p. 70.

38. Dodds, *The Greeks and the Irrational*, p. 287.

39. L. W. Leadbeater, "Aspects of the Philosophical Priesthood in Iamblichus' *De mysteriis*," *Classical Bulletin* 47 (1971): 91. On the official establishment of pagan priesthoods see Grant, "The Religion of Maximin Daia," pp. 157–60.

40. Dillon, *Iamblichi Chalcidensis*, pp. 14–15.

41. R. E. Witt, "Iamblichus as a Forerunner of Julian," in *Entretiens sur l'antiquité classique* 21: *De Jamblique à Proclus* (Geneva: Fondation Hardt, 1975), p. 40.

mine when a piece of literature has been written primarily for propaganda (the literary characters being mere pawns in the presentation of a thesis), and when its aim is primarily entertainment, though with sharp political overtones. There are no rules for solving such problems: one can only judge by the general tone of the work and by the prominence and definiteness of the political or sociological motives involved."[42] As we have seen in this chapter, though precise connections are difficult to make, the historical context of holy man biographies is suggestive of the biographers' propagandistic intentions. We know that biography functioned in a literary sense by mythologizing a man's life, that is, by using fiction to convey truth; and we know that as a literary form biography was suitable to the creation of caricatures, portraits so dominated by the ideals imposed by the biographer that history was distorted, if not actually lost.

The writers of the biographies considered here used the images of the holy philosopher current in their time to create ideal portraits of men significant in their own religious traditions. Through those portraits they attempted to interpret what was to them the most momentous event of their time, an increasing antagonism between pagans and Christians that had caused rifts in both communities. The biographies of Porphyry, and Iamblichus as well, can be read both as apologetic efforts to maintain allegiance to the pagan standard and as polemical manifestos, justifications of pagan supremacy based on the virtues inherent in its tradition and hallowed figureheads. Eusebius' biography too is both apologetic and polemical, attempting at once to close the Christian ranks and to refute pagan calumnies. In these biographies, the holy philosopher was depicted not as a passive figure but as a man with a mission. Whatever his historical mission might have been, in the biographies the mission was to a great extent dictated by the biographer himself.

Author as Prism

When we imagine that it is the prism-wielding biographer who dictates the active mission of his hero, it is actually the biographer whose activity we are emphasizing. It is he who has brought the silent mystery of his hero's life into active biographical expression. But from another perspective, it is the

42. Herbert Musurillo, ed. and trans., *The Acts of the Pagan Martyrs: Acta Alexandrinorum* (Oxford: Clarendon Press, 1954), p. 275.

biographer who is a silent mystery. He may be seen as the still prism brought to life by the active reflecting of ghostly shadows of his hero within himself. Then, a biography's holy man images would be the author's own faces.

In earlier chapters, we have suggested that for the biographers of Late Antiquity, history had become mythic—anything that could be judged likely or probable could be used as historical data. Eusebius declared himself "quite ready" to accept poetic ("highly colored") statements as valid history, and Porphyry too opened the doors of history to imaginative reconstruction.[43] In the biographers' hands, history had become a mythic in-between zone where the "air of truth" holds sway. From this perspective, the biographical text looks like a strange boundary that sustains a creative tension. This tension is the biography's mythic perspective, which arises from the author's willingness to let himself be a silent threshold through which the biographical elements of fact and fantasy, the text's active presences, move.

The movement of these presences involves a complicated interaction, for when the biographer breaks his silence to speak, what comes forth are images that figure those presences in such a way that fact is seen through fantasy and fantasy is seen through fact. Each is seen through the other in a single image. Eusebius, for example, presents two major images of Origen—the ascetic philosopher and the orthodox teacher—and in both we have seen the fantasy of the holy man and the facts of Origen's life interpreting each other. Porphyry's images of Plotinus as Socrates and Odysseus also depend upon the mutual illumination of historical fact and fantasies of holiness for their success as biographical characterizations. A biography's images give visible face to a process of seeing through.

The biographer dwells in this seeing through. Out of his silent dwelling comes his seeing, and this suggests that "threshold" and "prism" are metaphors that express two aspects of the biographical imagination. Thus when we imagine Eusebius as the one through whom the fantastic and factual aspects of Origen's life moved, we can call the author a threshold that sustains this interior coming and going. But when we read the biographical patterns that give expression to these interior encounters, we can call the author a prism whose work has reflected visible, textual images of the silent dynamic within. The threshold becomes a prism and, like Heraclitus' Lord

43. See chapter 3, pp. 63–64; chapter 4, pp. 73–74.

at Delphi, the biographer neither conceals nor reveals, but gives signs. He creates as he has himself been created by the interactions of factual and fantastic presences within. His biography's flow of "real beings," the striking image-signs that carry the hero's character, arise from a meditative mystery deep within the author himself. Prodded by the fire of imagination, the biographer breaks into speech, and the depths of his own soul become the matrix for his biographical speaking. As we have said often, the figures who come forth in these biographies are not Origen and Plotinus, but the "Eusebian Origen" and the "Porphyrian Plotinus": ghosts haunting other ghosts, making the biography a "*mise en abîme* of reflections within reflections."[44]

As critic, the reader of these biographies "cannot unscramble the tangle of lines of meaning, comb its threads out so they shine clearly side by side. He can only retrace the text, set its elements in motion once more, in that experience of the failure of determinable reading which is decisive here."[45] When, for example, we set the elements of Eusebius' biography of Origen in motion, we found a Janus-faced Origen, but we also found that this "determinable reading" failed to yield us an historical Origen. If we were to read that biography again, this time not from an historical perspective but from the perspective of "interior familiars" used to read Porphyry's biography of Plotinus (or, for that matter, if we were to read Porphyry's biography from the perspective of historical accuracy), we would have other "determinable readings," and other "failures."

What characterizes Eusebius' and Porphyry's biographical readings (and our own as well) might be described as a "law of shadowing."[46] Biographical myth is the story of a face reflected in many mirrors, the kind of history whose shadings and nuances reveal a divine *telos*, as Eusebius thought.[47] It is, as Pépin has remarked,[48] a deformation of historical reality, since its seeing is an imaginal seeing by way of tropes. However, as we have tried to suggest, it is just this tropical deformation that accounts for the success of a biographer's characterization of his hero as holy man. In other words, biographers live in that mythic middle realm peopled by daemonic presences, the tropes of antiquity. It is a place where "we are lived by Powers we

44. J. Hillis Miller, "The Critic as Host" in Harold Bloom, Paul de Man, Jacques Derrida, et al., *Deconstruction and Criticism* (New York: Seabury Press, 1979), p. 232.

45. Ibid., p. 248.

46. Ibid., p. 249.

47. See chapter 4, pp. 75–80.

48. Pépin *Mythe et allégorie*, p. 481.

pretend to understand," and it is the only place where meaningful discourse between the divine and the human unfolds.[49]

As Plato pointed out, daemonic conversation can happen both "in the waking state or during sleep."[50] By the time our biographers were writing, however, one theologian could say that "it is to dreams that the majority of mankind owe their knowledge of God."[51] The dream had become the *topos* of daemonic presence, and it was by dreaming that one entered that mythic middle realm where "false words"—daemonic images—"speak the truth" about the relations between the heavenly and the mundane.[52]

Were biographers dreamers? In an earlier chapter, we saw that many modern scholars have characterized the biographies of Late Antiquity as "aretalogies" because of their attention to the virtues (*aretai*) of their heroes. Their use of this term was based on a study that linked the *aretalogos* with the *oneirokritēs*, the judge of dreams. It was in the daemonic world of dreams that the gods spoke, and the task of the dream judge was to interpret how the gods were present in the dream's images.[53] Perhaps we can use the sense of this old cultic title to suggest a way of looking at the biographical imagination. A dream, we could say, names that realm of inner space, the interior geography of myth, where daemonic figures present themselves. It is here that fact and fantasy meet and intermingle, and it is this dreaming that the biographer "judges" when he names the dream's movements with images that give interpretative expression to the dialogue within the dreamer.

All of this suggests that the "dream" is what leads the biographer to give literary voice to what we called earlier a "charged atmosphere in which neither fact nor fiction prevails."[54] A biography is the biographer's interpretative judgment of his own dream. While he dreams, he is in that daemonic "world between," a threshold over which the magical and the banal, the mysterious and the mundane, cross and recross, interpreting each other and giving to their host his mythic perspective. When the biographer writes, he judges that dreaming by giving it concrete expression. He

49. This quotation, from W. H. Auden, is used by E. R. Dodds to introduce Chapter Two: "Man and the Daemonic World," of his *Pagan and Christian in an Age of Anxiety*.

50. Plato *Symposium* 202d–203a.

51. The statement is Tertullian's, in *De anima* 47.2, quoted by Dodds, *Pagan and Christian*, p. 38.

52. On dreams in Late Antiquity, see Dodds, *Pagan and Christian*, pp. 37–53.

53. See chapter 3, pp. 46–47.

54. Chapter 1, p. 7.

names the patterns of faces that reflect how he has conversed with the gods and with human reality, thus giving his hero's daemonic character a place to dwell.

Long ago, Heraclitus said, "a man's character is his daemon."[55] Character is daemonic. The biographies of Late Antiquity were living embodiments of the truth of that enigma.

55. Heraclitus fr. 94, Marcovich (119 Diels-Kranz).

Selected Bibliography

Ancient Authors

Aelius Theon. *Progymnasmata*. In *Rhetores Graeci*, vol. 2. Edited by L. Spengel. Leipzig: B. G. Teubner, 1854.

Ammianus Marcellinus. *History of the Roman Empire*. 3 vols. Edited and translated by John C. Rolfe. Loeb Classical Library. Cambridge: Harvard University Press, 1935–39.

Apollonius of Tyana. *Epistles*. In *Philostratus: Life of Apollonius of Tyana*, vol. 2. Translated by F. C. Conybeare. Loeb Classical Library. Cambridge: Harvard University Press, 1912.

Apuleius. *De deo Socratis*. In *Apulée: Opuscules philosophiques*. Edited and translated by Jean Beaujeu. Paris: Société d'Édition "Les Belles Lettres," 1973.

———. *De dogmate Platonis*. In *Apulée: Opuscules philosophiques*. Edited and translated by Jean Beaujeu. Paris: Société d'Édition "Les Belles Lettres," 1973.

Aristotle. *Nicomachean Ethics*. In *Basic Works of Aristotle*. Edited by Richard McKeon. New York: Random House, 1941.

Aristoxenus. *Fragmenta*. In *Die Schule des Aristoteles*. 10 vols. Edited by Fritz Wehrli. Basel: Benno Schwabe and Company, 1944–59. Vol. 2: *Aristoxenus* (1945).

Asclepius. In *Corpus Hermeticum*. 4 vols. Edited by Arthur Darby Nock. Translated by A.-J. Festugière. Paris: Société d'Édition "Les Belles Lettres," 1945. Vol. 2: *Asclepius*.

Athanasius. *Vita Antonii*. In *Nicene and Post-Nicene Fathers*, vol. 4: *St. Athanasius: Select Works and Letters*. Edited by Philip Schaff and Henry Wace. Grand Rapids, Michigan: Wm. B. Eerdmans Publishing Company, 1957.

Athenagoras. *Supplicatio pro Christianis*. In *Athénagore: Supplique au sujet des chrétiens*. Edited and translated by Gustave Bardy. Sources chrétiennes 3. Paris: Les Éditions du Cerf, 1943.

Cicero. *De finibus bonorum et malorum*. Translated by H. Rackham. Loeb Classical Library. London: William Heinemann, 1914.

———. *Tusculanae disputationes*. In *Cicéron: Tusculanes*. 2 vols. Edited by Georges Fohlen. Translated by Jules Humbert. Paris: Société d'Édition "Les Belles Lettres," 1964–68.

Clement of Alexandria. *Paedagogus*. Translated by Simon P. Wood. Fathers of the Church, vol. 23. New York: Fathers of the Church, Inc., 1954.

———. *Protrepticus*. Translated by G. W. Butterworth. Loeb Classical Library. London: William Heinemann, 1929.

———. *Stromata*. Edited by Otto Stählin. Die griechischen christlichen Schriftsteller der ersten drei Jahrhunderte, vols. 15 and 17. Berlin: Akademie-Verlag, 1970, 1972.

Clement of Rome. *Clementine Homilies*. In *New Testament Apocrypha*. 2 vols. Edited by Wilhelm Schneemelcher and Edgar Hennecke. Translated by R. McL. Wilson. Philadelphia: Westminster Press, 1963–64. Vol. 2: *Writings Relating to the Apostles, Apocalypses, and Related Subjects* (1964).

Dio Chrysostom. *Discourses*. Translated by J. W. Cohoon. Loeb Classical Library. London: William Heinemann, 1932.

Diocletian. *Edicts*. In *Roman Civilization*. 2 vols. Edited by Naphtali Lewis and Meyer Reinhold. New York: Harper and Row, 1966. Vol. 2: *The Empire*.

Diogenes Laertius. *Lives of Eminent Philosophers*. Translated by R. D. Hicks. Loeb Classical Library. London: William Heinemann, 1925.

Epictetus. *Discourses*. 2 vols. Translated by W. A. Oldfather. Loeb Classical Library. London: William Heinemann, 1926–28.

Epiphanius. *Panarion haeresis*. Edited by Karl Holl. Die griechischen christlichen Schriftsteller der ersten drei Jahrhunderte, vol. 3: *Epiphanius Werke*. Leipzig: J. C. Hinrichs, 1933.

Eunapius. *Lives of the Philosophers and Sophists*. In *Philostratus and Eunapius: Lives of the Philosophers and Sophists*. Edited and translated by Wilmer Wright. Loeb Classical Library. Cambridge: Harvard University Press, 1921.

Eusebius. *Contra Hieroclem*. In *Philostratus: The Life of Apollonius of Tyana*. 2 vols. Translated by F. C. Conybeare. Loeb Classical Library. Cambridge: Harvard University Press, 1912. Vol. 2: *The Life of Apollonius of Tyana, The Epistles of Apollonius, and the Treatise of Eusebius*.

———. *Demonstratio evangelica*. Edited by I. A. Heikel. Die griechischen christlichen Schriftsteller der ersten drei Jahrhunderte, vol. 23: *Eusebius Werke*. Leipzig: J. C. Hinrichs, 1913.

———. *Historia ecclesiastica*. 2 vols. Translated by Kirsopp Lake and J. E. L. Oulton. Loeb Classical Library. Cambridge: Harvard University Press, 1926–32.

———. *Martyrs of Palestine*. In *Eusebius: The Ecclesiastical History and the Martyrs of Palestine*. Trans. by H. J. Lawlor and J. E. L. Oulton. 2 vols. London: SPCK, 1927–28.

———. *Praeparatio evangelica*. Edited by Karl Mras. Die griechischen christlichen Schriftsteller der ersten drei Jahrhunderte, vol. 43. Berlin: Akademie-Verlag, 1956.

Gospel of Philip. In *The Nag Hammadi Library: In English*. Directed by James M. Robinson. New York: Harper and Row, 1977.

Gregory Thaumaturgus. *In Origenem oratio panegyrica*. In *Grégoire Thaumaturge: Remerciement à Origène*. Edited and translated by Henri Crouzel. Sources chrétiennes 148. Paris: Les Éditions du Cerf, 1969.

Heraclitus. *Fragments*. In *Heraclitus: Greek Text with a Short Commentary*. Edited and translated by M. Marcovich. Merida, Venezuela: The Los Andes University Press, 1967.

———. *Fragments*. In *The Presocratics*. Edited by Philip Wheelwright. Indianapolis: Bobbs-Merrill, 1960.

Herodotus. *The Persian Wars*. 4 vols. Translated by A. D. Godley. Loeb Classical Library. London: William Heinemann, 1920–24.

Homer. *Odyssey*. Translated by Robert Fitzgerald. Garden City, New York: Doubleday and Co., 1963.

Iamblichus. *De Mysteriis*. In *Jamblique: Les mystères d'Égypte*. Edited and translated by Edouard Des Places. Paris: Société d'Édition "Les Belles Lettres," 1966.

———. *Vita Pythagorica*. Edited by Ludovicus Deubner. Leipzig: B. G. Teubner, 1937.

Jerome. *De viris inlustribus*. In *Nicene and Post-Nicene Fathers*, second series, vol. 3. Edited by Philip Schaff and Henry Wace. New York: Christian Literature Company, 1892.

———. *Epistles*. In *Select Letters of St. Jerome*. Translated by F. A. Wright. Loeb Classical Library. London: William Heinemann, 1933.

———. "Praefatio" to *Onomasticon*. In *Jerome: Opera omnia*, vol. 3. Edited by D. Vallarsi. Venice: n.p., 1772.

———. "Prologus" to his translation of Origen, *Homiliae in Canticum Canticorum*. In *Origène: Homélies sur le Cantique des Cantiques*. Edited and translated by Dom Oliver Rousseau. Sources chrétiennes 37. Paris: Les Éditions du Cerf, 1966.

Justin. *Dialogue with Trypho*. Translated by A. L. Williams. London: SPCK, 1930.

Lactantius. *De mortibus persecutorum*. Translated by Sister Mary Francis McDonald. Fathers of the Church, vol. 54. Washington D.C.: Catholic University of America Press, 1965.

Lucian of Samosata. *Alexander the False Prophet*. Translated by A. M. Harmon. Loeb Classical Library. London: William Heinemann, 1925.

———. *The Cynic*. Translated by M. D. MacLeod. Loeb Classical Library. Cambridge: Harvard University Press, 1967.

———. *De morte Peregrini*. Translated by A. M. Harmon. Loeb Classical Library. London: William Heinemann, 1937.

———. *How to Write History*. Translated by K. Kilburn. Loeb Classical Library. Cambridge: Harvard University Press, 1959.

———. *Icaromenippus*. Translated by A. M. Harmon. Loeb Classical Library. London: William Heinemann, 1929.

———. *Menippus*. Translated by A. M. Harmon. Loeb Classical Library. London: William Heinemann, 1925.

———. *Philosophies for Sale*. Translated by A. M. Harmon. Loeb Classical Library. London: William Heinemann, 1929.

Maximus of Tyre. *Dissertationes*. In *Maximi Tyrii Philosophumena*. Edited by H. Hobein. Leipzig: B. G. Teubner, 1910.

Origen. *Commentariorum in Mattheum*. Edited by Erich Klostermann. Die griechischen christlichen Schriftsteller der ersten drei Jahrhunderte, Origenes Werke, vol. 10. Leipzig: J. C. Hinrichs, 1935.

———. *Contra Celsum*. Edited and translated by Henry Chadwick. Cambridge: Cambridge University Press, 1965.

———. *De principiis*. Edited and translated by G. W. Butterworth. New York: Harper and Row, 1966.

———. *Exhortation to Martyrdom*. In *Alexandrian Christianity*. Edited and translated by J. E. L. Oulton and Henry Chadwick. Library of Christian Classics 2. Philadelphia: Westminster Press, 1954.

———. *Homiliae in Genesim*. In *Origène: Homélies sur la Genèse*. Edited and translated by Louis Doutreleau. Sources chrétiennes 7. Paris: Les Éditions du Cerf, 1976.

———. *Homiliae in Jeremiam*. In *Origène: Homélies sur Jérémie* 1–11. Edited and translated by Pierre Nautin. Sources chrétiennes 232. Paris: Les Éditions du Cerf, 1976.

———. *Homiliae in Josuem*. In *Origène: Homélies sur Josué*. Edited and translated by Annie Jaubert. Sources chrétiennes 71. Paris: Les Éditions du Cerf, 1960.

———. *Homiliae in Leviticum*. In *Origenes: Homilien zum Hexateuch in Rufins Übersetzung, Die Homilien zu Genesis, Exodus, und Leviticus*. Edited by W. A. Baehrens. Die griechischen christlichen Schriftsteller der ersten drei Jahrhunderte, Origenes Werke, vol. 6. Leipzig: J. C. Hinrichs, 1920.

———. *Homiliae in Lucam*. In *Origène: Homélies sur S. Luc*. Edited and translated by Henri Crouzel, Francois Fournier, and Pierre Périchon. Sources chrétiennes 87. Paris: Les Éditions du Cerf, 1962.

———. *On Prayer*. In *Alexandrian Christianity*. Edited and translated by J. E. L. Oulton and Henry Chadwick. Library of Christian Classics 2. Philadelphia: Westminster Press, 1954.

———. *Selecta in Genesim*. In *Origenis opera omnia*, vol. 8. Edited by C. H. E. Lommatzsch. Leipzig: B. G. Teubner, 1836.

Pamphilus. *Apologia pro Origene*. In *Origenis opera omnia*, vol. 24. Edited by C. H. E. Lommatzsch. Leipzig: B. G. Teubner, 1846.

Philo. *De opificio mundi*. Translated by F. H. Colson and G. H. Whitaker. Loeb Classical Library. Cambridge: Harvard University Press, 1928.

———. *De vita Moisis*. Translated by F. H. Colson. Loeb Classical Library. Cambridge: Harvard University Press, 1935.

Philostratus. *Vita Apollonii*. In *Philostratus: The Life of Apollonius of Tyana*. 2 vols.

Translated by F. C. Conybeare. Loeb Classical Library. Cambridge: Harvard University Press, 1912.

———. *Vitae Sophistarum*. In *Philostratus and Eunapius: Lives of the Sophists*. Translated by Wilmer C. Wright. Loeb Classical Library. Cambridge: Harvard University Press, 1921.

Photius. *Bibliotheca*. In *Photius: Bibliothèque*. Edited and translated by R. Henry. Paris: Société d'Édition "Les Belles Lettres," 1969.

Plato. *The Collected Dialogues*. Edited by Edith Hamilton and Huntington Cairns. Bollingen Series 71. Princeton: Princeton University Press, 1963.

Pliny. *Natural History*. Translated by H. Rackham. Loeb Classical Library. Cambridge: Harvard University Press, 1945.

Plotinus. *Enneads*. In *Plotin: Ennéades*. 7 vols. Edited and translated by Émile Bréhier. Paris: Société d'Édition "Les Belles Lettres," 1924–38.

———. *Plotinus*. Translated and edited by A. H. Armstrong. Loeb Classical Library. 3 vols. Cambridge, Mass.: Harvard University Press, 1966–.

———. *Plotinus: The Enneads*. Translated and edited by Stephen MacKenna and B. S. Page. 3rd ed. London: Faber and Faber, 1962.

Plutarch. *Alexander*. In *Plutarch: Parallel Lives*, vol. 7. Translated by Bernadotte Perrin. Loeb Classical Library. London: William Heinemann, 1919.

———. *De defectu oraculorum*. In *Plutarch: Moralia*, vol. 5. Translated by Frank Cole Babbitt. Loeb Classical Library. Cambridge: Harvard University Press, 1936.

———. *De genio Socratis*. In *Plutarch: Moralia*, vol. 7. Translated by Phillip H. De Lacy and Benedict Einarson. Loeb Classical Library. Cambridge: Harvard University Press, 1959.

———. *De Isis et Osiris*. Edited and translated by J. Gwyn Griffiths. Swansea: University of Wales Press, 1970.

———. *Pericles*. In *Plutarch: Parallel Lives*, vol. 3. Translated by Bernadotte Perrin. London: William Heinemann, 1915.

———. *Pompey*. In *Plutarch: Parallel Lives*, vol. 5. Translated by Bernadotte Perrin. Loeb Classical Library. London: William Heinemann, 1917.

———. *Quaestiones convivales*. In *Plutarch: Moralia*, vol. 8. Translated by Paul A. Clement and Herbert B. Hoffleit. Loeb Classical Library. Cambridge: Harvard University Press, 1969.

———. *De Pythiae oraculis*. In *Plutarch: Moralia*, vol. 5. Translated by Frank Cole Babbitt. Loeb Classical Library. Cambridge: Harvard University Press, 1936.

Polemo. *Physiognomonica*. In *Scriptores Physiognomonici*. 2 vols. Edited by R. Förster. Leipzig: B. G. Teubner, 1893.

Polybius. *The Histories*. 6 vols. Translated by W. R. Paton. Loeb Classical Library. London: William Heinemann, 1922–27.

Porphyry. *Ad Marcellam*. Edited by Walter Pötscher. Leiden: E. J. Brill, 1969.

———. *Contra Christianos*. In *Porphyrius 'Gegen die Christen.'* Edited by Adolf Harnack. Abhandlungen der preussichen Akademie der Wissenschafter zu Berlin. Philosophisch-historisches Klasse, 1916, no. 1.

———. *De abstinentia*. In *Porphyrii philosophi platonici opuscula selecta*. Edited by A. Nauck. Leipzig: B. G. Teubner, 1886.

———. *De antro nympharum*. In *Porphyrii philosophi platonici opuscula selecta*. Edited by A. Nauck. Leipzig: B. G. Teubner, 1886.

———. *Vita Plotini*. In *Plotinus: Enneads*, vol. 1. Translated by A. H. Armstrong. Loeb Classical Library. Cambridge: Harvard University Press, 1966.

———. *Vita Pythagorae*. In *Porphyrii philosophi platonici opuscula selecta*. Edited by A. Nauck. Leipzig: B. G. Teubner, 1886.

Pseudo-Aristotle. *Physiognomonica*. In *Scriptores Physiognomonici*. 2 vols. Edited by R. Förster. Leipzig: B. G. Teubner, 1893. Vol. 2: *Pseudo-Aristoteles*.

Quintilian. *Institutio oratoria*. 2 vols. Translated by J. S. Watson. London: George Bell and Sons, 1875.

Seneca. *Epistulae morales*. 3 vols. Translated by Richard M. Gummere. Loeb Classical Library. London: William Heinemann, 1917–25.

Sextus. *Sentences*. Edited by Henry Chadwick. Cambridge: Cambridge University Press, 1959.

Socrates Scholasticus. *Historia ecclesiastica*. In *Nicene and Post-Nicene Fathers*, second series, vol. 2. Edited by Philip Schaff and Henry Wace. New York: Christian Literature Company, 1890.

Tacitus. *Annals*. Translated by John Jackson. Loeb Classical Library. Cambridge: Harvard University Press, 1951.

Thucydides. *History of the Peloponnesian War*. 4 vols. Translated by Charles Forster Smith. Loeb Classical Library. London: William Heinemann, 1919–23.

Modern Authors

Allemann, Beda. "Metaphor and Antimetaphor." In *Interpretation: The Poetry of Meaning*. Edited by Stanley Romaine Hopper and David L. Miller. New York: Harcourt, Brace and World, 1967. Pp. 103–23.

Armstrong, A. H. "The Background of the Doctrine 'That the Intelligibles Are Not Outside the Intellect'." In *Entretiens sur l'antiquité classique* 5: *Les sources de Plotin*. Geneva: Fondation Hardt, 1960. Pp. 391–425.

Atkins, J. W. H. *Literary Criticism in Antiquity*. 2 vols. Cambridge University Press, 1934. Vol. 2: *Graeco-Roman*.

Bardy, Gustave. "Aux origines de l'école d'Alexandrie." *Recherches des sciences religieuses* 27 (1937):69–90.

———. "'Philosophie' et 'philosophe' dans le vocabulaire chrétien des premiers siècles." *Revue d'ascétique et de mystique* 25 (April–December 1949):97–108.

Barnard, L. W. "The Date of S. Athanasius' *Vita Antonii*." *Vigiliae Christianae* 28 (September 1974): 169–75.

Barnes, T. D. "Origen, Aquila, and Eusebius." *Harvard Studies in Classical Philology* 74 (1968): 313–16.

———. "Porphyry *Against the Christians*: Date and Attribution of the Fragments." *Journal of Theological Studies*, n.s., 24 (October 1973): 414–42.

Beaujeu, Jean, ed. and trans. *Apulée: Opuscules philosophiques*. Paris: Société d'Édition "Les Belles Lettres," 1973.

Bernoulli, J. J. *Römische Ikonographie*. 2 vols. Stuttgart: W. Spemann, 1882–94.

Bertrand, F. *Mystique de Jésus chez Origène*. Paris: Aubier, 1954.

Bidez, Joseph. "La liturgie des mystères chez les Néoplatoniciens." *Academie Royale de Belgique, bulletins de la classe des lettres* (June 1919): 415–30.

———. "Le philosophe Jamblique et son école." *Revue des études grecques* 32 (1919): 29–40.

———. *Vie de Porphyre*. Ghent: n.p., 1913; reprint ed., Hildesheim: Georg Olms Verlagsbuchhandlung, 1964.

Bieler, Ludwig. *ΘΕΙΟΣ ΑΝΗΡ*. 2 vols. Vienna: Buchhandlung Oskar Höfels, 1935–36.

Bompaire, J. *Lucien Écrivain*. Paris: E. de Boccard, 1958.

Brown, Peter. *The Making of Late Antiquity*. Cambridge: Harvard University Press, 1978.

———. "The Religious Crisis of the Third Century A.D." In *Religion and Society in the Age of St. Augustine*. London: Faber and Faber, 1972. Pp. 542–58.

———. *The World of Late Antiquity*. London: Thames and Hudson, 1971.

Burckhardt, Jacob. *The Age of Constantine the Great*. Translated by Moses Hadas. New York: Pantheon Books, 1949.

Cadiou, René. *La jeunesse d'Origène*. Paris: Gabriel Beauchesne, 1935.

Cameron, Alan. "The Date of Porphyry's ΚΑΤΑ ΧΡΙΣΤΙΑΝΩΝ." *Classical Quarterly* 17 (1967): 382–84.

Caster, Marcel. *Lucien et la pensée religieuse de son temps*. Paris: Société d'Édition "Les Belles Lettres," 1937.

Chadwick, Henry. *Early Christian Thought and the Classical Tradition*. Oxford: Clarendon Press, 1966.

———, ed. *Sentences of Sextus*. Cambridge: Cambridge University Press, 1959.

Chesnut, Glenn F., Jr. "Fate, Fortune, Free Will and Nature in Eusebius of Caesarea." *Church History* 42 (June 1973): 165–82.

Corbin, Henry. *Corps spirituel et terre céleste*. Paris: Éditions Buchet/Chastel, 1979.

Coussin, J. "Suetone physiognomoniste dans les *Vies des XII Césars*." *Revue des études latines* 31 (1953): 234–56.

Crane, R. S. *Critical and Historical Principles of Literary History*. Chicago: University of Chicago Press, 1971.

Crouzel, Henri. *Bibliographie critique d'Origène*. The Hague: Martin Nijhoff, 1971.

———. "L'École d'Origène à Césarée." *Bulletin de littérature ecclésiastique* 71 (January–March 1970): 15–27.

———, ed. and trans. *Grégoire Thaumaturge: Remerciement à Origène.* Paris: Les Éditions du Cerf, 1969.

———. *Origène et la 'connaissance mystique.'* Paris: Desclée de Brouwer, 1961.

———. "Origène et Plotin élèves d'Ammonius Saccas." *Bulletin de littérature ecclésiastique* 57 (1956): 193–214.

———. *Théologie de l'image de Dieu Chez Origène.* Paris: Aubier, 1956.

Crouzel, Henri; Fournier, François; and Périchon, Pierre, eds. and trans. *Origène: Homélies sur S. Luc.* Sources chrétiennes 87. Paris: Les Éditions du Cerf, 1962.

Daniélou, Jean. *Origène.* Paris: La Table Ronde, 1948.

De Faye, Eugene. *Origène: sa vie, son oeuvre, sa pensée.* 3 vols. Paris: Éditions Ernest Leroux, 1923. Vol. 1: *Sa biographie et ses écrits.*

Delatte, Armand. *Études sur la littérature pythagoricienne.* Paris: Librairie Ancienne Honoré Champion, 1915.

Demetrakopoulos, Stephanie. "Hestia, Goddess of the Hearth." *Spring* (1979): 55–75.

Den Boer, Willem. *Some Minor Roman Historians.* Leiden: E. J. Brill, 1972.

Des Places, Edouard. "La Religion de Jamblique." In *Entretiens sur l'antiquité classique* 21: *De Jamblique à Proclus.* Geneva: Fondation Hardt, 1975. Pp. 69–101.

Dihle, Albrecht. *Studien sur griechischen Biographie.* Göttingen: Vandenbroeck and Ruprecht, 1956.

Dillon, John. "The Academy in the Middle Platonic Period." *Dionysius* 3 (December 1979): 63–77.

———, ed. and trans. *Iamblichi Chalcidensis: In Platonis dialogos commentariorum fragmenta.* Leiden: E. J. Brill, 1973.

———. *The Middle Platonists.* Ithaca: Cornell University Press, 1977.

Dodds, E. R. *The Greeks and the Irrational.* Berkeley: University of California Press, 1951.

———. "Numenius and Ammonius." In *Entretiens sur l'antiquité classique* 5: *Les sources de Plotin.* Geneva: Fondation Hardt, 1960.

———. *Pagan and Christian in an Age of Anxiety.* New York: W. W. Norton and Company, 1970.

———, ed. and trans. *Proclus: The Elements of Theology.* 2nd ed. Oxford: Clarendon Press, 1963.

Doty, William G. "The Concept of Genre in Literary Analysis." In *Working Papers of the Task Group on the Genre of the Gospels.* Missoula, Montana: Society of Biblical Literature, 1972. Pp. 29–64.

Drake, H. A. *In Praise of Constantine: A Historical Study and New Translation of Eusebius' Tricennial Orations.* University of California Publications in Classical Studies, vol. 15. Berkeley: University of California Press, 1976.

Evans, Elizabeth Cornelia. "Roman Descriptions of Personal Appearance in History and Biography." *Harvard Studies in Classical Philology* 46 (1935): 43–84.

———. "A Stoic Aspect of Senecan Drama: Portraiture." *Transactions and Proceedings of the American Philological Association* 81 (1950): 169–84.

———. "The Study of Physiognomy in the 2nd century A.D." *Transactions and Proceedings of the American Philological Association* 72 (1941): 96–108.

Festugière, A.-J. *La Révélation d'Hermès Trismegiste*. 4 vols. Paris: Librairie Lecoffre, 1944–54.

———. "Sur une nouvelle édition du 'De Vita pythagorica' de Jamblique." *Revue des Études Grecques* 50 (1937): 470–94.

Fischel, Henry A. "Story and History: Observations on Greco-Roman Rhetoric and Pharisaism." In *American Oriental Society, Middle West Branch Semi-Centennial Volume*. Edited by Denis Sinor. Asian Studies Research Institute, Oriental Series 3. Bloomington: Indiana University Press, 1969. Pp. 59–88.

Fowler, Alastair. "The Life and Death of Literary Forms." *New Literary History* 2 (1971): 202–12.

Frend, W. H. C. *Martyrdom and Persecution in the Early Church*. London: Basil Blackwell, 1965.

———. "Open Questions Concerning the Christians and the Roman Empire in the Age of the Severi." *Journal of Theological Studies*, n.s., 25 (October 1974): 333–51.

Grant, Robert M. "The Case against Eusebius, or, Did the Father of Church History write History?" *Studia patristica* 12 (1975): 413–21.

———. *The Earliest Lives of Jesus*. London: SPCK, 1961.

———. "Early Alexandrian Christianity." *Church History* 40 (June 1971): 133–44.

———. "Eusebius and His Lives of Origen." In *Forma Futuri: Studi in onore del Cardinale Michele Pellegrino*. Turin: Bottega d'Erasmo, 1975. Pp. 635–49.

———. "Porphyry among the Early Christians." In *Romanitas et Christianitas: Studies in Honor of Allen Wikgren*. Edited by William Den Boer. Amsterdam: North Holland Publishing Co., 1973. Pp. 181–87.

———. "The Religion of Maximin Daia." In *Christianity, Judaism, and Other Greco-Roman Cults: Studies for Morton Smith at Sixty*. Edited by Jacob Neusner. 4 vols. Leiden: E. J. Brill, 1975. Vol. 4: *Judaism after 70 and Other Greco-Roman Cults*. Pp. 143–66.

———. "The *Stromateis* of Origen." In *Epektasis: Mélanges patristiques offerts au Cardinal Jean Daniélou*. Edited by Jacques Fontaine and Charles Kannengiesser. Paris: Éditions Beauchesne, 1972. Pp. 285–92.

Grube, G. M. A. *The Greek and Roman Critics*. London: Methuen and Co., 1965.

Hadas, Moses and Smith, Morton. *Heroes and Gods: Spiritual Biographies in Antiquity*. New York: Harper and Row, 1965.

Hanson, R. P. C. "A Note on Origen's Self-Mutilation." *Vigiliae Christianae* 20 (June 1966): 81–82.

Harnack, Adolf. *Porphyrius 'Gegen die Christen.'* Abhandlungen der preussischen

Akademie der Wissenschaften zu Berlin. Philosophisch-historisches Klasse, 1916, no. 1.

Hillman, James. *The Dream and the Underworld*. New York: Harper and Row, 1979.

———. "The Fiction of Case History: A Round." In *Religion as Story*. Edited by James B. Wiggins. New York: Harper and Row, 1975. Pp. 123–73.

Hofmann, Karl-Martin. *Philema Hagion*. Gütersloh: Verlag C. Bertelsmann, 1938.

Holl, Karl. "Die schriftstellerische Form des griechischen Heiligenlebens." *Neue Jahrbucher für klassische Altertum* 29 (1912): 406–27.

Hopper, Stanley Romaine. "'Le Cri de Merlin!' Or Interpretation and the Metalogical." In *Yearbook of Comparative Criticism*, vol. 4: *Anagogic Qualities of Literature*. Edited by Joseph P. Strelka. University Park: Pennsylvania State University, 1971. Pp. 9–35.

Hornschuh, Manfred. "Das Leben des Origenes und die Entstehung der alexandrinischen Schule." *Zeitschrift für die Kirchengeschichte* 71 (1960): 1–25, 193–214.

Jones, A. H. M. "The Social Background of the Struggle between Paganism and Christianity." In *The Conflict between Paganism and Christianity in the Fourth Century*. Edited by Arnaldo Momigliano. Oxford: Clarendon Press, 1963. Pp. 17–37.

Kee, Howard. "Aretalogy and Gospel." *Journal of Biblical Literature* 92 (September, 1973): 402–22.

Kemp, E. W. "Bishops and Presbyters at Alexandria." *Journal of Ecclesiastical History* 6 (1955): 125–42.

Kermode, Frank. *The Genesis of Secrecy: On the Interpretation of Narrative*. Cambridge, Massachusetts: Harvard University Press, 1979.

Koester, Helmut. "One Jesus and Four Primitive Gospels." *Harvard Theological Review* 61 (1968): 203–47.

———. "Romance, Biography, and Gospel." In *Working Papers of the Task Group on the Genre of the Gospels*. Missoula, Montana: Society of Biblical Literature, 1972. Pp. 120–48.

Lawlor, H. J. and Oulton, J. E. L., trans. *Eusebius: The Ecclesiastical History and the Martyrs of Palestine*. 2 vols. London: SPCK, 1927–28.

Leadbeater, L. W. "Aspects of the Philosophical Priesthood in Iamblichus' *De Mysteriis*." *Classical Bulletin* 47 (1971): 89–92.

Leo, Friedrich. *Die griechisch-römische Biographie nach ihrer litterarischen Form*. Leipzig: B. G. Teubner, 1901.

Lévy, Isidore. *La légende de Pythagore de Grèce en Palestine*. Paris: Librairie Ancienne Honoré Champion, 1927.

———. *Recherches sur les sources de la légende de Pythagore*. Paris: Éditions Ernest Leroux, 1926.

Lubac, Henri de. *Histoire et esprit: L'intelligence de l'écriture d'après Origène*. Paris: Éditions Montaigne, 1950.

MacMullen, Ramsay. *Enemies of the Roman Order*. Cambridge: Harvard University Press, 1966.

Meredith, Anthony. "Asceticism—Christian and Greek." *Journal of Theological Studies*, N.S., 27 (October 1976): 313–32.

Miller, David L. "'I Know A Place . . .'." A lecture at the Symposium, "Religion after Freud and Jung." Sponsored by the Center for Twentieth-Century Studies, University of Wisconsin-Milwaukee. 15–16 April 1980. Manuscript.

———. "Utopia, Trinity, and Tropical Topography." A Lecture at the Colloquium on "Utopia." Sponsored by the Protestant Theological Faculty of the University of Human Sciences of Strasbourg and the Department of Religion of Syracuse University. 13–15 March 1980. Strasbourg, France. Manuscript.

Miller, J. Hillis. "Ariadne's Thread: Repetition and the Narrative Line." *Critical Inquiry* 3 (1976): 58–77.

———. "The Critic as Host." In Harold Bloom, Paul de Man, Jacques Derrida, et al., *Deconstruction and Criticism*. New York: The Seabury Press, 1979. Pp. 217–53.

Misener, Geneva. "Iconistic Portraits." *Classical Philology* 19 (1924): 97–123.

Momigliano, Arnaldo. "Christianity and the Decline of the Roman Empire." In *The Conflict between Paganism and Christianity in the Fourth Century*. Oxford: Clarendon Press, 1963. Pp. 1–16.

———. *The Development of Greek Biography*. Cambridge: Harvard University Press, 1971.

———. "Historiography on Written and on Oral Tradition." In *Studies in Historiography*. London: Weidenfeld and Nicolson, 1966. Pp. 211–20.

———. "Pagan and Christian Historiography in the 4th c. A.D." In *The Conflict between Paganism and Christianity in the Fourth Century*. Oxford: Clarendon Press, 1963. Pp. 79–99.

———. "Popular Religious Beliefs and the Late Roman Historians." *Studies in Church History* 8 (1972): 1–18.

Musurillo, Herbert A., ed. and trans. *The Acts of the Pagan Martyrs: Acta Alexandrinorum*. Oxford: Clarendon Press, 1954.

Nautin, Pierre. "La date des Homélies." In *Origène: Homélies sur Jérémie 1–11*. Edited by Pierre Nautin. Sources chrétiennes 232. Paris: Les Éditions du Cerf, 1976. Pp. 15–21.

———. *Lettres et écrivains chrétiens des IIe et IIIe siècles*. Paris: Les Éditions du Cerf, 1961.

———. "Origène prédicateur." In *Origène: Homélies sur Jérémie 1–11*. Edited by Pierre Nautin. Sources chrétiennes 232. Paris: Les Éditions du Cerf, 1976. Pp. 100–191.

———. *Origène: Sa vie et son oeuvre*. Paris: Éditions Beauchesne, 1977.

Nock, Arthur Darby. *Conversion*. Oxford: Oxford University Press, 1933.

Norden, Eduard. *Agnostos Theos: Untersuchungen zur Formengeschichte religiöser Rede.* Leipzig: B. G. Teubner, 1913.

O'Flaherty, Wendy Doniger. "Inside and Outside the Mouth of God: The Boundary between Myth and Reality." *Daedalus* 109 (Spring, 1980):93–125.

Pack, Roger. "The Volatilization of Peregrinus Proteus." *American Journal of Philology* 67 (1946):334–45.

Pearson, Lionel. *Early Ionian Historians.* Oxford: Clarendon Press, 1939.

Pépin, Jean. *Mythe et allégorie: Les origines grecques et les contestations judéo-chrétiennes.* 2nd ed. Paris: Études Augustiniennes, 1976.

———. "Porphyre, exégète d'Homère." In *Entretiens sur l'antiquité classique* 12: *Porphyre.* Geneva: Fondation Hardt, 1966. Pp. 229–72.

Petzke, G. *Die Traditionen über Apollonius von Tyana und das Neue Testament.* Studia ad corpus hellenisticum Novi Testamenti 1. Leiden: E. J. Brill, 1970.

Pötscher, Walter. "Porphyrios *Pros Markellan.*" *Philosophia antiqua* 15 (1969): 52–70.

Polman, G. H. "Chronological Biography and AKMĒ in Plutarch." *Classical Philology* 69 (July 1974):169–77.

Priessnig, A. "Die biographische Form der Plotinvita des Porphyrios und das Antoniosleben des Athanasios." *Byzantinische Zeitschrift* 64 (1971):1–5.

———. "Die literarische Form der Spätantiken Philosophenromane." *Byzantinische Zeitschrift* 30 (1929):23–30.

Rahner, Hugo. *Greek Myths and Christian Mystery.* Translated by Brian Battershaw. New York: Harper and Row, 1963.

Reinach, Salomon. "Les arétalogues dans l'antiquité." *Bulletin de correspondence hellénique* 9 (1885):257–65.

Reitzenstein, Richard. "Das Athanasius Werk über das Leben des Antonius." *Sitzungsberichte der Heidelberger Akademie der Wissenschaften* 8 (1914):26–57.

———. *Hellenistische Wundererzählungen.* Leipzig: B. G. Teubner, 1906.

Rohde, Erwin. "Die Quellen des Iamblichus in seiner Biographie des Pythagoras." *Rheinisches Museum* 26 (1871):554–78.

Schenkl, H. "Pythagoreersprüche in einer Wiener Handschrift." *Wiener Studien* 8 (1886):262–81.

Schmidt, W. "*Genethlios hēmera.*" *Real-Encyclopädie der klassischen Altertumswissenschaft* 13, cols. 1135–49. Edited by A. Pauly and G. Wissowa.

Schwartz, Eduard, ed. *Eusebius: Die Kirchengeschichte.* 3 vols. Die Griechisch-Christliche Schriftsteller 9. Berlin: J. C. Hinrichs, 1909.

Sirinelli, Jean. *Les vues historiques d'Eusèbe de Césarée durant la période prénicéene.* Dakar: Université de Dakar, 1961.

Smith, Andrew. *Porphyry's Place in the Neoplatonic Tradition.* The Hague: Martinus Nijhoff, 1974.

Smith, Jonathan Z. "Good News Is No News: Aretalogy and Gospel." In *Christian-*

ity, Judaism, and Other Greco-Roman Cults: Studies for Morton Smith at Sixty. Edited by Jacob Neusner. 4 vols. Leiden: E. J. Brill, 1975. Vol. 1: *New Testament*. Pp. 21–38.

Smith, Morton. "Prolegomena to a Discussion of Aretalogies, Divine Men, the Gospels, and Jesus." *Journal of Biblical Literature* 90 (June 1971): 174–99.

Stählin, Gustav. "*Phileō*." *Theological Wordbook of the New Testament*. Edited by Gerhard Kittel. Translated by Geoffrey Bromiley. 3: 119–23.

Starr, C. G. "Epictetus and the Tyrant." *Classical Philology* 44 (1949): 20–29.

Stuart, Duane Reed. *Epochs of Greek and Roman Biography*. Berkeley: University of California Press, 1928.

Syme, Ronald. *Emperors and Biography: Studies in the Historia Augusta*. Oxford: Clarendon Press, 1971.

Talbert, Charles H. "The Concept of Immortals in Mediterranean Antiquity." *Journal of Biblical Literature* 94 (September 1975): 419–36.

———. *What Is a Gospel? : The Genre of the Canonical Gospels*. Philadelphia: Fortress Press, 1977.

Telfer, W. "Episcopal Succession in Egypt." *Journal of Ecclesiastical History* 3 (1952): 1–13.

Tiede, David L. *The Charismatic Figure as Miracle Worker*. Society of Biblical Literature Dissertation Series 1. Missoula, Montana: Society of Biblical Literature, 1972.

Van Unnik, W. C. *Tarsus or Jerusalem?* Translated by George Ogg. London: Epworth Press, 1962.

Verbeke, G. *L'évolution de la doctrine du pneuma du Stoicisme à S. Augustin*. Paris: Desclée de Brouwer, 1945.

Wilken, Robert L. "Pagan Criticism of Christianity: Greek Religion and Christian Faith." In *Early Christian Literature and the Classical Intellectual Tradition*. Ed. by William R. Schoedel and Robert L. Wilken. Paris: Éditions Beauchesne, 1979. Pp. 17–34.

Witt, Rex E. *Albinus and the History of Middle Platonism*. Cambridge: Cambridge University Press, 1937.

———. "Iamblichus as a Forerunner of Julian." In *Entretiens sur l'antiquité classique* 21: *De Jamblique à Proclus*. Geneva: Fondation Hardt, 1975. Pp. 35–67.

Index

Designer:	Barbara Llewellyn
Compositor:	G&S Typesetters, Inc.
Text:	Linotron 202 Garamond
Display:	Phototypositor Garamond
Printer:	Braun-Brumfield, Inc.
Binder:	Braun-Brumfield, Inc.